Imaging Wisdom

Seeing and Knowing
in the Art of Indian Buddhism

BUDDHIST TRADITION SERIES

VOLUME 44

Edited by

ALEX WAYMAN

Imaging Wisdom

Seeing and Knowing in the Art of Indian Buddhism

Jacob N. Kinnard

MOTILAL BANARSIDASS PUBLISHERS
PRIVATE LIMITED • DELHI

First Indian Edition: Delhi, 2001

First Edition: U.K., 1999

ISBN: 81-208-1793-1

Also available at:
MOTILAL BANARSIDASS
236, 9th Main III Block, Jayanagar, Bangalore 560 011
41 U.A. Bungalow Road, Jawahar Nagar, Delhi 110 007
8 Mahalaxmi Chamber, Warden Road, Mumbai 400 026
120 Royapettah High Road, Mylapore, Chennai 600 004
Sanas Plaza, 1302 Baji Rao Road, Pune 411 002
8 Camac Street, Kolkata700 017
Ashok Rajpath, Patna00 004
Chowk, Varanasi 221 001

Printed in India
BY JAINENDRA PRAKASH JAIN AT SHRI JAINENDRA PRESS,
A-45 NARAINA, PHASE-I, NEW DELHI 110 028
AND PUBLISHED BY NARENDRA PRAKASH JAIN FOR
MOTILAL BANARSIDASS PUBLISHERS PRIVATE LIMITED,
BUNGALOW ROAD, DELHI 110 007

For Isabelle and Gideon

Foreword

This is a precious book that needs to be treated by chapter. The Chap. One on "Imagining Images" discusses how to get the 'presence' of the Buddha, and the problems this involves. Chap. Three "Imaging and Imagining the Buddha" takes up the problem of the initial images of the Buddha and the association with meditating on the Buddha. Chap. Four is on "The Image of Wisdom". By 'Wisdom' Kinnard means prajñā in Buddhism. And by 'image' he especially means the two representations of the Buddha-the 'earth-touching gesture' and the 'turning the wheel-of-dharma gesture'. While he seems to prefer 'Wisdom' for prajñā, he does recognize the meaning 'insight' because this implicates 'seeing'. This Chap. Four is full of interesting material. Chap. Five "Representing Prajñāpāramitā" is well illustrated with sculptures. It explains his title "Imaging wisdom" although he grants that such representations are some centuries later than the actual Prajñāpāramitā scriptures. His last chapter (Seven) entitled "Seeing and Knowing" shows the difference between 'seeing', e.g. a book on Prajñā, and the 'knowing' through the development of prajñā. The entire book is easy to understand, and makes an excellent addition to a Buddhist library.

Alex Wayman

Acknowledgments

A great many individuals assisted me during the research and writing of this book, and to all of them I owe my deepest gratitude. First, however, I would like to thank the Mellon Foundation for awarding me a postdoctoral fellowship that allowed me to complete this book, and also my colleagues at Northwestern University for creating an ideal environment in which to work.

While doing research in India, I was assisted by the Archeological Survey of India, which granted me permission to study and photograph at many sites under their care. The American Institute of Indian Studies Center for Art and Archaeology, in Varanasi, also provided me with advice and access to their large photo archive, and I am grateful to all of the officials of the A.I.I.S. for granting me permission to reproduce a number of images in their collection. Mr. R. Sharma, the Archivist, was especially helpful. Officials at the Patna Museum, Indian Museum, National Museum, and State Museum of Orissa were all most helpful.

Many people read drafts of chapters and offered valuable comments, and to all of them I am very grateful. Richard Cooler read and commented on early drafts of several chapters, and provided me with a comparative perspective that helped me focus on the specifics of the Pāla materials. John and Susan Huntington helped me see some specific Pāla issues with greater clarity; not only were they extremely generous with their time, but the Huntingtons also gave me free access to their large photo archive at Ohio State University, allowing me to reproduce several of their images here. I also want to thank Janice Glowski of the Huntington Archive at Ohio State, for helping me navigate through a tremendous number of photographs. Special thanks also go to Geri Malandra, who not only read and incisively commented on several chapters, but who also provided me with some timely and much-needed guidance in my research in India.

From my earliest thoughts on this project, Wendy Doniger, helped me to define - and pushed me on - issues that, at times, I was not even aware that I was raising. I am indebted to Janice Leoshko for so carefully reading and commenting on a number of manifestations of my manuscript, and for graciously allowing me to reproduce several of her photographs here. Steven Collins has served as a mentor for many years, and I thank him for being such a tough and demanding reader; I am also grateful to him for keeping me focused on Sanskrit thoughts, and I thank him for saving me from some particularly conspicuous translation howlers. Finally, Frank Reynolds has pushed and prodded, cajoled and en-couraged me throughout my work on this book. It was he who first encouraged me to work on things visual while I was at the University of Chicago, and it was he who deftly kept me motivated and focused throughout. Without his knowledge, his compassion, and his friendship this book would never have been written, and if there are glimmers of insight in these pages, they are largely is due to both his *prajñā* and his *karuna*.

Contents

List of Figures

Fig. 1. Stone Prajñāpāramitā, 9th century, Bihar, Avery Brundage Collection, photo courtesy of the Museum of Asian Art, San Francisco.

Fig. 2. Stone Prajñāpāramitā, 9th century, Bodhgayā, photo courtesy of Janice Leoshko.

Fig. 3. Bronze Prajñāpāramitā, 9th century, Nālandā, Nālandā Museum, photo courtesy of the American Institute of Indian Studies.

Fig. 4. Bronze Prajñāpāramitā, 9th century, Nālandā, Nālandā Museum, photo courtesy of the American Institute of Indian Studies.

Fig. 5. Bronze Mañjuśrī, 10th century, Bihar, National Museum, New Delhi, photo courtesy of the American Institute of Indian Studies.

Fig. 6. Stone Mañjuśrī, Nālandā, 10th century, Nālandā Museum, photo courtesy of the American Institute of Indian Studies.

Fig. 7. Bronze Mañjuśrī, 9th century, Nālandā, National Museum, New Delhi, photo courtesy the American Institute of Indian Studies.

Fig. 8. Stone Mañjuśrī, 11th century, Bihar, Indian Museum, Calcutta, photo courtesy of the American Institute of Indian Studies.

Fig. 9. Stone Mañjuśrī, 11th century, West Bengal, Bangiya Sahitya Parishad, photo courtesy of S. and J. Huntington.

Fig 10. Stone Avalokiteśvara, 8th century, Nālandā, Nālandā Museum, photo courtesy the American Institute of Indian Studies.

Fig. 11. Detail of stone Avalokiteśvara, 8th century, Nālandā, Nālandā Museum, photo courtesy the American Institute of Indian Studies.

Fig. 12. Stone *bhūmisparśamudrā* Buddha fragment, 9th century, Orissa, Kiching Site Museum, photo courtesy of the American Institute of Indian Studies.

Fig. 13. Stone *bhūmisparśamudrā* Buddha, 11th century, Orissa, Indian Museum, Calcutta, photo courtesy of the American Institute of Indian Studies.

Fig. 14. Stone Tārā, 10th century, Bangladesh, Dacca Museum, photo courtesy of Janice Leoshko.

Fig. 15. Stone *bhūmisparśamudrā* Buddha, 10th century, Bangladesh, Dacca Museum, photo courtesy of Janice Leoshko.

Fig. 16. Stone pedestal, Bodhgayā, 10th century, Lucknow State Museum, photo courtesy of the American Institute of Indian Studies.

Chapter One

IMAGINING IMAGES

> We all know that art is not truth. Art is a lie that makes us realize truth....
>
> Pablo Picasso[1]

This is a book about Buddhist images, about why Buddhists at a particular time and in a particular place made images, about why these Buddhists looked at and venerated such images, and about what such Buddhists did with and thought about the images that they made. This is also a book about how we, as students and scholars of religion, deal with religious images; or, to be more precise, it is a book about how we have tended *not* to deal with images. At the heart of our own scholarly approach to images is the thorny question of the presence of the divine in apparently inanimate objects. This is, to be sure, a very old issue. Indeed, historians and anthropologists and sociologists of religion have been grappling with, and fighting about, this basic issue at least since the nineteenth-century discussions of totemism in the works of William Robertson Smith, Emile Durkheim, and Sigmund Freud. However, as with so many contested issues in academe, we have come to something of a theoretical and methodological impasse, with two distinct, opposed, and monothetic camps solidifying and defending their respective positions: either the object in question - be it a totem, a sculpture, wine, or a cucumber - really is considered *to be* or to *embody* the thing represented (the divine, the sacred, a/the god); or the object in question is considered to be a *representation* of the divine, a *symbol* or *signifier*.

The problem, however, is that such an impasse merely serves

---

[1]Quoted in Herschel B. Chipp, *Theories of Modern Art* (Berkeley: University of California Press, 1968), p.264.

to reify what is, I believe, a fundamentally facile dichotomy, a dichotomy that is more about our own particular preconceptions and biases at any given moment than it is about the actual understandings and attitudes of the objects of our inquiries, the actual people who think about, construct, and utilize images. This is a dichotomy, furthermore, that is especially pronounced in scholarly discussions of images of the Buddha. We are not entirely lost yet, though. Recent work in ritual theory, most significantly that of Pierre Bourdieu and those immediately following his insights, points in fruitful directions, suggesting strategies for moving beyond the simple, and I think false, either/or dichotomy and moving toward a dialectic sense of *both*. What I shall do here, then, following and developing Bourdieu, is to formulate an approach to images in general and Buddhist images in particular that focuses on the ongoing process of contestation and negotiation involved in the motivations for and responses to any particular religious image.

Thus, in this initial chapter, I first lay out what I believe are the most critical and most pressing issues involved in the general scholarly debate about *presence*; I then sketch out the directions in which the theoretical positions of Bourdieu and others working in ritual point us. It will become clear as this chapter progresses, I think, that this rather general methodological discussion lays the groundwork for my examination of some of the broad concepts involved in the Buddhist creation and use of artistic images. And it is this theoretical groundwork that, in turn, underlies the specific focus of this study: the complex web of ideas and practices surrounding the visual representation of a single, central concept, *prajñā*, or wisdom, in medieval north India.

The existence of two levels of contested discourse - to use a distinction I borrow from linguistic anthropology, the *emic* (internal) level of the long-running Buddhist debate about presence, and the *etic* (external) level of our own scholarly discourse on this topic - makes this particular instance of the problem of presence an important subject for exploration, one that sheds new light not only on the specific Buddhist context, but also on the broader context of religious studies in general. Therefore, although this discussion is ultimately intended to serve as the methodological frame for my specific discussion of Buddhist visual practices in medieval North India, I also wish to assert a more broadly applicable point: namely, that by re-positioning a specific instance of "divine" presence in its larger cultural context, it is possible - indeed, following Bourdieu, I would say that it is necessary - to see not a single, *mono*vocal discourse, but rather a multiplicity of discourses operating simultaneously, with unified, established rules and doctrines both conflicting and interacting with more fluid beliefs and practices. Indeed, if we are to take seriously what the anthropologist Clifford Geertz once said was the intellectual poverty of "impeccable depictions of formal order in whose actual existence nobody can quite believe,"[2] then we must descend, if not actually into the turbulent waters of chaos, at least into the muck of disorderly praxis.

I. The Paramparā: From the Primitive Mentality to *Habitus*

> ***Paramparā***: f. an uninterrupted row or series, order, succession, continuation, mediation, tradition; lineage, progeny...received by tradition.
>
> Sir Monier Monier-Williams[3]

> People know what they do; they frequently know why they do what they do; but what they don't know is what what they do does.
>
> Michel Foucault[4]

One of the first scholars of religion to consider seriously the question of the presence of the divine in inanimate objects - outside of the Christian theological context, at any rate - was the Scottish biblical scholar William Robertson Smith. In his 1889 opus, *Lectures on the*

---

[2]Clifford Geertz, *The Interpretation of Cultures* (New York: Basic Books, 1973), p. 18.
[3]Sir Monier Monier-Williams, *A Sanskrit-English Dictionary* (Oxford: Oxford University Press, 1899).
[4]Quoted in H.L Dreyfus and P. Rabinow, *Michel Foucault: Beyond Structuralism and Hermeneutics* (Chicago: University of Chicago Press, 1982), p. 187.

Religion of the Semites, Smith took up the embodiment of the sacred, what he called the "immanent" divine, in such things as trees, the earth, tombs, and a host of other objects. His comments about water are emblematic of his position: "the sacred waters are instant with divine life and energy....impregnated, so to speak, with the vital energy of the deity to which it is sacred."[5] Primitive, premodern man saw the sacred embodied in such objects; the totem animal, the rock, a tree, all of these objects were instances of a perceived ontological presence of the divine. One might well ask, however, why there is the need to invoke a century-old text, seldom read by anyone besides graduate students preparing doctoral exams and the idly curious; Smith's discussion is certainly not now taken seriously. James Frazer, however, took Smith very seriously (even if he did not always agree with him), and Durkheim based much of his theory of the origin of religion on his reading of Smith, and Freud's concept of the oedipal complex - and indeed his entire notion of religion - is firmly rooted in Smith's account of the *Ur*-sacrifice and the primal horde, and so on.

My point here is perhaps self-evident: the issues we scholars now find important, and our knowledge about them, are handed down in a regular succession, a lineage, a *paramparā*, with considerable alterations, certainly - as in the children's game of telephone - but in a more or less continuous line. The issues involved in "presence" may seem, at first blush, then, to be mere curiosities, dead ideas relegated to dusty tomes (or tombs) and obscure footnotes, but in fact they are still very much with us, and reexamining such a lineage may help us, as Tomoko Masuzawa has recently put it, to "venture a little further into the present epistemic mire, into our own time."[6] Indeed, as we will see, even a scholar such as Gregory Schopen, himself on the very cutting edge of Buddhist studies, not only uses language nearly identical to Smith's, but also seems to inherit, perhaps unwittingly, some of Smith's preconceptions in his discussions of presence in the

---

[5]William Robertson Smith, *Lectures on the Religion of the Semites* (London: Adam Black, 1889), p. 173. See also pp. 194-95, p. 518, and p. 544 for other examples of the immanent divine.

[6]Tomoko Masuzawa, *In Search of Dreamtime: The Quest for the Origin of Religion* (Chicago: University of Chicago Press, 1993).

context of Buddhist relics.

This idea of a *paramparā* is very much central to this book, both in terms of my overall methodological position and in terms of my specific understanding of the representation of wisdom in medieval Buddhist art. Indeed, as I shall maintain throughout this study, it is impossible to understand the dynamics - how and why it was made, how it was perceived - of a tenth-century Buddha image without also understanding something of the complex layers of thought and practice that preceded such a specific image. In this regard, it is perhaps helpful to introduce another Indian image, that of a text and its commentaries; traditionally, a Sanskrit text is printed along with its various commentaries, such that any interaction with the "original" text always involves an interaction with many layers of interpretation of that text. To encounter the text in the present is, in a very important sense, inextricably bound up with the ways others have encountered that text in the past.[7]

Returning now to the issue of presence, Catherine Bell has recently reviewed some of the fundamental, dominant views of ritual in Western scholarship, from Durkheim to the present. What she has found, whether in the work of Durkheim, Lévi-Strauss, Victor Turner, or Clifford Geertz, is the positing of a basic opposition between thought and action. Rituals thus "dramatize, enact, materialize, or perform a system of symbols.... [B]y enacting the symbolic systems, ritual was said [by such scholars] to integrate two irreducible aspects of symbols, the conceptual (worldview) and the dispositional (ethos)."[8] Additionally, rituals enable the theorist to abstract conceptual categories and cultural particularities:

> The opposition of the theorist and the ritual object becomes homologized with two other oppositions, namely, the opposition that differentiates ritual

---

[7]For a very useful collection of essays on these matters, see Jeffrey R. Timm, ed., *Texts in Context: Traditional Hermeneutics in South Asia* (Albany: State University of New York, 1992).

[8]Catherine Bell, *Ritual Theory, Ritual Practice* (New York: Oxford University Press, 1992), p. 31.

> (beliefs versus activities) and the opposition of two fundamental sociocultural forces that it resolved by ritual (conceptual versus dispositional forces).... In the end, a model of ritual that integrates opposing sociocultural forces becomes homologized to a mode of theoretical discourse that reintegrates the dichotomy underlying the identification of a thinking theorist and an acting object.[9]

The theorist then maintains and projects, whether explicitly or implicitly, a basic thought-action dichotomy, with the (all-knowing) theorist subject doing the thinking, and the (un-knowing) native object doing the acting. Ritual activity, in this theoretical world, is thus not meaningful to the participant in ritual (or at least not in any conscious way), but to the observing theorist who uses it as a window into cultural activity.

Such a basic dichotomous stance can be seen in any number of critical positions - Freud-influenced theories of unconscious motivation, Malinowskian functionalism, Lévi-Straussian structural models. Bell's analysis of this critical position, this mostly unarticulated dichotomy between thought and action is incisively to the point. As she puts it, a "closed and highly structured discourse may be necessary *only* to an attempt to generate and secure bodies of knowledge that have a particular function with regard to the knower and the known: they set up a relationship based on differentiating one from the other while inscribing the basis for this differentiation into the nature of the object itself, that is, the reality of ritual."[10] Such a critique, although not entirely novel,[11] is certainly relevant, pointing as it does to the persistent tendency of allowing - or perhaps more commonly, of forcing - the theory to govern the phenomenon.

With specific regard to the presence of the divine, this

---

[9]Ibid., p.32.

[10]Ibid., p. 48; Bell is specifically talking about Geertz here, but her comments are more broadly applicable.

[11]Dan Sperber has a similar, though ultimately less admonishing, thing to say about Lévi-Strauss in his *Rethinking Symbolism* (Cambridge: Cambridge University Press, 1975), p. 84.

tendency is most evident in the two opposing monothetic views of presence to which I have already alluded. Those scholars situated in the immediate Robertson Smith/Frazer lineage, most notably and most notoriously Lucian Levy Bruhl, see in the primitive worship of inanimate objects a pre-logical (or really non-logical) mentality at work. The primitive simply does not, and is not able to, cognize the difference between the god/sacred and the object. He or she sees instead only affinity and identity, an ontological presence. For those scholars following in the lineage of Freud, there is in contrast only a symbolic (or semantic, in the Peircian sense of signifiers, signifieds, and indexes) presence at play, by which the devotee is not worshipping the god/sacred *in* the tree (or *as* the tree), but worshipping the tree as a symbol, or a signifier, or simply a reminder of the god/sacred which is elsewhere. What is most pertinent here is not which side is *true*, or even at this point which side is more methodologically sound (although I shall have more to say on this shortly). Rather, it is precisely the dichotomy that is the issue for the moment; that is, it is the existence and perpetuation of the two monothetic theoretical camps that needs to be called into question.

Several scholars in the history of religions have, I think, gone a long way in breaking down this dichotomy. Jonathan Smith, for instance, has in several of his works greatly complicated (his own self-professed scholarly *raison d'être*) the dominant views of ritual, arguing that in fact ritual actors are not unknowing dupes simply going through the agreed-upon motions, but instead conscious agents who often know not only what they are doing but also why, even if they are acting out an idealized view of the world in ritual.[12] The anthropologist Stanley Tambiah, following a similar line of argument, has also called into question the Durkheimian stance, arguing that ritual does not serve to evoke feelings in individuals that allow them to act out deep social and cultural values in any direct way

---

[12]Smith first articulated this position in his important "The Bare Facts of Ritual," in *Imagining Religion* (Chicago: University of Chicago Press, 1982), pp. 53-65. In the course of the twenty years since he first wrote this article Smith has considerably enriched this analysis; see in particular *To Take Place: Toward Theory in Ritual* (Chicago: University of Chicago Press, 1987).

(antistructure, *communitas*); rather, Tambiah argues, there is a distancing effect in ritual that allows for the articulation and dramatic reflection of attitudes of institutionalized communication.[13]

A perhaps more notable, and certainly more overlooked, exception to the dichotomy between thought and action is found in E.E. Evans-Pritchard's work on the Nuer. Evans-Pritchard's analysis of the presence of the divine in Nuer religion, specifically his discussion of the ritual substitution of objects in sacrifice, has generated considerable debate and controversy over the years - including a heated debate that ran in the journal *Man* - but his basic insights are still pertinent, and, perhaps more importantly, in my view still valid. In a section of *Nuer Religion* entitled "The Problem of Symbols," Evans-Pritchard attempts to explicate what it is, exactly, that is operative when Nuer make statements such as "crocodile is Spirit." What is immediately striking about Evans-Pritchard's work is his consistent attempt to get at indigenous categories, to recognize that there may, in fact, be a difference between the way *they* see the world and talk about the world and the way that *we* do, and that this difference need not be cast in dichotomous "rational/non-rational" terminology. Thus when a Nuer says "crocodile is Spirit," he or she is not, according to Evans-Pritchard, simply stating an erroneous ontological affinity, but is in fact engaging in an indigenous mode of critical reflection and interpretation. The Nuer "is not saying that the crocodile is Spirit - it is not so for him - but that certain people so regard it."[14] For instance, in certain sacrificial contexts, the Nuer substitute a cucumber for the more traditional (and desirable) ox:

> In doing so they are asserting something rather more than that it takes the place of an ox. They do not, of course, say that cucumbers are oxen, and in speaking of a particular cucumber as an ox in a sacrificial situation they are only indicating that it may be thought of as an ox in that particular situation; and

---

[13]See in particular Tambiah's article "A Performative Approach to Ritual," *Proceedings of the British Academy* 65 (1979): 113-69. Also see Bell, *Ritual Theory, Ritual Practice* pp. 41-42.
[14]E.E. Evans-Pritchard, *Nuer Religion* (London: Oxford University Press, 1956), p.127.

> they act accordingly by performing the sacrificial rites as closely as possible to what happens when the victim is an ox. The resemblance is conceptual, not perceptual. The "is" rests on qualitative analogy. And the expression is asymmetrical, a cucumber is an ox, but an ox is not a cucumber.[15]

This passage could, of course, be read simply as an example of what I have been calling symbolic/semantic presence. The cucumber is the signifier, pointing beyond its ontological presence as the ritual object to the signified presence of the sacred (or, in this context, Spirit). Be that as it may - although such an interpretation does an injustice to the subtleties and nuances of Evans-Pritchard's discussion - what is interesting here is Evans-Pritchard's attention to the indigenous exegesis that goes on, the *conscious* and intentional act of ritual substitution, and the contested nature of that substitution. The actors here are not unknowing objects, but knowing subjects, and they are negotiating their own ritual acts and the significance of those acts.

Turning now to Bourdieu, let me first say, as a caveat, that Bourdieu's theoretical stance defies easy summation, and any attempt to do so is to risk radically simplifying and misrecognizing (to use one of his own terms) the complexity of his analysis. Furthermore, much of Bourdieu's work is very much context-specific. Nonetheless, it is possible to extract aspects of his various works and some of the more useful insights he offers, and to apply them outside of the specific contexts in which he discusses them; indeed, as I shall maintain, Bourdieu's conceptions of *habitus*, strategy, and field are especially germane to understanding medieval Indian Buddhist representations of wisdom.

In his development of the concept of *habitus*, Bourdieu moves beyond the theoretical tenets of both functionalism and structuralism - which have dominated thought about ritual for half a century - and develops a theory of practice which, while not entirely abandoning either stance, establishes a dramatically different, fundamentally

---

[15]Ibid., p. 128.

dialectical position. Here Bourdieu is writing of kinship in particular, but his position is more generally applicable to any number of specifically religious phenomena as well:

> To treat kin relationships as something people *make*, and with which they *do* something, is not merely to substitute a "functionalist" for a "structuralist" interpretation, as current taxonomies might lead one to believe; it is radically to question the implicit theory of practice which causes the anthropological tradition to see kin relationships "in the form of an object or an intuition," as Marx puts it, rather than *in the form of the practices which produce, reproduce, and use them* by reference to necessarily practical functions.... [T]hey are the product of *strategies* (conscious or unconscious) oriented towards the satisfaction of material and symbolic interests and organized by reference to a determinate set of economic conditions. Once one forgets all that is implied in extracting from the product the principles of its production...one condemns oneself to proceed as if the regular product had been produced in accordance with the rules.[16]

Structures, in the sense of established rules, exist for Bourdieu, but they exist only in so far as there are agents to use them, to manipulate them, and even to ignore them; and the degree to which these strategies actually *work* "rises with the degree to which they actually or potentially fulfill functions indispensable to them or, to put it less ambiguously, the extent to which they do or can satisfy vital material and symbolic *interests*."[17]

Given the slipperiness of Bourdieu, and given his context-specific analyses, I think it important to stress that Bourdieu offers a

---

[16]Pierre Bourdieu, *Outline of a Theory of Practice* (Cambridge: Cambridge University Press, 1977), pp. 35-36, emphasis added.
[17]Ibid., p. 38.

broadly-applicable way of looking at structures such as rules and doctrines that allows one to explicate how individuals (and complexes of individuals) both follow such things, and also how they manipulate them, how they negotiate with and contest these rules and doctrines.[18] This is what makes his concept of *habitus* so rich. As systems of what he calls "durable, transposable *dispositions*," these are not simply fixed and unchanging structures that govern individual and collective behavior. The system is not static, but dynamically dialectical; things are always in a state of flux.. *Habitus* refers to those systems which "function as structuring structures, that is, as principles of the generation and structuring of practices and representations which can be objectively 'regulated' and 'regular' without in any way being the product of obedience to rules...." Such systems, or principles, thus enable "agents to cope with unforeseen and ever-changing situations," in a manner that is neither predetermined nor unconscious, but always a matter of tension.[19]

It is this kind of tension, I want to suggest, that is at play in the Buddhist conceptions of the absence/presence of the Buddha in images. Practicing Buddhists are able to maintain *at once* that the Buddha is present in such things as relics, sculptures, and paintings, *and at the same time* able to hold the conflicting (and seemingly contradictory) view that it is only the emblem, or reminder, of the no-longer-present Buddha that they worship. In other words, they are able *simultaneously* to maintain an ontological and a semantic/symbolic position on the presence of the Buddha. And, what is more, as I shall argue shortly, they use sculptural images as a means of reflecting on the tensions between these two simultaneously held positions.

---

[18]Talal Asad has pointed out that Bourdieu's conception of *habitus* bears a striking resemblance to one formulated by Marcel Mauss in an essay entitled "Body Techniques." Mauss chooses this Latin term over the French "*habitude*" in order to get at the variability of such "habits." "These 'habits' do not vary just with individuals and their imitations; they vary especially between societies, educations, proprieties and fashions, prestige." Quoted in Asad, *Genealogies of Religion: Discipline and Reasons of Power in Christianity and Islam* (Baltimore: The Johns Hopkins University Press, 1993), p.75.

[19]Bourdieu, *Outline of a Theory of Practice*, p. 72.

II. The Problems with Images: From Idolatry to Iconoclasm

> For pictorial representation is made use of in Churches for this reason; that such as are ignorant of letters may at least read by looking at the walls what they cannot read in books.
>
> Gregory the Great[20]

The history of religions discipline could easily be characterized as, to use Lévi-Strauss' familiar trope, the *bricoleur*'s discipline *par excellence.* Historians of religions, like Lévi-Strauss' jack-of-all-trades, have a striking range of available methodologies and a vast array of materials on which to work. But while historians of religions have utilized an impressive array of theoretical tools in their studies, they have also worked almost exclusively on literary materials, only seldom making use of religiously significant visual materials such as sculptures, paintings, and architecture in their attempts to reconstruct the patterns and varieties of religious experience. Even those scholars who have considered visual data, and there have been some notable exceptions to the rule,[21] have tended to do so in light of the available literary materials, and the visual is frequently said to "illustrate" the textual. This disciplinary literary bias is particularly evident in the specific context of Buddhism: scholars have described, analyzed, and constructed a Buddhism which is almost exclusively contained in texts.

Although this literary focus certainly has facilitated the examination of the vastly complex doctrinal and intellectual systems of Buddhism, it has also created an incomplete picture that obscures some vital aspects of Buddhist thought and practice. If one of the

---

[20]In Philip Schaff and Henry Wace, eds., *A Select Library of Nicene and Post-Nicene Fathers of the Christian Church*, second series, vol. 13 (Edinburgh: T. and T. Clark, 1989), p. 23.

[21]See for instance Paul Mus, *Barabudur: Esquisse d'une histoire du bouddhisme fondée sur la critique archéologique textes* (Hanoi: Imprimerie d'Extrême-Orient, 1935); S.G.F. Brandon, *Man and God in Art and Ritual: A Study of Iconography, Architecture and Ritual Action as Primary Evidence of Religious Belief and Practice* (New York: Scribners, 1975); and Kay Read, "Binding Reeds and Burning Hearts: Mexica-Tenochca Concepts of Time and Sacrifice." Ph.D. dissertation, University of Chicago, 1991.

underlying disciplinary goals of the history of religions is to create the most complete picture of a religious tradition as is possible, then we must find room in our academic toolboxes for the visual. For this reason, then, the present study is perhaps as much an attempt to demonstrate a methodology that would facilitate such an expansion as it is an attempt to expand our understanding of Buddhism.

Before moving into the details of the kind of presence involved in Buddhist artistic images, therefore, it is worthwhile and important first to consider the very place of such images in the history of religions and art history disciplines. It should, I think, raise few academic eyebrows to point out that the history of religions has traditionally been a text-oriented discipline. If Max Müller can be considered the great founder of the discipline as we know it, his *Ur*-methodology is dominated by philology. In short, for Müller and the generations of scholars who followed in his footsteps, the history of religions is fundamentally about texts. There are, to be sure, good reasons for this focus on texts. Texts speak to us in ways that rituals and music and images simply cannot; they speak in complex languages, and often they speak to one another. Furthermore, texts often contain explicit keys for their decipherment in the form of commentaries and intertextual glosses. Texts, in a sense, speak about themselves. Images, in contrast, are hardly so loquacious. Indeed, they are essentially mute. As Giulio Carlo Argan has put it, the work of visual art is silent: "It is always the scholar alone who speaks in the presence of the work of art, and his entire problem consists in deciding what kind of talking he should do."[22]

In so consistently relying on written texts, however, historians of religions have frequently overlooked some of the serious limitations such a methodology imposes. Gregory Schopen, for one, has charged that the history of religions' textual bias has created the illusion that textual data represent what *real* (or *average*) people *really* do (or did). Writing specifically about Charles Thomas, G.F. Snyder, and Mircea Eliade, but more generally about the underlying assumptions of the history of religions as a discipline, Schopen argues that scholars have

---

[22]Giulio Carlo Argan, "Ideology and Iconology," in W.J.T. Mitchell, ed., *The Language of Images* (Chicago: University of Chicago Press, 1980), p.20.

categorically refused to consider data outside of the realm of texts: "[T]he relationship of what early Christian people," for example, "actually did, or actually believed, to 'the literary material' falls outside the purview of the historian of Christianity. Christianity - like Buddhism - apparently only exists in texts."[23]

There is perhaps no more clear example of the textual bias in the study of religion than in the case of Buddhism. From the moment Buddhism was "discovered" by the West, it was accepted that the true religion was contained in its textual traditions.[24] By virtually ignoring other forms of Buddhist practice - which were seen to be syncretistically corrupted by Hinduism and indigenous cults - Buddhism was, essentially, made into a rarified taxonomic object. As Philip Almond aptly puts it:

> Buddhism, by 1860, had come to exist, not in the Orient but in the Oriental libraries and institutes of the West, in its texts and manuscripts, at desks of the Western savants who interpreted it. It had become a textual object, defined, classified, and interpreted through its own textuality.... By the middle of the century, the Buddhism that existed "out there" was beginning to be judged by a West that *alone* knew what Buddhism was, is, and ought to be.[25]

This "ought to be" is what is contained in the doctrinally recognized (or sanctioned) texts. Ironically, however, even Schopen - himself so critical of this textual bias - indirectly illustrates just how methodologically pernicious this bias is.

---

[23]Gregory Schopen, "Archaeology and Protestant Presuppositions in the Study of Indian Buddhism," *History of Religion* 31(1991): 1-23, p.18.

[24]Eugène Burnouf, who is generally considered to be the "founder" of Buddhist studies, had this to say in his 1844 volume, *Introduction a l'histoire du buddhisme indien* (Paris: Impremerie Royal, 1844): "Il résultera de cet examen, que les éléments fondamentaux et véritablement antiques du Buddhisme devront être cherches dans ce qu'auront conserve de commun les deux redactions des livres religieux...," p. 31.

[25]Philip Almond, *The British Discovery of Buddhism* (Cambridge: Cambridge University Press, 1988), p. 13. See also the essays in Donald Lopez, ed., *The Curators of the Buddha: The Study of Buddhism Under Colonialism* (Chicago: University of Chicago Press, 1995).

Schopen's general critique concludes with the suggestion that the textual bias of historians of religions rests upon, indeed *covers up*, what to him looks very much like "a religious or theological position." "Embedded, for example, in apparently neutral archaeological and historical method might very well be a decidedly nonneutral and narrowly limited Protestant assumption as to where 'religion' is actually located."[26] Historians of religions, according to Schopen, have "inherited" basic religious and ideological doctrines that have, seemingly without their awareness, drastically skewed their methodologies. "It is possible," writes Schopen, "that what was in origin a sixteenth-century Protestant conception of where 'true' religion is located has been so thoroughly absorbed into the Western intellectual tradition that its polemical and theological origins have been forgotten and that it is now taken too often entirely as a given."[27]

Schopen's critique of this academic *paramparā* certainly should be taken seriously by historians of religions, and by anyone writing about Buddhism, although it is worth pointing out that he is hardly the first to assert that the history of religions discipline my be undergirded by a crypto-theological agenda. Indeed, this has become something of a hackneyed refrain in critical discussions of Eliade. In his own constructive work, Schopen goes a long way in breaking away from the confines of the textual bias, but at the same time he embraces - quite self consciously, I think - what might be called a "verbal bias." Indeed, so many of his attempts to illustrate, as he puts it, "what religious people of a given community actually did and how they lived,"[28] rely almost exclusively on philological minutiae. Thus although I rely heavily on Schopen's methodological insights and his

---

[26]Schopen, "Protestant Presuppositions," p.19.

[27]Ibid., p.22.

[28]Gregory Schopen, "Burial '*Ad Sanctos*', and the Physical Presence of the Buddha in Early Indian Buddhism: A Study in the Archeology of Religions," *Religion* 17 (1987): 193-225, p. 194. Margaret Miles makes an almost identical point in her *Image As Insight* (Boston: Beacon Press, 1985) when she writes that verbal texts, "almost exclusively the product of culturally privileged, highly educated, male, and most frequently monastic authors, constitute the great bulk of the literary products of Christianity before the modern period. From these writings, we can learn a great deal about how their authors thought, something about how they felt, and sometimes a bit about how they lived. But we cannot expect to learn from them how the large majority of the people in their cultures thought, felt, and lived," pp. 9-10.

general position in much of my analysis in this book, I shall also attempt to move away from, or move beyond, this verbal bias and thus help to broaden our scope to include the visual.

Of central relevance to the present study, then, is the specific problem of how the history of religions discipline (and religious studies in general) has - or more properly, has not - dealt with visual images. Just as rituals have, until rather recently, largely been farmed out to anthropologists, so too have images been largely left to the specialists - art historians. Schopen argues that what underlies this academic buck passing is a deep vein of Protestantism; historians of religions, children of the Enlightenment, are fundamentally suspicious when it comes to visual images, because images are about error, about confusing the illusion with the reality.[29] In this ironically neo-Tylorian view, historians of religions exhibit what might be called iconoclastic *survivals*, deeply rooted holdovers (or hangovers) from the vicious iconoclasm of the Reformation. Let me pause for a moment, then, and briefly consider what is at stake here.

The art historian and theorist W.J.T. Mitchell has aptly described iconoclasm in language that, at least in spirit if not in letter, could easily be applied to many historians of religions' approaches to visual images:

> [I]conoclasm typically proceeds by assuming that the power of the image is felt by somebody *else*; what the iconoclast sees is the emptiness, vanity, and impropriety of the idol.... The rhetoric of iconoclasm

[29] The early study of Buddhism, in particular, is marked by a consistent devaluation of ritual practices in general; the Buddha is portrayed as a rational reformer, akin to Luther, and ritual practices such as relic and image veneration are portrayed as a late corruption and degeneration of the "authentic" teachings of the Buddha. As Almond has noted, part of this anti-ritualistic portrayal of Buddhism was fueled by the general Victorian sentiment toward Catholicism; see Almond, pp. 123-26. See also Kevin Trainor's discussion in his *Relics, Ritual, and Representation in Buddhism: Rematerializing the Sri Lankan Thervāda Tradition* (Cambridge: Cambridge University Press, 1997), particularly Chapter One; and see Jonathon Silk's "The Victorian Creation of Buddhism," *Journal of Indian Philosophy* 22 (1994): 171-96. It is worth noting that this anti-ritualistic characterization of Buddhism is still very much with us; witness Walpola Rahula's statement in his *What the Buddha Taught* (New York: Grove Press, 1974) - the standard text in countless introductory Buddhism courses - that the Buddhist path "has nothing to do with belief, prayer, worship or ceremony," p. 49.

> is thus a rhetoric of exclusion and domination, a caricature of the other as one who is involved in irrational, obscene behavior from which (fortunately) we are exempt.... The images of the idolatrous...must be declared "dumb," "mute," "empty," or "illusory." *Our* god, by contrast - reason, science, criticism, the Logos, the spirit of human language and civilized conversation - is invisible, dynamic, and incapable of being reified in any material, spatial image.[30]

The history of iconoclasm in the West is well documented,[31] and carries with it all manner of theological baggage. It is worth briefly mentioning, however, one of the giants of the debate, Gregory the Great. What makes Gregory relevant here is his articulation, some twelve hundred years ago, of an attitude toward images which is very much still with us. According to Gregory, images are the *libri idiotarum*, the "books of the illiterate." In a letter to Serenus, Bishop of Massila, Gregory writes: "For pictorial representation is made use of in Churches for this reason; that such as are ignorant of letters may at least read by looking at the walls what they cannot read in books. Your Fraternity therefore should have both preserved the images and prohibited the people from adoration of them...."[32] This stance is echoed by Thomas Aquinas - images are "for the instruction of the unlettered, who might learn from then *as if from books*" - and countless others.[33] Both Bonaventure and John of Damascus, in quite

---

[30]W.J.T. Mitchell, *Iconology: Image, Text, Ideology* (Chicago: University of Chicago Press, 1986), p.113.

[31]See for instance Sergiusz Michalski, *The Reformation and the Visual Arts: The Protestant Image Question in Western and Eastern Europe* (London: Routledge, 1993), especially Chapter 3, "Iconoclasm: Rites of Destruction," pp. 75-98; Jaroslav Pelikan, *The Christian Tradition: A History of the Development of Doctrine* 5 Volumes, *Volume II: The Spirit of Eastern Christendom (600-1700)* (Chicago: University of Chicago Press, 1974), especially Chapter 3, "Images of the Invisable," pp. 91-145; David Freedberg, *The Power of Images: Studies in the History and Theory of Response* (Chicago: University of Chicago Press, 1989), Chapter 14, "Idolatry and Iconoclasm," pp. 378-428; and Joseph Gutmann, ed., *No Graven Images: Studies in Art and the Hebrew Bible* (New York: Katv, 1971).

[32]In Philip Schaff and Henry Wace, eds., *A Select Library of Nicene and Post-Nicene Fathers of the Christian Church*, p. 23.

[33]David Freedberg, *The Power of Images*, p.166.

different contexts, develop this basic notion into the concept that images are an aid in "seeing" what is to the eye invisible, that is Christ. As Bonaventure puts it, "since the divine is not at all sensible, susceptible to the normal responses of the senses, but only exists on the level of pure spirit, we can only perceive it by means of objectification in the form of images."[34]

I will return to this notion of the image as the visual form of the invisible in the next chapter, in my discussion of the presence of the Buddha in visual images, for there are significant similarities between certain Buddhist interpretations of presence and those of Bonaventure, John of Damascus, and others. The point I wish to stress here, however, is the degree to which the legacy of Gregory's *libri idiotarum* has allowed us, if not unconsciously forced us, to see images as *merely* visual texts to be read. Again, we see the *paramparā* in action, and the degree to which seemingly long-dead ideas and biases are alive and well.

I began this section by noting that historians of religions are at best "visually challenged," and I have proceeded to suggest that they are at worst iconoclastically motivated. If historians of religion are unable to adequately discuss images, though, art historians - the visual specialists - ought to be able to provide some guidance. However, art history has its own forms of textual biases to combat. Indeed, perhaps the most influential art historian of this century, Erwin Panofsky, had this to say about what would become art history's dominant methodology, iconology:

> While we believe ourselves to identify the motifs on the basis of our practical experience pure and simple, we really *read* "what we see" according to the manner in which objects and events were expressed by forms under varying historical conditions. In doing this, we subject our practical experience to a controlling principle which can be called history of style. Iconographical analysis, dealing with images,

[34]Ibid., p. 166.

> stories and allegories instead of with motifs, presupposes, of course, much more than that familiarity with objects and events which we acquire by practical experience. It presupposes a familiarity with specific themes or concepts *as transmitted through literary sources*, whether acquired by purposeful *reading* or by oral tradition.[35]

The goal of iconology, to see through the work of art into the mental landscape that produced it, is certainly laudable, and the spirit of Panofsky's insistence on situating a work of art in its proper social and historical contexts fundamentally informs my own methodological position; it is his methodological presuppositions and the uses to which his methods have been put which should raise our suspicion.

In the introduction to a recent volume of essays that discusses some of the problematics of Panofsky's legacy, Brendan Cassidy writes: "He swept up in his wake scores of eager young historians in thrall to the sheer intellectual excitement of his approach. In attempting to emulate the master's erudition many abandoned themselves to an orgy of text hunting in the indices of the *Patrologia Latina*, in search of that textual nugget that would reveal the secret of a Netherlandish triptych or an Italian fresco."[36] This all has resulted in a kind of "iconographical malpractice," with texts, and not the images that they are meant to illuminate, once again dominating the scene. "This may be understandable," Cassidy notes,

> since the written word provides the milieu in which academics, even art historians, are most comfortable. The visual is more intractable, offering only ambiguous answers to many of the questions that the text-bound historian is inclined to ask. However, it is

[35]Erwin Panofsky, *Studies in Iconology: Humanistic Themes in the Art of the Renaissance* (New York: Oxford University Press, 1939), p. 11, emphasis added.

[36]Brendan Cassidy, "Introduction: Iconography, Texts, and Audiences," in Brendan Cassidy, ed., *Iconography at the Crossroads: Papers from the Colloquium Sponsored by the Index of Christian Art, Princeton University, 23-24 March 1990* (Princeton: Department of Art and Archaeology, Princeton University, 1993), pp. 6-7.

> not the appeal to texts for clarification of the meaning of an image that is the issue, for iconography would scarcely be possible without texts. *It is rather the tendency to reduce art to illustration of particular kinds of texts* and the inclination to account for medieval and Renaissance images *as if they were verbal statements made by non-verbal means*. Equally problematic is the failure to appreciate the complexity of the relationships between words and images.[37]

Cassidy's analysis of the problem seems to me to hit the mark exactly, not only in the context of art history, but also in the history of religions.

There is no question that images are, in some sense, texts, but the real issue here is not the "text as image" language so readily assumed by historians of religions and art; rather, it is the reduction of the visual image to the status of the verbal. The methodology I advocate here is not, therefore, one based on the outright abandonment of texts. Rather, what I propose is a methodology that rethinks and reformulates how historians of religions use texts *in relation* to visual objects. For certainly, scholars of religion cannot be expected simply to give up texts, even when dealing with things visual; indeed, texts provide invaluable insight into the original contexts in which a particular visual object was located. But as Cassidy notes, such scholars "must also know when to let go of their texts and approach images on their own terms and on terms that would have been familiar to their creators."[38]

Cassidy's gentle imperative, "to let go of their texts and approach images on their own terms...," is, however, too seductive not to arouse at least some suspicion. What exactly, one might ask, is an image's "own terms"? By following such advice, are we necessarily led into the methodologically tricky - some would say treacherous - waters of aesthetics? In a trio of books explicitly attempting to

---

[37]Ibid., emphasis added.
[38]Ibid., p. 10.

navigate precisely these waters, Robert Plant Armstrong develops a methodology that completely rejects the "image as language" or "image as symbol" approach. "Such things [visual images] are not, at base, symbols of something else (a symbol beings something that has arbitrary form and is held by convention to 'stand for' something else): they *are* whatever they are."[39] Images are:

> [A]n estate of human consciousness, a unique binding together in human cognition of objective phenomena and of subjective values concerning them.... The *presence* achieved in a work is the sum total of all those powers that excite it, quickening it from its core to its flanks, charging it with significant perusals - the affirmations and interrogations - of consciousness. Thus, inasmuch as power is variable in degree and in intensity, it follows that so also is presence.[40]

Armstrong thus sees in visual images a fundamental power, a power that taps into something basic in the human consciousness.

David Freedberg focuses on similar issues in his massive *The Power of Images*, and like Armstrong, he sees an inherent power in images that transcends cultural, geographical, and historical contexts:

> I proceed in the belief that however much we intellectualize, even if that notion is spontaneous, there still remains a basic level of reaction that cuts across historical, social, and other contextual boundaries. It is at precisely this level - which pertains to our psychological, biological, and

[39]Robert Plant Armstrong, *The Powers of Presence: Consciousness, Myth, and Affecting Presence* (Philadelphia: University of Pennsylvania Press, 1981), pp. 5-6. See also Armstrong's two earlier works, *The Affecting Presence: An Essay in Humanistic Anthropology* (Urbana: University of Illinois Press, 1971), and *Wellspring: On the Myth and Source of Culture* (Berkeley: The University of California Press, 1975). In these studies, Armstrong develops a complex theory of the status, function, and power of visual images through an extended examination of what he calls the "aesthetic of invocation" and the "aesthetic of virtuosity," the necessary conditions, or means, for the power of images.

[40]Armstrong, *The Powers of Presence*, pp.14-16.

> neurological status as members of the same species - that our cognition of images is allied with that of all men and women, and it is this still point which we seek.... [W]e may think that our responses are culturally conditioned; but we also know that we cannot, by thinking in this way, wholly subvert or repress the psychological processes that lead us to invest images with powers that make them work, with qualities that make them seem lively, with the ability to rouse us to empathy, incite us to action, and provide us with a mode of articulating the recollection that fades.[41]

Armstrong and Freedberg offer important methodological insights into the dynamics of imagery, and I will have reason to return to them both at various points in my subsequent discussion of representations of *prajñā.* But both of them too easily slip into a kind of wooly trans-culturalism at the expense of context. Certainly, I would contend, we must pay attention to the kinds of emotive power inherent in visual images; we must heed the power of images to provoke very strong, very real reactions - in the same way that we must recognize the same sort of power in the written and spoken word. But in so doing we must not forget that images are always located in a specific context: all images are local.

There is, however, a final general issue that must be dealt with here, and that is the very question of the visual image as a sort of *language* or *text*. For even though we must to some degree admit that images are not, or at least not always, exactly *texts* to be *read*, we must also recognize that they do involve something like a *language*. As Freedberg notes at the end of his book: "However much we may strive to do so, we can never entirely extract ourselves from our sense of the signified in the sign; and our responses are irrevocably informed by that."[42] Freedberg here uses the language of semiotics almost, it seems, without being aware of it. The use of semiotic terminology -

---

[41]David Freedberg, *The Power of Images*, pp. 22-23, p. 47.
[42]Ibid., p. 436.

the sign, the signifier, the signified, and so forth - has become so common in discussing images that it is rarely questioned. Indeed, even those scholars who take the "image as language" trend to task seem comfortable with semiotic terminology. Keith Moxey, in a short article entitled "The Politics of Iconology," writes: "The study of the historical horizon becomes the study of the ways in which various signifying systems percolated through works of art, as well as through the societies in which they were produced. Works of art become systems of signification that are contiguous to and continuous with the systems that articulate and structure all other aspects of social life."[43] Although he does not develop it further, Moxey's use of Saussure's language, via Peirce, is extremely useful, and I will further make use of it below when I turn specifically to the Buddhist discourse on "presence" in visual images. As a methodological caveat, however, it is, I think, necessary to emphasize that although visual images do "signify," they do so in a way that is considerably different than the way words signify.

One thing that makes images different from languages is the complexity of the signifier/signified relationship. *What* is signified by any given image necessarily depends on the context in which the image is situated. "Images are not just a particular kind of sign," writes W.J.T. Mitchell, "but something like an actor on the historical stage, a presence or character endowed with legendary status, a history that parallels and participates in the stories we tell ourselves about our own evolution from creatures 'made in the image' of a creator, to creatures who make themselves and their world in their own image."[44] As Mitchell argues, images are not stable, static, or in any metaphysical sense permanent. Rather, they are perceived differently by different viewers, and they perform, I would add, very different functions in different contexts. Images involve what Mitchell calls "multisensory apprehension and interpretation;"[45] indeed, as I will

---

[43]Keith Moxey "The Politics of Iconology," in Cassidy, ed., *Iconography at the Crossroads*, pp. 29-30.

[44] Mitchell, *Iconology*, p.9.

[45]Ibid., pp. 13-14.

argue, they also involve multiple *misinterpretations* and *misapprehensions*.

My broad methodological point, then, is that visual images *are* something like a language, but they are not *merely* language. When, for instance, a West African ceremonial mask is describe as being "just cloth," or "merely a material object," or "only a symbol for," or a "signifier of," such descriptions entirely miss the point. As Freedburg points out, "this, of course, is just what the mask is not.... The image, once properly prepared, set up, adorned, and decorated, becomes the locus of the spirit. It becomes what it is taken to represent."[46] The image, in this sense, is *ontologically dialectical*, depending on the very complex, very dynamic contexts in which it is situated. "The essence of the dialectical image is its polyvalence - as object in the world, as representation, as analytic tool, as rhetorical device, as figure - most of all as a Janus-faced emblem of our predicament, a mirror of history, and window beyond it."[47]

One of the great dangers inherent in visual images is mistaking the image for the prototype, confusing the signifier with the signified. It is, in short, the fear of such an error that fuels iconoclasm. But it is also the very *possibility* of such an error that invests visual images with such power.

---

[46]Freedberg, *The Power of Images*, p. 31.
[47]Mitchell, *Iconology*, p. 205.

Chapter Two

PRESENT PRESENCE, PRESENT ABSENCE

> The padres gave us bonbons and stroked our hair to show us that they loved us. But they would also say to us constantly: "Look at your mud image. You are worshipping clay."
>
> Anagarika Dharmapala[1]

The question of the presence of the Buddha in physical objects - relics, *stūpas*, sculptures - is very much centered on the kinds of issues I have just been discussing, and it is a question that is at the heart of the use and production of artistic images in medieval Indian Buddhism. To begin with the general, there are two basic, overlapping levels of discourse here: first, there is that of various Buddhists in various geographical and historical milieus; second, there is that of the mostly Western scholars who write about them. The first discourse has, as we shall see, been developed since the Buddha's own lifetime. The scholarly debate, in turn, was initiated at the very beginnings of Buddhist studies in the mid-nineteenth century and is, not coincidentally, coeval with the broader discussions about the presence of the divine that I have been discussing in the previous chapter. I want to focus here on the latter of these two discourses, for I will turn to the specifics of the Buddhist case in Chapter Two. It is helpful, however, to give a general orientation, at least, and to lay out the basics of the Buddhists' own discourse now.

The Buddhist position can be divided roughly into a Hīnayāna, or for my purposes a Theravāda, and a Mahāyāna position.[2] The

---

[1]Anagarika Dharmapala, *Return to Righteousness*, Ananda Guruge, ed. (Colombo: Government Press, 1965), p. 683.

[2]For a useful survey of the main traits of the early Buddhist schools, see Nalinaksha's *Buddhist Sects in India* (Calcutta: Firma KLM, 1970). Let me say that I am using the distinction between Theravāda and Mahāyana quite tentatively here, thus attempting to avoid the very complex range of theoretical issues that arise in attempting to validate such a distinction.

Theravādin position, on its face at any rate, is relatively straightforward: the Buddha was an extraordinary man who lived in the sixth century BCE; he was endowed with certain extra-human powers, but was nonetheless a mortal who was born, lived, and died. As Steven Collins puts it: "Cognitively, the Buddha was a man who attained final enlightenment some 2500 years ago, and who, being both dead and during his life a preacher of the most extreme self-reliance in religious practice, is no longer available to assist the this-worldly or other-worldly aspirations of present-day Buddhists."[3] Therefore, to look for the presence of the Buddha in stones, relics, sculptures, etc., is to look in vain. These are merely reminders of the Buddha, and they thus serve to signify the Buddha who is himself no longer present, but whose life and teachings serve as both, to use Geertz' well known terms, a *model of* and a *model for* the ideal life.

The Mahāyāna position is more difficult to summarize briefly. Basically stated, though, without the many layers of philosophical complexity which constitute it, the various Buddhas were not merely mortals, but semi-divine beings who, although perhaps physically dead, remain in the world as active forces. Thus Mahāyāna Buddhists frequently maintain that the Buddha is indeed present in physical, otherwise inanimate objects, although from a philosophical point of view this presence is ultimately an illusion, an absence in the sense of *śūnyatā*, or emptiness. Malcolm David Eckel articulates this point in his *To See the Buddha* in this way: "From one point of view, the manifestation is an illusion, but, in a world where everything finally is an illusion, a manifestation can work just as efficiently as anything else to bring about a 'real' effect."[4] Already, I think, we can see the complexity we are in for.

---

[3]Steven Collins, *Selfless Persons: Imagery and Thought in Theravāda Buddhism* (Cambridge: Cambridge University Press, 1982), p. 18; as we will see, however, the Thevavāda discourse on presence and absence is considerably more complex and multivocal than Collins' summary statement lets on. See Trainor's *Relics, Ritual, and Representation* for an extended discussion of the complexities and ambiguities of the Theravāda context.

[4]Malcolm David Eckel, *To See the Buddha* (San Francisco: Harper/Collins, 1992), p. 85. It is significant here that the concept in question, *nirmāṇa*, connotes a manifestation precisely in the sense of a magically created *illusion*, in contrast to, say, the Brahmanical concept of the *avatāra*. For a rather complex discussion of *nirmāṇa* and its relation to *pariṇāma* and *adhiṣṭhāna*, see Eckel, pp. 90-92. I will return to Eckel's discussion of presence below.

The scholarly discourse on "presence" in the Buddhist context, although obviously more recent than the indigenous discourse, is perhaps no less involved than that of the Buddhists themselves, and it necessarily interweaves (and overlaps) the indigenous discourse. A particularly sharp exchange on this issue took place in the early 1980s between Richard Gombrich and Stanley Tambiah. This debate is well known and frequently cited in Buddhist studies, but it is particularly germane here and I think worth briefly reviewing, in part because it highlights precisely the sort of dichotomous impasse I have been discussing. It began with Gombrich's study of hill country Buddhism in contemporary Sri Lanka, *Precept and Practice*. In that book, Gombrich maintains that there are two distinct and conflicting modes of Buddhist practice, the cognitive and the affective (roughly coincidental with Gombrich's titular division). Cognitively, according to Gombrich, Buddhists know that the Buddha is not actually present in relics and *stūpa*s and sculptures; this is the position in accord with the "official" doctrinal position in the Pāli Canon. Affectively, however, Buddhists pay little attention to doctrinal strictures; in reality, they act *as if* the Buddha is really present. What people say they believe is the cognitive level; what people *really* do, often in spite of what they *say* they do, is the affective level.[5]

Tambiah, in his *The Buddhist Saints of the Forest and the Cult of Amulets*, argues a position diametrically opposed to Gombrich's. Indeed, Tambiah castigates Gombrich, calling his precept/practice dichotomy "simpleminded," "arbitrarily imposed," and "theoretically untenable."[6] According to Tambiah, there is ample evidence throughout the vast corpus of Theravāda literature that the Buddha was thought to be present in images and relics. As Tambiah puts it, these objects were endowed with the "radiance" and "fiery energy" of the Buddha himself.[7] Tambiah, however, does not himself argue for

---

[5]Richard Gombrich, *Precept and Practice: Traditional Buddhism in the Rural Highlands of Ceylon* (Oxford: Clarendon Press, 1971), pp. 4-5.
[6]Stanley Tambiah, *The Buddhist Saints of the Forest and the Cult of Amulets* (Cambridge: Cambridge University Press, 1984), p. 375, n. 11.
[7]Ibid., p. 203.

any sort of ontological presence, but instead introduces and applies Charles Peirce's concept of the "indexical symbol."[8] By this Tambiah means that sculptures and other physical objects are both associated with the represented object (the Buddha) by conventional semantic rules, and at the same time related in a pragmatic, existential manner to what they represent.[9] "The Buddha's words, said long ago, are partially captured and clothed in the *Dhamma* texts and are vehicles of instruction and remembrance; the Buddha's presence manifest long ago is 'indexically' present...in images and relics and other icons and indices, but they too are vehicles that aid human understanding."[10] Here Tambiah is also developing Paul Mus' position that images, relics, and other icons serve as reminders of the Buddha's absence, and are thus objects intended for meditation on the Buddha's teaching, particularly the fundamental truth of impermanence.[11]

These two positions have served to frame, both explicitly and implicitly, many subsequent discussions of Buddhist practice generally, and the Buddha's presence specifically. The problem, however, is that what have, again, is a false dichotomy. Schopen, in an influential series of articles developing the "archaeological" methodology I have already mentioned, has implicitly challenged both Gombrich and Tambiah. He presents a body of evidence that suggests that the idea of the Buddha's presence was as much a cognitively held monastic doctrine as an affective lay practice - thus calling into question the very existence of a precept/practice dichotomy - and that

---

[8]See C.S. Peirce, "The Icon, Index, and Symbol," in *Collected Works*, Charles Hartshorne and Paul Weis, eds., vol. 2 (Cambridge: Harvard University Press, 1931-58); and Arthur Burks, "Icon, Index, and Symbol," *Philosophy and Phenomenological Research* 9 (1949): 673-89. For a particularly interesting discussion of the Peircean concepts as they relate to Buddhism, see Janet Gyatso, "Letter Magic: A Peircean Perspective on the Semiotics of Rdo Grub-chen's Dhāranī Memory," in Gyatso, ed., *In the Mirror of Memory: Reflections on Mindfulness and Remembrance in Indian and Tibetan Buddhism* (Albany, NY: SUNY, 1992), pp. 173-214.

[9]For further elucidation of this difficult concept, see Tambiah, *The Buddhist Saints of the Forest*, pp. 4-5, p. 132, and p. 204.

[10]Ibid., p. 204.

[11]This position is most cogently presented in Mus' magnum opus, *Barabudur*; see also Tambiah, *The Buddhist Saints of the Forest*, p. 205.

this presence was not about signs and indices but about embodiment.[12] Schopen argues that such inanimate objects undergo a kind of ontological transformation; the relics of the Buddha, for instance, are "'informed,' 'perfumée,' 'saturated,' 'pervaded,' 'imbued' with just those characteristics which defined the living Buddha."[13]

The gist of Schopen's argument is that when Buddhists - or, more specifically for him, sixth-century Buddhists in particular Indian locales - worship physical relics of the Buddha, they do not make some kind of symbolic (or signifying) conceptual link between the object (the relic) and the subject (the once-present-but-now-absent Buddha Śākyamuni), as Tambiah's invocation of Peirce suggests. The relic does not signify the Buddha, but actually *is* the Buddha, re-creating his *real* presence for the devotee/practitioner. As Schopen puts it, "there is no distinction between a living Buddha and a collection of relics - both make the sacred person equally present as an object of worship...." In an inscription from the South Indian Buddhist site of Nāgārjunikonda, for instance, the Buddha is spoken of as "enclosed in the relic chamber."[14] Schopen argues that this is not a metaphorical sense of "enclosed," but a literal one: the Buddha was really thought to be in the relic chamber, to be physically contained within the *stūpa*.

Yet another take on this same issue is offered by John Strong, in his study of the Indian Buddhist saint Upagupta. Unlike Schopen, Strong is not particularly concerned with Buddhism on the ground, with the archaeological evidence of what real people apparently really did, but rather with the Buddhism recorded in legends and stories as reflective of actual practice. Furthermore, rather than the kind of implicitly ontological position Schopen maintains, Strong argues for a view of presence more congruent with that put forth by Mus and

---

[12]See Gregory Schopen, "Burial 'Ad Sanctos';" see also his "On the Buddha and His Bones: The Conception of a Relic in the Inscriptions of Nāgārjunikonda," *Journal of the American Oriental Society* 108 (1988): 527-37; and "Protestant Presuppositions."

[13]It is important to note that Schopen's argument focuses on relics, and not specifically on artistic images. The two are, indeed, very different objects; but methodologically, Schopen's argument can easily be extended to include a wide range of objects. See Schopen, "Burial 'Ad Sanctos'," p.204; see also his "On the Buddha and His Bones," p. 535.

[14]Schopen, "On the Buddha and His Bones," p.535. Here the verbal form in question is "parigahita."

Tambiah. What I will argue, though, is that it is not only possible, but I think also *desirable* to read the very data Strong presents rather differently. For Strong sees the central question facing Buddhists throughout history as, "What is to be done now that the Buddha is no longer present in the world?" The basic answer is: To come to a deeper understanding of the nature of his absence. This, however, seems to preclude the very possibility than an ontological presence may also be maintained.

Upagupta, a quasi-historical Buddhist saint whose career extends from second century India to modern Thailand, is a figure of great complexity, grounded at once in doctrinal discourse and popular practice. As Richard Davis has nicely described him, Upagupta is "a complex and paradoxical figure...a 'multivocal' or 'polysemous' symbol, standing for several different referents and eliciting a variety of associations depending on the context."[15] In a particularly relevant passage in Strong's book, in a chapter entitled "Upagupta and Māra: Bhakti and the Buddha Body," Strong recounts what is perhaps the single most famous and significant event in Upagupta's life, his defeat of Māra, the Buddhist embodiment of evil.[16] More specifically, it is Upagupta's request of Māra to display the Buddha's *rūpakāya*, literally his "form body," which concerns us here. Let me then summarize the main events of the encounter between Upagupta and Māra which lead up to this request.

It begins when Māra creates a series of disturbances while Upagupta is giving a *dharma* talk to a group of monks. Māra showers the assembly first with pearls, then gold, and finally produces a celestial theatrical performance, all of which is intended to distract the gathered monks from the matter at hand, the discourse on the *dharma*. Upagupta, angered at Māra's treachery, in turn tricks him and subsequently ties him up, binding him with what at first appears to be a garland of flowers but which turns out to be a string of snake carcasses, a dead dog, and a human corpse. Māra is so impressed by

---

[15]As quoted in John Strong, *The Legend and Cult of Upagupta: Sanskrit Buddhism in North India and Southeast Asia* (Princeton: Princeton University Press, 1992), note 75.

[16]Māra is most prominently associated with death, as his name implies (from the Sanskrit root mr, "die"), but he is also the great creator of illusion as well as the lord of the world of lust.

this magical one-upmanship that he converts to Buddhism on the spot and pledges to amend his evil ways of trickery and deceit.[17] Before Upagupta will release him from the fetid garland, though, he asks Māra to apply his illusionary magic one last time: Upagupta wants to see the physically present Buddha:

> Although I have seen the Dharma-Body [dharmakāya]
> I have not seen the physical body [rūpakāya]
> of the Lord of the Triple World
> who resembles a mountain of gold.
> Thus, in return for this "very greatest favor"
> [of introducing you to the venerability of the Buddha
> I want you] to make manifest here
> the physical form of the Buddha.
> Truly, nothing would be more pleasing to me
> than this, for I am eager [to see]
> the body of Daśabala.[18]

As Strong puts it, Upagupta has been suffering from a "rūpalogical" deficiency,[19] for he has never actually seen the Buddha, and it this is a deficiency which confines him to what Strong calls the karmic slow track, a course that leads to enlightenment only after many rebirths.

There is an inherent danger for both Upagupta and Māra here, however: if Upagupta mistakes Māra's illusion for the truly - one might even say *ontologically* - present Buddha, if he actually bows down and worships the chimera, Māra will burst into seven pieces;[20] Upagupta, likewise, knows that the situation is inherently dangerous for him, not only since Māra is by his very nature (promise of conversion or no) not to be trusted, but also because Upagupta risks mistaking what is fundamentally impermanent and not real (the

---

[17]Ibid., pp. 93-104.

[18]Ibid., p. 105.

[19]Strong's use of the "rūpalogical" language refers to the well-known Buddhist doctrine of the "bodies of the Buddha": 1) the dharmakāya, or the body of the Buddha's teachings, 2) the sambhogakāya, or the enjoyment body, and 3) the rūpakāya, the physical form of the Buddha.

[20]Ibid., p. 108; this is a standard effect of "idolatrous" behavior stated in a variety of Buddhist texts.

appearance of the Buddha's physical form) for something stable and eternal. Significantly, however, Upagupta does not avoid these pitfalls. Indeed, when he see the illusion he falls down, "like a tree cut off at the root," and worships Māra.[21]

Māra, however, curiously remains whole despite the potential danger, and he is quick to remind Upagupta of their agreement. Upagupta's response is:

> Of course, I know that the Best of Speakers
> has gone altogether to extinction,
> like a fire swamped by water.
> Even so, when I see his figure,
> which is pleasing to the eye,
> I bow down before that Sage.
> But I do not revere you![22]

Indeed, Upagupta insists that what he is doing is analogous to what worshippers do when they worship clay images of gods, "knowing that what they worship / is the god and not the clay."[23] Strong, heavily relying on Mus suggests that this episode involves "a double realization: that the Buddha's body, his *rūpakāya*, is impermanent in its activity (since it is no longer present); and that, paradoxically, it still exists (since it is in the past, where it can be re-cognized)."[24]

Malcolm David Eckel's examination of the sixth-century Buddhist philosopher Bhāvaviveka presents a particularly detailed and roughly parallel account of just this sort of "double realization." Eckel formulates two distinct aspects of the Buddhist presence/absence debate. There is, in his words, the "diachronic problem posed by the fact that the Buddha once was active in a certain way and now is not, and there is a synchronic problem posed by the fact that any particular representation of the Buddha (including the

[21]Ibid., p. 110.
[22]Ibid.
[23]Ibid., p. 111; what is particularly interesting about this response, though, is that it begs the very question at hand.
[24]Ibid., p. 112.

physical Buddha himself) is inadequate to represent the Buddha in the deepest sense."[25] For Bhāvaviveka, or more precisely for Eckel's reading of Bhāvaviveka, it is the reality of *śunyatā*, of emptiness, that is dominant, and therefore the question of the Buddha's presence is in fact always a question of absence. Thus a physical representation of the Buddha is a self-conscious reminder of both the Buddha's absence and all that this absence signifies. As Eckel puts it, an image of the Buddha "was an empty center where a person could appropriate the Buddha's power, be reminded of the Buddha's message, and gain a paradoxical vision of the Buddha's manifested presence."[26] Put another way, in seeing what the Buddha is *not*, that is physically present, the devotee could see what the Buddha *is*, that is absent or empty.

On the surface, this is strikingly similar to the views of many "negative," or apophatic theologians in both the Christian and Muslim contexts. Indeed, as we have already seen, such early Church figures as Gregory the Great and John of Damascus championed the use of visual images in religious practice precisely because, in the words of Gregory, "We do no harm in wishing to show the invisible by means of the visible."[27] The visible image, in fact, served to heighten the invisibility and practical inaccessibility of God. As Freedberg writes, specifically about Bonaventure, "since the divine is not at all sensible, or susceptible to the normal responses of the senses, but only exists on the level of pure spirit, we can only perceive it by means of objectification in the form of images."[28] Dionysius the Areopagite articulated the importance of images in the following manner:

> The essences and orders which are above us...are incorporeal, and their hierarchy is of the intellect and transcends our world. Our human hierarchy, on the contrary, we see filled with the multiplicity of visible symbols, through which we are led up hierarchically

---

[25]Eckel, *To See the Buddha*, p.72.
[26]Ibid., p. 49.
[27]See Freedberg, *The Power of Images*, p.164.
[28]Ibid., p. 166.

> and according to our capacity to the unified Deification, to God, and to divine virtue.... We are led up, as far as possible, through visible images to contemplation of the divine.[29]

A more recent account of the position of images in Christianity has been developed by the French philosopher and theologian, Jean Luc Marion, in his *God Without Being*.

In the opening section of this book, Marion examines the differences between an idol and an icon.[30] An idol, for Marion, is the visible form of the divine, such as we find in statues, paintings, names, etc. Marion puts great emphasis on the *visibility* of the idol; indeed, it is the act of *gazing* that creates the idol for Marion. "The idol thus acts as a mirror, not as a portrait: a mirror that reflects the gaze's image, or more exactly, the image of its aim and of the scope of that aim."[31] The idol acts as a mirror in that it reflects *the gazer's* limited capacity to conceive of the divine. The idol *freezes* the gaze, in the sense that it fixes one's vision of the divine in an image. In a word, it *limits* the *un*limited God.

> Consequently, the genuineness and the limits of the idol can be defined: in the idol, the divine actually comes into the visibility for which human gazes watch; but this advent is measured by what the scope of particular human eyes can support, by what each aim can require of visibility in order to admit itself fulfilled.... That god whose space of manifestation is measured by what portion of it a gaze can bear - precisely, an idol.[32]

---

[29]Quoted in Freedberg, *The Power of Images*, p. 165.
[30]Jean-Luc Marion, *God Without Being*, Thomas Carlson trans. (Chicago: University of Chicago Press, 1991). Although Marion's use of the terms idol and icon is very much within the standard Christian sense of these things, there is also a certain novelty to his use of the terms.
[31]Ibid., p. 12.
[32]Ibid., pp. 13-14.

No physical image can make the divine visible for Marion, precisely because God is necessarily what Marion calls *invisable*, by which he means that which cannot be taken into view, that which cannot be aimed at.

Idolatrous behavior, for Marion, is not sheer folly; certainly, he admits, it would be foolish to suggest that the idol does not reflect the divine.[33] But rather than reflect the true nature of the divine, it reflects only the limited human capacity to see (or conceptualize) the divine. "Because the idol allows the divine to occur only in a man's measure, man can consign the idolatrous experience to art and thus keep it accessible....art attempts, then, to consign materially, on a second level, and by what one habitually calls an idol, the brilliance of the god."[34] The defining characteristic of the idol, therefore, is that it *limits* God. The idol merely attempts to make what is necessarily invisible visible. It therefore confines the divine to the human realm. "In a word, the divine is figured in the idol only indirectly, reflected according to the experience of it that is fixed by the human authority...."[35]

The icon, for Marion, is fundamentally different in nature, although the idol and the icon may be "contained" in the same material form. The idol and the icon are, rather, "two modes of apprehension of the divine in visibility. Of apprehension, or also, no doubt, of reception."[36] The icon, as it were, inverts the phenomenology of the idol; the idol *contains* the gaze, whereas the icon *liberates* the gaze. "The icon does not result from a vision but provokes one. The icon is not seen, but appears...."[37] Here Marion invokes Saint Paul's *eikon tou theou tou aratou* ["icon of the invisible God"] and John of Damascus' *pasa eikon ekphantorike tou kruphiou kai deiktike* ["every icon manifests and indicates the secret"]. In the icon, therefore, the invisible divine remains invisible.

---

[33]Ibid., p. 28.
[34]Ibid., p. 15.
[35]Ibid., p. 28.
[36]Ibid., p. 9.
[37]Ibid., p. 17.

> The icon...attempts to render visible the invisible *as such*, hence to allow that the visible not cease to refer to an other than itself, without, however, that other ever being reproduced in the visible. Thus the icon shows, strictly speaking, nothing, not even in the mode of the productive *Einbildung*.... The gaze can never rest or settle if it looks at an icon; it always must rebound upon the visible, in order to go back in it up the infinite stream of the invisible. In this sense, the icon makes visible only by giving rise to an infinite gaze.[38]

The icon allows for the gazer to transcend the limits of his or her own vision; it "offers an abyss that the eyes of men never finish probing."[39] This "abyss," this "infinite depth" that the icon makes available is indeed very similar to the kind of "vision of emptiness" that Eckel sees in Bhāvaviveka's quest for a vision of the Buddha. The physical image of the Buddha does very much seem to be an icon in Marion's sense, in that it gives rise to contemplation of the Buddha's infinite *śunyatā*.

Marion's idol/icon distinction is, I would suggest, a particularly insightful and useful way of thinking about the phenomenology of Buddhist images. I will leave to others the potentially fruitful task of comparing Marion's *beyond* being discourse with the various intricacies of *śunyatā*.[40] The distinction between the idol and the icon is useful here in that it provides a way of discussing the representation of what is, necessarily, *un*representable: God cannot be made *visible*, only his *invisibility* can be made visible. In

---

[38]Ibid., p. 18, emphasis added.

[39]Ibid., p. 21.

[40]Marion argues that to discuss God in terms of ontology, even in Heidegger's sense of Being, is to limit God. He calls for a discussion that will go beyond such limitations, a discussion which will "in short no longer attempt to think God in view of being, because one will have renounced, to begin with, thinking him on the basis of Being....to think God without pretending to inscribe him or to describe him as a being," ibid., p. 45. He then goes on to argue that it is love, agape, that provides the key to discuss God; God gives the gift of out of this love. A particularly fruitful comparison would be between Marion's conception of a God not limited to being and *śunyatā* in light of, respectively, *agape* and *karuna*.

the same way, from a doctrinal standpoint, the Buddha himself is not what the sculpture makes visible; rather, the sculpture highlights and opens for contemplation the Buddha's *śunyatā*.

Returning to Upagupta, then, it may be possible to interpret the Upagupta/Māra episode in light of Bhāvaviveka's sense of "seeing" *śunyatā*: Māra's manifestation of the Buddha's form is thus a kind of negative signifier, making visible the reality of invisibility - *invisibility as such*, as Marion would put it. Eckel's Bhāvaviveka avoids what we might call idolatrous behavior by operating purely in the realm of the icon. The image for Bhāvaviveka is there to open up vision; in Marion's words, the image "imbalances human sight in order to engulf it in infinite depth...."[41] But whereas Bhāvaviveka's philosophical quest is to "see" the Buddha in the sense of to gain a *cognitive* realization of the reality of emptiness, Upagupta's goal is rather different. He longs to be in the actual, *physical* presence of the Buddha. Upagupta is seeking to correct, as Strong puts it, a *rūpalogical* deficiency, literally a deficiency of *form*. Thus whereas for a philosophical figure such as Bhāvaviveka there is no conflict between precept and practice - precisely because practice *is* precept, because "to see" the Buddha is all about mental vision - for Upagupta the two modes are very much in tension. For Upagupta, "to see" the Buddha is in effect to see an icon. But it is also to see an idol, *not* in the sense of a limited *representation*, but in the sense of a vision that puts him in the *real* presence of the *real* Buddha. Upagupta, as it were, has one foot in the realm of representation and one foot in the realm of ontology.

Strong's "double realization" is, in my opinion, very helpful in resolving this tension, but it is precisely this push toward resolution that I wish to call into question. For in the end, Strong's analysis ultimately explains the apparent contradiction too neatly, and what we are left with is an episode which does, in fact, reflect the fundamental, doctrinal (here specifically Sarvāstivādin) position. I would posit that it is more fruitful, and I think more accurate, to see this episode not as an expression of the congruence of doctrine (precept) and practice, but

[41] Ibid., p. 24.

rather as *a self-conscious reflection on their incongruence*. Thus the episode does not simply explain away the apparent contradiction; rather, it codifies it. By this I mean that the Buddhist tradition has preserved this episode rather than alter or remove it from the ongoing process of the Upagupta legend. The tension between the doctrinal position and actual practices is thus preserved in the textual tradition, and it is precisely this tension that, to borrow Ricoeur's phrase, gives rise to thought.[42]

I am not suggesting that exactly this level of complex reflection is present for all Buddhist at all times. On the contrary, I would argue that it is precisely the ambiguity of the *habitus* of the image of the Buddha that allows for a broad range of thought and self-conscious reflection on the absence/presence issue, thought and reflection that varies considerably according to the historical or cultural context, say, or according to the individual actor's particular motivations. My basic point, however, is that we can expand Strong's somewhat binary analysis considerably by applying some of the insights of Bourdieu. This situation is analogous to Bourdieu's discussion of parallel-cousin marriage structures, in the past so frequently taken by anthropologists as the structuralist ground *par excellence*. Bourdieu recognizes that the highly structured logical relations of kinship

> exist in practice only through and for the official and unofficial uses made of them by agents whose attachment to keeping them in working order and to making them work intensively - hence, through constant use, ever more easily - rises with the degree to which they actually or potentially fulfill functions indispensable to them or, to put it less ambiguously, the extent to which they do or can satisfy vital material and symbolic *interests*.[43]

---

[42]See Paul Ricoeur, *The Symbolism of Evil* (Boston: The Beacon Press, 1969), in particular the concluding chapter of that work, "The Symbol Gives Rise to Thought," pp. 347-57.
[43]Bourdieu, *Outline*, p. 38.

Methodologically, what is important for our discussion is that the rules, and doctrines, do not in and of themselves govern behavior; there is not a static doctrinal position, but a dialectical process, a dynamic relationship - and not merely an implied contradiction - between precept and practice. Indeed, such an analysis calls into question the very validity of such a dichotomy; precept and practice are not two distinct categories, but two overlapping discourses that mutually inform one another. It is in this way that I suggest we interpret the Upagupta/Māra episode, and more importantly, as we shall see, Buddhist sculptural images in general. That is, I suggest that we see such instances as part of the process of the dialectics of presence.

Thomas Kasulis has described a similar process in his discussion of "metapractical discourse,"[44] a discussion that is particularly germane here. Kasulis begins his discussion by focusing on the Greek word *pneuma*, "breath" or "wind," and the variety of ways it has been translated, most significantly as "spirit." As he puts it:

> A theory of spirit raises ontological and metaphysical questions whereas a theory of spirituality raises issues more existential and practical. In so cavalierly translating *pneuma* as "spirit," are we either consciously or inadvertently concealing the practical and the existential in favor of the theoretical and metaphysical? Is our translation, and ultimately our reading, of *pneuma* colored by Neoplatonic assumptions about mind and spirit? Is our facile move from the Greek word *pneuma* to the English rendering "the spirit," and by extension, "the Holy Spirit" a residue of Trinitarian and Christological debates in, say, the fourth century? Are we failing in the attempt to capture the life of the text as it breathed in the early second century...? As scholars

[44]Thomas P. Kasulis, "Philosophy as Metapraxis," in Frank Reynolds and David Tracy, eds., *Discourse and Practice* (Albany: State University of New York Press, 1992), pp. 169-95.

> of religion, we should be concerned how religious thought relates to praxis.[45]

It is this practice of questioning how religious thought relates to religious practice, and asking not only *what* is done, but *why*, that is the basis of metapractical reflection.

Metapraxis as Kasulis describes it exists on the same two levels as the debate about the Buddha's presence; namely, it exists on the level of Buddhist discourse about Buddhist practice, and on the level of scholarly discourse about Buddhist practice (and about Buddhist discourse about Buddhist practice). Thus Upagupta, in his response to Māra, is engaging in metapractical discourse, reflection on how what he knows to be the official, doctrinal stance relates to what his own practice is. This is necessary in the context because Māra, in an odd turn as the upholder of Buddhist doctrine, has pointed out to him that his actions contradict his statements (which are doctrinally correct). This is where the notion of metapractice is especially helpful, for as Kasulis puts it, "metapractical reflection arises out of questions about the purpose and efficacy of the religious praxes.... Metapractical reflection inquires into the purpose and efficacy of the practice in terms of these participatory and transformative functions.... Metapraxis analyzes and evaluates that happening."[46]

Kasulis' broad methodological point in developing this concept of metapraxis - and here it is worth recalling Bell's critique of the dominant approaches to ritual - is to counter what he sees as an all too prevalent readiness to divide religious phenomena into *either* metaphysics *or* praxis. Instead of this basic dichotomy, which is again roughly analogous to the thought-action dichotomy Bell sees as dominant in anthropological and religious theory, Kasulis proposes a dialectical methodology: "Whenever we find a historical issue that seems to be only about praxis or only about metaphysics or only about metapraxis, *we might do well to look more carefully at the materials*

---

[45]Ibid., p. 172.
[46]Ibid., p. 178.

to see if there are interrelated phenomena in the other two dimensions."[47]

It might be reasonable to ask at this point why a response such as Upagupta's cannot be seen as a simple rationalization, or justification - in the same way that Gombrich's monks and educated middle class Buddhists offer rationalizations and justifications - of action that is not quite in line with doctrine. Although such an interpretation may appeal to the "Occam's razor" impulse in all of us, I think that it both oversimplifies and misrepresents what is going on. Rather than justification, the redactors of the Upagupta legend seem to be involved in precisely the sort of metapractical reflection described by Kasulis. The metaphysical level, which can here be said to be doctrine - particularly the fundamental tenet of *anitya*, or impermanence - is what Upagupta is supposed to do. The praxis is of course what Upagupta actually does, that is he bows down to Māra's illusion. The metapractical reflection is, on one level, Upagupta's own account of his actions, and on a further level the tradition's reflection on the incident as a whole (which is, after all, consciously preserved in the texts). We can now see Upagupta's response to Māra as reflective of the dynamic interplay between metaphysics, praxis, and metapraxis: "Of course, I know that the Best of Speakers has gone altogether to extinction [metaphysics]....I bow down before that Sage [praxis]. But I do not revere you! [metapraxis]."

The philosopher Hans-Georg Gadamer articulates a similar position, and one that is directly concerned with visual images, in his *Truth and Method*.[48] Although there is much of interest in Gadamer's discussion - especially his rejection of the position that a work of art can be taken merely on aesthetic terms, and his discussion of the concept of "play" as it relates to art objects - what is particularly relevant about Gadamer's discussion is his suggestion that the relation of the picture, which for Gadamer includes both sculpture and architecture, and the original is complex and dynamic. It is not merely

[47]Ibid., p. 185, italics added.

[48]Hans-Georg Gadamer, *Truth and Method* (New York: Seabury Press, 1975); specifically, see the section "First Part: II. The ontology of the work of art and its hermeneutical significance," pp. 91-152.

that the picture is a copy (this misunderstands the dynamics of "mimesis"), but rather that the picture acts as a kind of ontological commentary on the original. He uses the example of the performance of a play: "The world which appears in the play of representation does not stand like a copy next to the real world, but is the latter in heightened truth of its being."[49] The work of visual art is not a mere copy of the original (or, better, the prototype); rather, it "*says something about the original*."[50] The picture thus has ontological significance in its own right; it is an "ontological event,"[51] and it also serves to "complete" - to add to, to alter, to comment on - the ontology of the prototype. "The picture then has an independence that also effects the original."[52] The work of art is in what Gadamer calls "ontological communion" with the original; it "shares in what it represents."

Although this is not the place to delve into the specifics of Gadamer's position on the question of ontology, his discussion of the ontology of the work of art is useful in that it highlights a fundamental aspect of my examination of Buddhist art: these sculptures do not simply *re*present the Buddha and the various deities in the Mahāyāna pantheon, and they do not simply *re*produce the doctrinal positions found in the corpus of Mahāyāna manuscripts; rather, they are dynamically involved in the production of such meaning. As we have seen in the Upagupta episode, as well as in Bhāvaviveka's writings, the image of the Buddha produces the realization - and I would argue also the reality - of *both* the absence and the presence of the Buddha. Absence and presence, in this regard, are thus a set; the one necessitates the other. A sculptural representation of the Buddha is therefore in a kind of "ontological communion" with the original Buddha in that the image at once heightens the reality of his *absence* (and therefore graphically embodies *śunyatā*), while at the same time makes available his *presence*.

---

[49]Ibid., p. 121.
[50]Ibid., p. 124, italics added..
[51]Ibid., p. 127.
[52]Ibid., p. 125.

Finally, then, let me reiterate one of the basic problems I have tried to address in this chapter: Given that Mahāyāna Buddhists, in particular medieval Indian Buddhists, maintain the absolute emptiness of the Buddha, why would they make images of him? On the most obvious level, one could answer that they do so in order to "remember" the now-gone Buddha. I say "most obvious" because, like most things obvious, such an interpretation avoids both the vexing problems and the interesting incongruities in the Buddhist use of images. Gombrich is right, after all, to highlight the degree to which what people do does not always, nor *simply*, mesh with what people *say they* do. Gombrich is wrong, however, to see in this incongruity merely a static dichotomy.

What I have attempted, then, is to go in the opposite direction of Gombrich, to move, as Bourdieu puts it, away from rule - and the inherent danger of "breaking the rules" - and towards strategy.[53] I have tried in these first two chapters to demonstrate that for the participants in rituals and textualized discourses, the embodied presence of the divine is never a simple, invariable either/or phenomena: either it really *is* the divine in the stone or the stone *symbolizes* or *refers to* the divine. Rather, such phenomena involve *both* positions, *both* presence *and* absence. Ann Gold, in a study of contemporary Rajasthani pilgrimages, uses the felicitous phrase "simultaneous understandings" to describe the feelings and motivations of the pilgrims about whom she writes. "Simultaneous understandings - pilgrimage is ascetic versus pilgrimage is quite fruitless - form the fundamental and essentially stable ground of belief among the peasant journeyers...."[54] Although I would alter Gold's "essentially stable ground," it is with this basic methodological conviction that I now turn to the specifics of how the concept of *prajñā* is visually represented. What I will argue in the following pages is that Buddhist images were intended to function as what we

[53]Strategy "is the product, not of obedience to a norm explicitly posited and obeyed or of regulation exerted by an unconscious 'model;" rather, strategy involves the whole range of social, historical, economic, genealogical, intellectual, etc. relationships. See Bourdieu, *The Logic of Practice* (Stanford: Stanford University Press, 1990), pp. 15-16.

[54]Ann Gold, *Fruitful Journeys* (Berkeley: University of California Press, 1988), p. 265.

might call *metapractical objects*, involving and invoking a range of strategies with which Buddhists could work through the incongruities and complexities, and even the contradictions, of precept and practice

Chapter Three

IMAGING AND IMAGINING THE BUDDHA

> His instructing was limited by time; after some years, the great voice fell silent and the Wheel of the Law ceased to turn, for the Master himself entered Nirvāṇa, "like a lamp going out when the oil is exhausted." From then on, he was out of sight.
>
> Étienne Lamotte[55]

In this chapter, I turn to an examination of the various strategies available to medieval Indian Buddhists for making the Buddha present. In particular, I shall consider the surprisingly few references to making and worshiping visual images of the Buddha in both early (that is, in Pāli and espousing a basically Theravāda worldview) and later texts (that is, in Sanskrit and espousing a basically Mahāyāna worldview). I am also concerned, however, with a closely related subject: the importance placed on being *in the physical presence* of the historical Buddha in this literature, and with the strategies employed when this *physical presence* is no longer available. I will then turn to the concept of *buddhānusmṛti* (Pāli *anussati*), or "recollecting the Buddha." Although this technique is explicitly meditational, and therefore involves a *cognitive* or imaginative act of "making present" the Buddha in the mind, I want to argue that it too is an essential part of the Pāla-period *habitus* of Buddha images. These layers are necessary components of the larger field of Buddhist artistic representation in medieval northeast India. Or, to put it another way, they are all components of the devotional and intellectual *paramparā* relating to Buddhist images.

The actual images that I shall discuss in the second half of this book were all produced relatively late in the history of Indian Buddhism, in what I have up to now loosely referred to as "medieval

[55]Étienne Lamotte, *History of Indian Buddhism from the Origins to the Śaka Era*, Sara Webb-Boin, trans., Publications de l'Institut Orientaliste de Louvain, vol. 36 (Louvain-la-Neuve: Institut Orientaliste, 1988), p. 614.

Indian Buddhism." In fact, the images I shall discuss can be situated within an even more specific context, what has been traditionally called the "Pāla period." The Pālas were a lineage of kings who ruled over substantial parts of northeastern India from the middle of the eight century until the end of the twelfth. Thus one of my tasks in this chapter is to give a brief account of the Buddhism of this period.

On its face, certainly, this is a period of tremendous change in the Buddhist world: there were significant developments in the conception of Buddhahood in this period, a great variety of Buddhas and Bodhisattvas arise, and artistically, this is a period of iconographic expansion and innovation, with the introduction of countless new figures into the Buddhist pantheon. It may seem odd, then, to direct our gaze *back* to the early Pāli texts, as I shall do in part of this chapter. But it is precisely these earlier conceptions and expressions of the presence of the historical Buddha in artistic images, I argue, that inform and underlie the later production and use of sculptures and paintings. Thus what I attempt here is a kind of archaeology - not in Foucault's sense, but in the sense of Bourdieu's methodological conviction that the *field* of art at any given time is constructed on, or through, a complex system of beliefs and practices made up of many layers of prior, inherited beliefs and practices. It is this layered system, this field, which allows for the recognition, in the deepest sense, of the object; it is the field that creates the "belief which knows and acknowledges it as a work of art."

I should note at the outset of this chapter, however, that my discussion of this field, and the *habitus* that constitutes it, is necessarily limited in scope. My primary concern here is thus with specifically Buddhist discourse, and, further, discourse that is contained within texts. Without such limitations we would quickly find ourselves in a kind of infinite regress of context. As such, then, other aspects of the *habitus* that fall outside of this scope - the unrecorded oral tradition in which images might have been situated, for instance, or the emotional motivations and orientations toward the veneration of images that were part of their ritual context, the economic incentives to make and to venerate images, the various contemporary non-Buddhist conceptions of images, and so on - go largely unexamined here.

I. The Field of Pāla-Period Buddhism

> [D]uring the 'Pāla Period' of its history Buddhism itself was already in a phase wherein it was *heavily adulterated* by the Tāntric cult and its magic spells and practices.... The effect of this on its old cultural standards was to stunt their catholicity of intellectual interests - in fact to reduce culture to a cult.
>
> Sukumar Dutt[56]

> Buddhism under the Pālas differed essentially from what it was even in the time of Hiuen Tsang in the seventh century A.D. There was no trace, not only of the ancient schools of the Hīnayāna system, but even of the pure form of Mahāyāna.
>
> R.C. Majumdar[57]

Let me say right away that delineating a period of religious and artistic development on the basis of a lineage of kings is a mostly arbitrary act, and one upon which we probably should gaze with a certain degree of methodological suspicion. In the case of the Pālas, in particular, there has been a tendency among historians of India who have focused on them to attribute too readily a link between their political rule and the oscillations of the Buddhist institutions that were located within their dynastic domain. The actual evidence to support such a link is in fact rather scant. This is not to say that the Pālas did not support Buddhism at all; rather, I wish only to emphasize that their patronage of Buddhism was never to the exclusion of Brahmanical traditions, nor was it ever limited to any single Buddhist sect. Thus during the over four hundred years of Pāla suzerainty, some of the Pālas seem to have supported Buddhists exclusively, others seem to

---

[56]Sukumar Dutt, *Buddhist Monks and Monasteries of India: Their History and their Contribution to Indian Culture* (Delhi: Motilal Banarsidass, 1962), p. 344-45, emphasis added.
[57]R.C. Majumdar, *History of Ancient Bengal* (Calcutta: G. Bharadwaj and Co., 1971), p. 378.

have supported Vaiṣṇavas exclusively, while the majority seem to have supported both. It is even more problematic to attribute to the Pālas any direct involvement in the production of art; there are, for instance, many inscribed images mentioning a particular date in a particular king's reign, but none of these gives any clear indication that the king in question was a patron.

My use of the term "Pāla period" is not entirely arbitrary, though. In addition to evidence that does allow us to infer that the Pāla kings did at times directly lend support to the Buddhist monasteries and universities within their realm, using "Pāla period" to describe the artistic developments is in line with the indigenous strategies for marking sculpture and architecture. Unlike the common stylistic divisions created by art critics and historians and applied to Western art, such as "Gothic," or "Renaissance," or "Rococo," let alone such divisions as "ancient," or "medieval," or "modern," Indian artists and their patrons, as well as Indian historians, themselves used dynastic divisions to date their work.[58] Furthermore, although the Pāla period does not represent a clear break with previous artistic production, any more than it marks a definite break with prior Buddhist practice and thought, concomitant to the ascension of the Pālas there was a noticeable consolidation of styles and subjects in northeast India. Indeed, as Frederick Asher has demonstrated, the period directly preceding the Pāla period is marked by a variety of locally dictated styles, subjects, and materials. Given the evidence that does survive, it is impossible to demonstrate a definite causal link here; but with the ascension of the Pālas, and perhaps as *a result of* the more unified and stable political climate that the early Pālas effected, this localism gave way to a more defined and consistent artistic tradition.[59]

There has been an overwhelming tendency amongst scholars writing about Buddhism in the medieval period in general and the Pāla period to emphasize what is new. That is, they have largely focused

---

[58]See Frederick Asher, *The Art of Eastern India, 300-800 A.D.* (Minneapolis: University of Minnesota Press, 1980), p. 6, for a discussion of this methodological point.
[59]Ibid., pp. 100-101; see also the remarks of Susan Huntington on the subject in her *The "Pāla-Sena" Schools of Sculpture*, Studies in South Asian Culture, vol. 10 (Leiden: E.J. Brill, 1984).

on the rise of esoteric (i.e. Vajrayāna) Buddhism and its many ritual and artistic innovations. But this focus on what was obviously new - new *mantra* and *maṇḍala* practices, say, or the numerous new deities that were added to the Buddhist pantheon - I want to argue, significantly skews our understanding of the character of Pāla-period Buddhism. For this emphasis on innovation eclipses not only the continuity of Buddhist practice in this period, but it also obscures evidence of another equally significant kind of *newness* in the Pāla milieu. For in addition to the tantric and Vajrayāna *ācarya*s (teachers) working in and around the Pāla monastic complexes, major figures concerned with interpreting the very old *Prajñāpāramitā* discourse - Śāntideva, Prajñākaramati, Haribhadra, and Abhayākaragupta, to name only a few - were also active in Pāla-period monastic establishments, and a tremendous amount of energy was put into copying and promulgating the *Prajñāpāramitā* texts that had been composed many centuries before. The character of Pāla-period Buddhism, then, is not only marked by the rise of new Vajrayāna practices, but also by a *re*newed focus on the very old *Prajñāpāramitā* genre.

Bourdieu's notion of the *field* is relevant in this regard, particularly as it applies to the specific realm of art. In his, "The Field of Cultural Production, or: The Economic World Reversed," Bourdieu emphasizes the *relational* nature of artistic production and reception. He rejects Foucault's concept of the *épistemè*, because Foucault "refuses to look outside the 'field of discourse' for the principle which would cast light on each of the discourses within it....he thus refuses to relate works in any way to their social conditions of production, i.e. to positions occupied within the field of cultural production."[60] Bourdieu also argues explicitly against Kant's "pure gaze" aesthetic and the notion that there is some independent, intrinsic quality in the work of art. insisting instead that the "work of art is an object which exists as such only by virtue of the (collective) belief which knows

[60]Pierre Bourdieu, "The Field of Cultural Production, or: The Economic World Reversed," in Randal Johnson, ed., *The Field of Cultural Production: Essays on Art and Literature* (New York: Columbia University Press, 1993), p. 33.

and acknowledges it as a work of art."[61] Thus in order to understand the work of art in the terms in which it was understood in its original context, it is necessary to reconstruct the *field* in which that work was situated, a field that according to Bourdieu, was made up of a whole range of strategies of production *and* reception. Such strategies did not simply burst, fully developed, onto the scene; they too were passed on, modified, and adapted. *Paramparā*, again.

The Pāla period, as I have noted, has typically been described by historians of India and Buddhism as a time of great changes, of tremendous innovations: "Buddhism under the Pālas differed essentially.... There was no trace...of the ancient schools." There has been a marked tendency to focus on what was new, and there was indeed much that was new to the Pāla period: the rise and increased development of the *tantra*s, the emergence of Vajrayāna, and the concomitant iconographic innovations that went along with, and no doubt contributed to, such developments.[62]

This tendency to focus on change and innovation, however, has I think skewed our understanding of Buddhism in the Pāla period; it is as if Pāla-period Buddhists had somehow managed simply to wipe clean the slate of Buddhist thought and practice. Either wiped clean, or completely sullied. Take, for instance, Dutt's remark that "during the 'Pāla Period' of its history Buddhism itself was already in a phase wherein it was *heavily adulterated* by the Tāntric cult and its magic spells and practices."[63] Although there is little question that there was a great deal of ritual *innovation* in this milieu, there was also a decidedly *conservative* character to Pāla-period Buddhism, and, as I shall seek to demonstrate in subsequent chapters, as much as Pāla-

---

[61]Ibid., p.35. See also, in the same volume, the article "Outline of a Sociological Theory of Art Perception," pp. 215-37.

[62]For a general survey of the Buddhist literature of the Pāla period, one that betrays this rather one-sided view of the Buddhism of the period by focusing almost exclusively on the tantras, see S.K. De, "The Buddhist Tantric Literature (Sanskrit) of Bengal," *New Indian Antiquary* 1 (1938-39): 1-23.

[63]Dutt, *Monks and Monasteries of India*, p. 344, emphasis added. Dutt's language is actually rather muted, when compared to some of the other characterizations of Pāla-period/tantric Buddhism. De la Vallée Poussin, for instance, refers to the "disgusting practices both obscene and criminal" that characterize this genre of Buddhist literature; see his "Tantrism," in *Hastings' Encyclopedia of Religious Ethics*, vol. 12 (Edinborough, 1908-26), p. 195.

period Buddhism might be seen to anticipate the fully developed esoteric Buddhism of Tibet, it also echoes and continues, and indeed, as I shall argue, *emphasizes* the traditions that had been prevalent in Magadha for the preceding millennium.

Part of the problem with attempting to characterize Pāla-period Buddhism in any general way is that the very rubric "Pāla Period," which too conveniently encompasses a number of disparate elements. "Pāla-period Buddhism" can legitimately refer to anything from the Sarvāstivādin and Theravādin philosophical and ideological convictions that fueled the production of many of the sculptures of mid-eighth century Bodhgayā, say, to the mainstream Mahāyāna convictions behind the particularly abundant images of Avalokiteśvara and Mañjuśrī from tenth-century Nālandā, to the Vajrayāna and *tantra* notions that seem to have informed the production of some of the surviving images from twelfth-century Bangladesh.

This, then, is a highly complex field of practice, and it would take several book-length studies to explore adequately the doctrinal and ritual character, or characters, of Buddhism in this period. I should stipulate, therefore, that I am not interested in attempting to construct anything like a comprehensive history here. Indeed, on the contrary, part of what I wish to do here is to *limit*, quite intentionally, the scope of my discussion. My focus throughout this study will be on what I shall call "mainstream Mahāyāna," by which I mean primarily the *Prajñāpāramitā* genre of textual discourse and the ritual and artistic traditions that seem most closely linked to this genre. I shall make reference to a variety of Buddhist genres that seem to have existed in the medieval Indian milieu. However, I will argue that the *Prajñāpāramitā*, with its dominant emphasis on the practical and soteriological aspects of wisdom, continues to be a central component in Pāla-period Buddhist praxis. More importantly, I shall demonstrate in the chapters that follow that we see this mainstream Buddhist character, with its consistent emphasis on *prajñā*, borne out by a significant number of sculptures that were created and used in the Pāla milieu. Certainly some Pāla-period Buddhist sculpture does evince tantric and Vajrayāna practices, but it would not be an overstatement to say the majority of Pāla-period Buddhist sculpture is decidedly mainstream in character.

Virtually all of the major monastic centers - the so-called "Buddhist universities" about which a great deal has been written[64] - of the Pāla realm display evidence of what might be called a "poly-sectarian environment," an environment in which certain monastic complexes, at certain times, perhaps leaned toward one school or another, but also an environment very much characterized by what we might call "a fluidity" of ritual and philosophical concerns. This fluid environment is attested to by a variety of pre- and post-Pāla period sources: by the pre-Pāla period Chinese pilgrims, Faxian, Xuanzang, and Yijing; by the Tibetan historian Tāranātha; by various inscriptions, particularly by the many stones and images inscribed with *dhāraṇī* s (or magical formulas) that survive from the period, about which I will have much more to say in Chapter Five; by the various extant manuscripts from the period; and, perhaps most importantly for the present study, as I have just noted, by the diversity of sculpture that survives from the various sites. In the midst of all of this fluidity, however, is one constant: *prajñā*.

Perhaps the single most commonly cited source for the Pāla period has been Tāranātha, who wrote his unambiguously Vajrayāna-centric *History of Buddhism in India* in Tibet in 1609. Tāranātha begins his description of this period with an account of the ascent of Gopāla, and he makes the Vajrayāna sympathies of this first Pāla king quite clear. Before ascending the throne, Tāranātha tells us, Gopāla "received *abhiṣeka* from an *ācārya* with instructions to propitiate the goddess Cundā," and, having "attained *siddhi* of goddess Cundā....he became the king on the next day."[65] In the remainder of Tāranātha's account of this first Pāla king there are several other allusions to the Vajrayāna; he mentions a variety of *siddhi*s and *sādhana* practices, implying, although not actually stating, that Vajrayāna was practiced at the highest level of this first Pāla king's realm. The prominence of

---

[64]General surveys of these institutions abound. See G.S. Majumdar, *Buddhism in Ancient Bengal* (Calcutta: Navana, 1983), particularly pp. 119-42; S. Dutt, *Monks and Monasteries of India*; Puspa Niyogi, Buddhism in Ancient Bengal, and also "Organization of Buddhist Monasteries in Ancient Bengal and Bihar," *Journal of Indian History* 54 (1976): 273-98; and A.K. Warder, *Indian Buddhism* (Delhi: Motilal Barnarsidass, 1970), pp. 462-513.

[65]Chimpa and Chattopadhyaya, *Tāranātha's History of Buddhism in India*, pp. 257-58.

Vajrayāna in Tāranātha's account of the subsequent Pāla kings is equally striking.

Tāranātha's account gives an unambiguous description of the Pāla period as being dominated by the three classes of *tantra* and, in particular, by the Vajrayāna teachings and practices as described in the *Guhyasamāja* and other *anuttarayoga* texts. There are, however, serious problems with viewing Tāranātha as anything like an "objective historian," which is precisely how he is frequently treated. Tāranātha clearly had a sectarian axe to grind, and part of his historiographical exercise was to legitimize his own preferred brand of Buddhist practice. As David Templeman nicely puts it, "Tāranātha's purpose....was not to paint a completely accurate portrait of the Dharma and its adherents but to glorify them, to make them serve as inspirations to the Buddhists of Tibet...."[66] Thus the mainstream Mahāyāna, as exemplified by the *Prajñāpāramitā* genre, is frequently present in his *History of Buddhism in India* only as a kind of lesser partner to the *tantras*. And the many *śrāvakas* (by which he means Theravadins) who were present in the Pāla realm at this time, particularly at Bodhgayā, are mentioned only as iconoclasts who go so far as to melt down consecrated images and turn them into coins. However, it is worth noting that even Tāranātha, with his *tantra* sympathies, includes the *Prajñāpāramitā* as being widely propagated in the Pāla milieu, such as when he says, in his account of Dharmapāla, that the king "filled all directions with the Prajñā-pāramitā and the Sri Guhya-samāja."[67]

The seventh-century Chinese pilgrims, Xuanzang and Yijing, both of whom travelled in India, visiting important pilgrimage places and monastic centers, and collecting a wide range of Buddhist texts, are also frequently cited as sources for understanding the Pāla-period Buddhist milieu. Although they were perhaps no less polemically motivated than Tāranātha - they were, after all, on a mission to collect *vinaya* texts and Mahāyāna *sūtras* - they were at least chronologically much closer to the Pāla period than was Tāranātha, and furthermore, they provide a useful contrast to Tāranātha, presenting a Buddhist

---

[66]David Templeman, "Tāranātha the Historian," *Tibet Journal* 6 (1981): 41-46, p. 45.
[67]Chimpa and Chattopadhyaya, *Tāranātha's History of Buddhism in India*, p. 274.

milieu in which a number of sects, particularly *mainstream* Buddhist sects, coexisted.[68]

Yijing, for instance, describes a Pāla region in Northeast India that is dominated by the Sarvāstivādins and other so-called Hīnayāna schools: "In Northern India and the islands of the Southern Sea," he reports, "they generally belong to the Hīnayāna...."[69] He sees, however, no definitive differences between the various schools extant in the seventh-century milieu, and writes: "We can reasonably practise both the Mahā(yāna) and the Hīna(yāna) doctrines in obedience to the instruction of the Merciful Honoured One, preventing small offences, and meditating upon the great Doctrine of Nothingness."[70] In short, one comes away from Yijing's report, and also away from Xuanzang's slightly earlier account, with the impression that the milieu in seventh-century Northeast India was, in contrast to Tāranātha's portrayal, decidedly mainstream.

My point here is not to engage in a lengthy discussion of the historiographic merit of these sources, but rather to emphasize that a certain skepticism should be exercised when one encounters the Pāla period= *tantra*/Vajrayāna equation - as for instance in Conze's, where the author writes, echoing the language we have already seen Dutt use, that the Pāla period was "the period of Tantric influence and of absorption into magic (600 to 1200)."[71] The *tantra*s and Vajrayāna were both very much "in the air" in the Pāla period, as we know from a great variety of sources.[72] But their preeminence during this period has, I would suggest, been overly emphasized. We know, for example, that a large number of manuscripts were copied during the Pāla period,

---

[68]A great deal has been written on these Chinese pilgrims, more on Xuanzang than Yijing; for a good discussion of Xuanzang in particular, see Kenneth Ch'en, *Buddhism In China: A Historical Survey* (Princeton: Princeton University Press, 1964), pp. 235-40, and also his extensive bibliographical references.

[69]J. Takakusu, trans., *A Record of the Buddhist Religion as Practised in India and the Malay Archipelago* (A.D. 671-695) by I-tsin (Oxford: The Clarendon Press, 1896) p. 14.

[70]Ibid., p. 51.

[71]Edward Conze, *The Prajñāpāramitā Literature* (The Hague: Mouton and Co., 1960), p. 9.

[72]We know, for instance, that a number of Chinese pilgrims to India were particularly interested in tantric texts. See Jan Yün-hua, "Buddhist Relations Between India and Sung China," *History of Religions* 6 (1966): 24-42; and "Buddhist Relations Between Indian and Sung China, Part II," *History of Religions* 6 (1966): 135-68.

both by pilgrims such as Xuanzang,[73] and by Indian monks in the Pāla milieu. Indeed, this was a primary occupation in the Buddhist establishments located within the Pāla sphere. Furthermore, the majority of the copied manuscripts that survive from the period are Prajñāpāramitā texts, particularly *Astasāhasrikāprajñāpāramitā* texts.[74]

The prevalence of surviving *Aṣṭasāhasrikā* manuscripts from the Pāla period does not, in itself, mean that these were necessarily the dominant texts of the Pāla period. As we shall see in subsequent chapters, the ideology of these texts is decidedly self referential and, I would say, self preservational;[75] the reader/practitioner is repeatedly exhorted to learn, venerate, and *copy* the text as both a means and a measure of religious progress, and so it makes sense that a large number of these copies would have been produced and would have subsequently survived. I think, however, that we can safely infer from these extant manuscripts that this genre of Buddhist literature, and the mainstream Mahāyāna expressed by it, was of particular importance in the Pāla milieu,[76] especially when we consider that several important commentaries on the *Aṣṭasāhasrikā* and other *Prajñāpāramitā* texts - the most important of which is Haribhadra's eighth-century

[73]See, for instance, Leon Hurvitz, "Hsüan-tsang (602-664) and the Heart Scripture," in Lewis Lancaster, *Prajñāpāramitā and Related Systems: Studies in Honour of Edward Conze* (Berkeley: Berkeley Buddhist Studies Series, 1977), pp. 103-21.

[74]Frustratingly little has been written about the surviving Pāla-period manuscripts, and no one to my knowledge has attempted anything like a comprehensive study of this subject. Although it is clearly beyond the scope of my own discussion, a kind of Annales School accounting - including Indian, Tibetan, and Chinese sources - of the actual texts that were used and copied in the Pāla milieu would greatly enhance our understanding of the Buddhism of this period. For a partial list of Pāla-period manuscripts, most of which are in fact copies of the *Aṣṭasāhasrikā*, see S.K. Saraswati, "East Indian Manuscript Painting," in *Chhavi: Golden Jubilee Volume* (Banaras: Bharat Kala Bhavan, 1971): 243-62; see also S.B. Dasgupta, *Eastern Indian Manuscript Painting* (Bombay: D.B. Taraporevala Sons & Co. Pvt. Ltd., 1972), pp. 29-31, and p. 45. For a more sketchy, although still useful, discussion, see Jeremiah P. Losty, *The Art of the Book in India* (London: The British Library, 1982), pp. 18-36; see also, in the same general vein, Pratapaditya Pal and Julia Meech-Pekarik, *Buddhist Book Illuminations* (New York: Ravi Kumar Publishers, 1988).

[75]I will have considerably more to say about the self-referential discourse of the Prajñāpāramitā, particularly in Chapter Five, where I discuss the so-called "cult of the book" and its relevance to Pāla period visual practices.

[76]It is not insignificant that a substantial number of the texts brought from India to China were Prajñāpāramitā genre texts. See P. B. Bagchi, *India and China: A Thousand Years of Cultural Relations* (Calcutta: Saraswat Library, 1981), especially pp. 169-79.

Abhisamayālamkāra - were in fact composed during the Pāla period.[77] In other words, not only were *Prajñāpāramitā* manuscripts being copied for religious merit, they were also continuously being taught and apparently re-interpreted in the Pāla milieu.

It is certainly striking that the *Astasāhasrikā*, a text composed at least as early as the first century, should rather suddenly gain such prominence. Striking, but also, as I shall argue throughout this study, indicative of the Pāla-period emphasis and focus on the intricacies of wisdom, the practical and soteriological effects of *prajñā*. In other words, although this *prajñā*-centered discourse is not new to medieval Buddhism, it gains a preeminence in the Pāla period that *is* new. And as we shall see in the chapters that follow, this emphasis on *prajñā* was not simply textual, but was also visual; indeed, there is a remarkable correlation between the textual and visual discourses in the Pāla period. Finally, and perhaps most importantly, the *explicit* visual emphasis on wisdom *is* very much new, and it is precisely the dynamics of this visual emphasis on *prajñā* that I shall play out in the rest of this study.

II. Image Talk

> Honor the eldest member of the community, the Bodhi tree, an image, a shrine.
>
> Buddhaghosa[78]

---

[77]According to Tāranātha, Dharmapāla actually directly patronized Haribhadra; see Chimpa and Chattopadhyaya, *Tāranātha's History of Buddhism in India*, p. 277. See also A. K. Warder's discussion of Haribhadra and those immediately following him, in his Indian Buddhism, pp. 478-482.

[78]*Samantapāsādikā: Buddhaghosa's Commentary on the Vinaya Pitaka*, vol. 4, J. Takakusu and M. Nagai, eds. (London: Pali Text Society, 1924-38), p. 623; *Cetiyam patimam bodhim sanghattheram vandathā ti.*.

II. A. Seeing the Buddha.

> Beings become contented by seeing the Buddha; they attain deathlessness having heard (his) spoken utterance.
>
> *Buddhavamsa*[79]

A great deal of ink has been spilled on the topic of Buddha images. Beginning in the first quarter of this century with the debate between Ananda Coomaraswamy and Alfred Foucher over the indigenous or exogenous origins of the Buddha image,[80] and progressing through the more recent debates about the so-called "aniconic" period in early Buddhism,[81], scholars have been wrangling over two very basic questions: 1. *When* did Buddhists begin representing the Buddha in

---

[79]*Buddhavamsa and Cariyāpiṭika*, N.A. Jayawickrama, editor (London: Pali Text Society, 1975), p. 41 *Dassanena pi ti tam buddham tositā honti pānino / Vyāharantam giram sutvā amatam pāpunanti te.*

[80]See Alfred Foucher, "L'Origine grecque de l'image du Bouddha," *Annales du Musee Guimet* (Chalon-sur-Saone: Bibliotheque de vulgarisation, 1913), pp. 231-72. In this highly influential article, Foucher first articulates the view that the origins of the earliest Buddha images were Greek; see also Foucher's "The Beginnings of Buddhist Art," in his *The Beginnings of Buddhist Art and Other Essays in Indian and Central Asian Archaeology* (Paris: Paul Geuthner, 1917), pp. 1-29 . Perhaps the most vocal opponent of this theory was Ananda Coomaraswamy; see his "The Origin of the Buddha Image," *The Art Bulletin* 9 (1927): 1-43; and also see his "The Indian Origin of the Buddha Image," *Journal of the American Oriental Society* 46 (1926): 165-70.

[81]See Susan Huntington, "Early Buddhist Art and the Theory of Aniconism," *Art Journal* 49 (1990): 401-07, for a useful survey of the relevant points here. See also Vidya Dehejia, "Aniconism and the Multivalence of Emblems," *Ars Orientalis* 21 (1992): 45-66; and S. Huntington's response, "Aniconism and the Multivalence of Emblems: Another Look," *Ars Orientalis* 22 (1993): 111-56 [and Dehejia's brief response, on p. 157]. Also see A.K. Narain, "First Images of the Buddha and Bodhisattvas:. Ideology and Chronology," in A.K. Narain, ed. *Studies in Buddhist Art of South Asia* (New Delhi: Kanak Publications, 1985), pp. 1-21; see also John Huntington's article, in the same volume, "The Origin of the Buddha Image: Early Image Traditions and the Concept of Buddhadarśanapunyā," pp. 24-58. One of the most fruitful discussions on this subject, and one that has been far too often ignored, is found in Paul Mus' article, "The Iconography of an Aniconic Art," *RES* 14 (1987): 5-28. Mus argues that the early "aniconic" period was karmically motivated: "What one comes to experience (if one can attain it) is not so much 'the joy to be felt in contemplating the Buddha' as in this very joy, which acts as a detector of something of his presence, the certainty of having encountered him karmically.... Leaving the place vacant, representing the Master by his absence, meant setting the stage for future viewers to attain, beyond the convention of the work of art, the realism of an evocatory religious act," pp. 12-13; see also pp. 22-23.

sculptures, drawings, and paintings? and 2. *Why* did they do this? The first question, one would think, would be relatively straightforward - given the precision of modern dating techniques - and for the most part it is, except that some art historians have recently begun to introduce "new" data that would push the date back in time.[82]

Turning the second question - *Why* did Buddhists begin making images of the Buddha - as I have argued, they did so in order to negotiate the *gap* between the absence and the presence of the Buddha. Indeed, as I have suggested, images are perhaps best seen as a means toward and a mode of metapractical reflection on this gap. But why is it so important to be in the presence of the Buddha? To answer this question, we must first consider the significance that is placed on *being in the presence of the Buddha* in the Pāli canonical literature - because it is this discourse, I wish to argue, that in part constitutes the *field* of the later conceptions of and reactions to images, and the ways in which they function to mediate between presence and absence.

On the most basic level, the Buddha's disciples wish to be in the teacher's presence in order to hear the *dhamma* directly from him, in order to receive his direct guidance. We see variations of this throughout the Pāli Canon: a would-be disciple learns that the Buddha is preaching the *dhamma* somewhere, and resolves to go hear it directly for himself or herself. This is also implicitly emphasized by the familiar opening of so many of the *sutta*s: *Evaṃ me sutaṃ*, "Thus have I heard." The text that follows this stock beginning is, at least on a very superficial level, made legitimate, or invested with authority, by the fact that it was heard directly from the mouth of the Buddha - it is *buddhavacana*, the Buddha's very own words.[83]

One of the most well-known and often-cited expressions of this general theme involves the Buddha's chief disciple and companion, Ānanda, and his tearful lament in the *Mahāparinibbāna*

---

[82]See for instance J.E. van Lohuizen-de Leeuw, "New Evidence with Regard to the Origin of the Buddha Image." In Herbert Hartel, ed., *South Asian Archaeology 1979* (Berlin: Dietrich Reimer Verlag, 1981).

[83]There are many places in both the Canon and the commentaries in which this point is emphasized. For a useful discussion of *buddhavacana* in the Pāli Theravāda context, see George Bond, *The Word of the Buddha* (Colombo: M.D. Gunasena and Co., 1982), pp. 1-33.

Sutta when he knows that the Buddha's death is imminent. He is found alone, leaning on a pillar in a corner of the monastery, crying: "Alas! I am still in want of training, but a learner, one who has [more] work to do. And the teacher is about to pass away from me - he who is so compassionate to me!"[84] Ānanda here is expressing several layers of distress, not the least of which is the deep emotion of losing a dear companion. What is perhaps most emphasized in the passage, though, is Ānanda's fear that without the *present* Buddha there to teach and to guide him, his progress on the Path will stop; he fears that he will remain a mere learner, and will thus never attain enlightenment.

In this instance, the Buddha assures him that he can, and indeed must, proceed on his own. First, he must be diligent and earnest in his own efforts - he must be "a lamp unto himself." Second, Ānanda and the other disciples must realize that after he is physically gone, it is the Buddha's teaching that will endure. As the Buddha puts it: "Oh Ānanda, that *dhamma* and *vinaya* has been made known and taught to you by me; after me (after I'm gone) that is your teacher."[85]

The matter, however, is not quite so easily resolved, for as we have already seen in the later cases of both Upagupta and Bhavaviveka, the desire to see the Buddha, to be in his physical presence, persists. Indeed, even in the early context we see not just the emphasis on hearing the Buddha's words directly from the Buddha's mouth, but also a certain emphasis on *seeing* him as well. Thus, in the episode preceding Ānanda's tearful lament, the gods who have heard that the Buddha is about to pass from the world come in order to see him (*tathāgataṃ dassānaya*) one last time.

Lamotte links this desire to see the Buddha and to behold his miraculous qualities to an essentially lay-devotional impulse that took place *after* the Buddha had died:

---

[84]The Pāli reads: *Āhañ ca vat' amhi sekho sakaraṇīyo, Satthu ca me parinibbānaṃ bhavissati yo mamaṃ anukampako ti*. *Dīgha Nikāya*, vol. 2, T.W. Rhys Davids and J. Estlin Carpenter, eds. (London: Pali Text Society, 1949-1960), p. 13.

[85]See *Dīgha Nikāya*, vol. 2, p. 145, and p. 154; the Pāli for the latter reads, *Yo vo Ānanda mayā Dhammo ca Vinayo ca desito paññatto, so vo mam' accayena Satthā.*

> If monks, devoted to a life of study and meditation, are able to resign themselves to regarding their founder only as a sage who had entered Nirvāṇa, lay followers, who are exposed to the difficulties of their times, require something other than a "dead god" of whom only the "remains" (*śarīra*) could be revered. They want a living god, a "god superior to the gods" (*devātideva*) who will continue his beneficial activity among them, who can predict the future, perform wonders, and whose worship (*pūja*) will be something more than mere recollection (*anusmṛti*).[86]

Leaving aside the problems of seeing the devotional aspect of early Buddhism as a lay affair,[87] Lamotte is probably correct in emphasizing the relative lateness of this tradition, although there are certainly earlier strata which emphasize the importance of *seeing* the physical Buddha.

In the *Vaṇṇu-patha Jātaka*, for instance, a young member of a Sāvatthi family, after being admitted to the first stage of the Saṅgha, and after having been given a topic of meditation by the Buddha, goes off to the forest to meditate. After living there for three months, however, he makes no progress, and was not able to obtain even a hint or a glimmer of insight. He then thinks to himself: "'I will go back to the teacher, and having gone to the presence of the teacher, I will live looking at his most excellent body and listening to his honey-sweet teaching.'"[88] When he learns of this, however, the Buddha admonishes

---

[86]Étienne Lamotte, *History of Indian Buddhism from the Origins to the Śaka Era*, p. 645.

[87]Gregory Schopen has argued that this is a fundamental misconception about Indian Buddhism. See his "On Monks, Nuns and 'Vulgar' Practices: The Introduction of the Image Cult into Indian Buddhism" *Artibus Asiae* 46 (1988): 153-68. According to the evidence Schopen presents, it was the monastics who "initiated and disproportionately supported the cult of images at Sārnāth [among other places] in the early periods.... A picture of the actual Indian Buddhist monk and nun is gradually emerging, and these monks and nuns differ markedly from the ideal monk and nun which have been presented on the basis of textual material alone. The actual monk, unlike the textual monk, appears to have been deeply involved in religious giving and cult practice of every kind from the very beginning," p. 155 and p. 167.

[88]*Jātakā: Together with its Commentary*, vol. 1, V. Fausboll, ed. (London: Pali Text Society, 1962-64), pp. 21. The Pāli reads: *Satthu-santikam gantvā rūp'-agga-ppattam Buddha-sarīram olokento madhura-dhamma-desanam suṇanto vihārissāmiti.*

the young monk for giving up so easily, and then delivers a story about the need for perseverance in which the now-remiss *bhikkhu* is shown to have been in his former life an energetic young man. The young monk thus sees the error of his ways and all is made right: "Having delivered this *dhamma* discourse, he made known the four truths; at the end of this the remiss *bhikkhu* was established in the highest fruit, arahantship."[89]

Although the intent of this *Jātaka* is quite clearly to emphasize the need for perseverance, it is also noteworthy for its dual emphasis on seeing and hearing, and for the especially efficacious effects of this sight and sound. The young Sāvatthin in the story does not want merely to receive the Buddha's words; he also wants to *look at* the Buddha, to be in his physical presence. There is, indeed, a rather striking emphasis on the physical body of the Buddha here; not only do we get the stock phrase "having gone to the presence of the teacher" [*Satthu-santikam gantvā*], but also the phrase "looking at the body of the Buddha" [*Buddha-sarīram olokento*]. The emphasis in this episode is thus placed equally on hearing the *dhamma* and on *seeing* the physically present Buddha.

Another early expression of this desire to see the living Buddha is found in a version of the story of Vakkali, as it occurs in the *Samyutta Nikāya* of the Pāli Canon.[90] In this version, Vakkali is a rather frail monk who has fallen ill and is visited by the Buddha, who is concerned about Vakkali's health. When the Buddha asks him how he is faring, however, Vakkali replies that he has long desired to see the Blessed One (*Bhavantam dassanāya*), but due to his illness he has been unable to satisfy this desire. The Buddha sharply rebukes him:

---

[89]Ibid.; *Evam imam dhammadesanam dassetvā cattāri saccāni pakāsesi, Saccapariyosāne ossatthaviriyo bhikkhu aggaphale arahatte patitthāsi.* I have translated the Pāli "*ossatthaviriyo bhikkhu*" as "remiss *bhikkhu*," although the compound "*ossatthaviriyo* means literally "one whose energy (*viriyo*) is let loose (*ossattha*)." It would make equal semantic sense to translate this phrase as "diligent *bhikkhu*," since the *ossattha* can also have the sense of "put forth." The redactors of this *Jātaka* are obviously playing on this compound, although it is difficult to say, exactly, how they intend it to be taken. Either the young monk achieves *arahant* status as a result of his *former* diligence (i.e. in his previous life), or he achieves it - rather paradoxically, in my opinion - as a result of seeing and hearing the Buddha.

[90]There are several versions of this story, in the *Anguttara Nikāya*, as well as the commentary on the *Dhammapada*.

"Enough, Vakkali! What is the sight of this putrid body to you? He who sees the *dhamma*, Vakkali, he sees me; he who sees me, he sees the *dhamma*."[91] As in the *Jātaka* story above, the point of this passage is quite clear: attachment to the physical body of the Buddha is pointless - if not actually a hindrance - since the vision of the Buddha and the "vision" of the *dhamma* are equal. As we shall see, this equation of vision and knowledge is a central component in Pāla-period sculptural representation.

In the version of the same story that occurs in the *Dhammapada* commentary, however, the message of the Vakkali story is somewhat more ambiguous. In this version, Vakkali is a young Brahmin who one day sees the Buddha and is so struck with his appearance that he joins the *Saṅgha* in order to see the Blessed One constantly. As a monk, he is so attached to the physical form (*sarīrasampattiṃ*) of the Buddha that he follows him everywhere, to the point that he neglects his *dhamma* study and meditational exercises. The Buddha upbraids him with the *Saṃyutta* verse that we have just noted, equating seeing the Buddha with seeing the *dhamma*, but the visually obsessed Vakkali is unable to leave the Buddha's side. The Buddha finally attempts to cure Vakkali by forbidding the young monk to accompany him on the rains retreat; Vakkali, however, responds by vowing to hurl himself off a cliff. In order to save him, the Blessed One creates an image of himself for Vakkali.[92] Vakkali is overjoyed at the sight of this image, and once the Buddha sees that Vakkali is out of danger, he delivers a short sermon and Vakkali is cured of his visual obsession and attains the status of an *arahant*.

Again, although the most obvious message of this episode is the danger of becoming too attached to the physical form of the Buddha, there is also a kind of celebration of the joy one receives from

---

[91]The Pāli reads: *Alaṃ Vakkali kiṃ te iminā pūtikayena diṭṭhena. Yo kho Vakkali dhammaṃ passati so mam passati, yo mam passati so dhammam passati*, *Samyutta Nikāya*, vol. 3, Leon Feez, ed. (London: Pali Text Society, 1960), p. 120. The episode concludes with Vakkali, committing suicide, although the Buddha then declares that, in fact, Vakkali had already been *parinibutto* at the time of his death. For more on such suicides, see Martin G. Wiltshire, "The 'Suicide' Problem in the Pāli Canon." *Journal of the International Association of Buddhist Studies* 6 (1983): 124-40.

[92]The Pāli is *obhāsam*, the most immediate sense of which is "appearance." This, however, refers to a kind of "aura" more than an actual physical image such as a sculpture.

a vision of the Buddha. It is, after all, the *sight* of the Buddha that immediately saves Vakkali in the *Dhammapada* commentary version of the story and which thus enables him to absorb the Buddha's wisdom. Much more could be said about the dynamics of vision in the Buddhist context, and I shall return to this topic later.[93] What is most relevant for the moment, though, is that *seeing* the Buddha is linked to progress on the Path, with a true understanding of the *dhamma*.

However, there is also a tension that is maintained in these examples, a tension between seeing that is salvifically *efficacious* and seeing that is a salvific *hindrance*. It is not enough just to see the Buddha, but to see him *in the correct way*. It is in the context of just this tension, and the need to mediate between proper and improper vision, that I would suggest Buddhist images are located.

In this sense, we can again draw a fruitful analogy with various Christian conceptions of images, if we, in a sense, blur our vision slightly, or at least attempt to think somewhat along the lines of Marion's discussion of the idol and the icon, by which I mean that the two can be contained in the *same object*. Certainly, the Western and Eastern churches are divided with regard to images. In spite of this division - which is centered on two very different Christological positions, but which also involves multiple layers of social and political discourse - there is also a fundamental conceptual *agreement* underlying both the Eastern and Western take on images that I have already noted in: the image itself is clearly *not* considered to be divine in either case. The Eastern church unquestionably does *not* hold that images *are* God; this would be idolatry writ large. On the contrary, the iconoduals of both the Eastern and Western churches see the image as a *means* through which the *ultimate invisibility* of God can be comprehended. Recall Bonaventure's words: "since the divine is not at all sensible, susceptible to the normal responses of the senses, but only exists on the level of pure spirit, we can only perceive it by

---

[93] See, for instance, Ananda Coomaraswamy's interesting article, "*Saṃvega*, 'Aesthetic Shock'," *Harvard Journal of Asiatic Studies* 7 (1942-43): 174-79; Alex Wayman, "The Buddhist Theory of Vision," in George Elder, ed., *Buddhist Insight: Essays by Alex Wayman*, (Delhi: Motilal Banarsidass, 1984), pp. 153-61; Stephan Beyer, "Notes on the Vision Quest in Early Mahāyāna," in Lewis Lancaster, ed., *Prajñāpāramitā and Related Systems*, pp. 329-40.

means of objectification in the form of images."[94] For the iconoclasts, part of the problem with images is deeply theological: images involve a misunderstanding of the nature of God. In the words of Calvin: "Since God has no similarity to those shapes by means of which people attempt to represent him, then all attempts to depict him are an impudent affront...to his majesty and glory."[95] However, between the lines of such critiques, including those of Luther, Zwingli, Wyclif, and others, "we can infer a criticism of luxury and unnecessary expenditure;" what was most dangerous was "the misguided desire to gain salvation through endowing images and sculptures."[96] The danger is in the *use* of such images, and the potential for the grave error of mistaking the object (the image) for the divine.[97]

Such errors of perception are inherently present in Buddhist images as well; to attach oneself to the image is, as we have just seen, to mistake what is fundamentally illusory and *impermanent* for something real and *permanent*. In the Buddhist discourse on images, however, we do not see two divided positions, so much as a single field. It is, to be sure, a complex field (although, I think, no less complex than the Christian case). What is more, images are situated in a field fundamentally characterized by something very much like Kasulis' notion of *metapraxis*; they are, quite intentionally, objects that mediate between *presence* and *absence*, and which, again to paraphrase Ricoeur, are intended to give rise to thought.

II.B. Seeing Images.

> Om, salutations to the Buddha. When the blessed Buddha was staying at the Jetavana monastery, having returned

---

[94]In Freedberg, *The Power of Images*, p. 166.
[95]Quoted in S. Michalski, *The Reformation and the Visual Arts*, p. 62.
[96]Ibid., p. 5 and p. 7.
[97]The basis for this Christian iconoclastic position is, of course, shared by both Judaism and Islām. It is important to note, however, that iconoclasm is rarely *simply* motivated by theology. Witness, for instance, the iconoclastic riots of the mid-16th century in the Netherlands, which had as much to do with the social and political milieu as with any theological stance. See Sergiusz Michalski, *The Reformation and the Visual Arts*, for the Protestant context; see also, for the early Israelite context, Tryggve N. D. Mettinger, *No Graven Image? Israelite Aniconism in its Ancient Near Eastern Context* (Stockholm: Almqvist and Wiksell, 1995).

> from most excellent Tusita heaven after having instructed his mother in the *dharma*, Śāriputra said this to the Blessed One: "Oh, Blessed One! When you have gone, or when you have entered *parinirvāṇa*, what is [to be] the proper behavior by the faithful sons of good families?" The Blessed One replied: "Oh Śāriputra, when I have gone or when I have entered *parinirvāṇa*, an image with the circumference of a banyan tree is to be made.... The image is to be made for the purpose of reverence and worship."
>
> *Pratimālakṣaṇam*[98]

Despite the sometimes heated scholarly debates over the earliest Buddha images and the origins of these images, there are suprisingly few textual references to images and image making in early Buddhism. In all of the Pāli Canonical literature there is not a single reference to images of the Buddha. This is a striking fact, but it is also an understandable one, I think. The Pāli Canon is, after all, largely concerned with events contemporaneous with the living Buddha. Certainly shortly before and immediately after his death there is discussion of his corporeal remains, but there is simply no mention of images.[99] This lack of image talk indicates, at least on an intuitive level, that images of the Buddha are unnecessary except in his absence. This, then, leads us to look more closely at *why* images of the Buddha are made.

Although an exhaustive analysis of the vast body of Pāli commentarial literature is clearly beyond the scope of my discussion,

---

[98]Jitendra Banerjea, "*Pratimālakṣaṇam*," *Journal of the Department of Letters, University of Calcutta* 23 (1933): 1-85; *oṃ namo buddhāya / buddhobhagavāñjetavane viharati sma / tuṣitavarabhavanānmātudharma-deśanādāgatakālasamaye śāriputro bhagavantametadavocat // bhagavan bhagavati gate parinirvate vā śraddhaiḥ kulputraiḥ kathaṃ pratipattavyaṃ / bhagavānāha // śāriputra mayi gate parinirvate vā nyagrodhaparimaṇḍalaṃ kāyaṃ kartavyaṃ ....pūjāsatkārārthampratimā kartavyā /*. Banerjea prints a translation as well as the text of the "*Pratimālakṣaṇam*," although the translation here is my own. It is noteworthy, I think, that *kāya* (body) and *pratimā* (image) are used interchangeably here, although I am hesitant to draw any conclusions about the relationship between the two on the basis of this passage alone.

[99]The earliest textual references to images seems to be from the Mathurā inscriptions; see H. Lüders and K.L. Janert, *Mathurā Inscriptions* (Göttingen, 1961), numbers 4, 9, 29, 74, 135, 167, and 180, among others.

there are a few specific references that I wish to examine because they demonstrate that images were in part made to fill the void left by the absent Buddha. They were intended, in contrast to Lamotte's "out of sight" remark, to bring him back in to sight.

In the extra-canonical *Samantapāsādikā*, the commentary on the *Vinaya,*[100] there are several references to two of the most common Pāli terms for images, *viggaha* and *paṭimam.*[101] The precise distinction

---

[100]It is perhaps significant that these references occur in the *Vinaya* commentary, since much of the fuel behind the *aniconic* thesis about early Buddhist art has been a purported ban on images in the *Vinaya*. In fact, only one such passage occurs, in the *Mulasarvāstivādin Vinaya*, where the Buddha is said to have explicitly prohibited the use of images; see the "appendix" to Arthur Waley's article, "Did the Buddha Die of Eating Pork?" *Mélanges chinois et bouddhiques* 1 (1932): 352-54. See also G. Roth, "The Physical Presence of the Buddha and its Representation in Buddhist Literature," in *Investigating Indian Art* (Berlin: Museum für Indische Kunst, 1987), pp. 291-312. One of the most commonly cited passages to support the purported ban on images is the *Kalingabodhi Jātaka* (*Jātaka*, vol. 4, p. 228). Stanley Tambiah, in his *The Buddhist Saints of the Forest*, has seen in this passage "an early Buddhist view against the representation of the Buddha in human form," p. 201. In this *Jātaka*, Anāthapindika learns that while the Buddha is away from Jetavana on pilgrimage, the people of Sāvatthi, in the absence of the Buddha, leave garlands and wreaths at the gateway of the Buddha's chambers. Anāthapindika goes to Ānanda and tells him that the monastery is "unsupported" (*nipaccaye* - this would appear to mean without alms, since there is no place for the lay-people to deliver them, or no Buddha to receive them) while the Buddha is on pilgrimage. He asks Ānanda to speak to the Buddha in order to find out whether there is a place for such offerings (*pūjanīyaṭṭhānassa sakkuṇeyyabhāvaṃ vā asakkuneyyabhāvam vā...*). The Buddha informs Ānanda that of the three kinds of memorials (*cetiyani*), a bodily memorial (*sarīrakaṃ*) is not proper because the Buddha is not dead; an *uddesikaṃ* memorial is not proper because it depends on imagination (*uddesikaṃ avatthukam manamakattena hoti*); a Bodhi tree (here, presumably, a *pāribhogikaṃ* shrine), however, is fit for worship. The Buddha thus allows Ānanda to have a Bodhi tree planted. Tambiah has suggested that the Buddha rejects "personalized" (i.e. *uddesika*) symbols "because such are 'groundless and merely fanciful,' that is, they are only artificially, arbitrarily, and by convention referable to the absent being," pp. 201-02. Tambiah is placing a great deal of emphasis on the word *avatthukaṃ* here. Literally, this means "without ground." This, however, is not some general indictment of image worship (or an iconoclastic "precedent," as Tambiah suggests on p. 202). No images are, in fact, mentioned in this passage. Rather, the specific discussion is about what sort of structure would be most appropriate to allow lay people to bring alms and flowers to the monastery in the Buddha's absence. For a detailed discussion of some of the textual problems with this *Jātaka* passage, see Steven Collins' unpublished manuscript, "Some Remarks on Time in Two Pali Buddhist Texts," footnote 29.

[101]Other terms for images are *rūpa*m ("form," often as *buddharūpam* - see the particularly interesting episode in the *Samantapāsādikā* in which Aśoka convinces a Nagārājā to create an image of the Buddha for him to see, at which point the text reads: *Buddha-rūpam passanto satt-divasāni akkhi-pūjam nāma akāsi*, *Samantapāsādikā*, vol. 3, pp. 43-44; *bimba* and *paṭibimba*, see Ñāṇamoli Bhikkhu, trans., *The Path of Purification (Visuddhimagga)* (Colombo: Buddhist Publication Society, 1975), p. 140, as well as in the *Vimāna-vatthu*, E.R. Gooneratne, ed. (London: Pali Text Society, n.d.), p. 50; and occassionally *śarīra*, such as *Jātaka*, vol. 5, p. 398.

between the two is not at all clear. *Viggaha* (Sk. *vigrāha*) derives from the Vedic root *grah*, "grasp, grab, seize," with the prefix "*vi*" here serving as an intensifier. Hence the *viggaha* "seizes" that which it depicts - or it enables the viewer to seize on to it. *Paṭimā* (Sk. *pratimā*) comes from the verbal root *mā*, "measure," with the suffix *pati* functioning here as a comparison, as in that which is "measured against" the original, or copied. Most of the occurrences of these terms are not of particular interest, in that they fail to explain *why* Buddhists made images; however, there are two that are particularly worthy of note.

The first, which we have already encountered, is embedded in a list of objects deserving of veneration: "Honor the eldest member of the community, the Bodhi tree, an image, a shrine."[102] Here we will have to examine the actual Pāli original, "*cetiyaṃ paṭimaṃ bodhiṃ saṅghattheram vandathā ti*," in order to understand its significance. What is most striking is the inclusion of the word "*paṭimaṃ*," or "image," as an object of veneration. Indeed, Walpola Rahula has gone so far as to suggest that "the Buddha image, though in existence at the time, was not given a place in the scheme of worship by the Pāli Commentaries....the image is completely ignored."[103] The other objects are rather obviously worthy of respect and veneration: a shrine, or "*cetiyaṃ*," contains the physical remains of the Buddha, and thus, as Schopen has argued, is in some way involved with his presence; the bodhi tree, likewise, has a direct connections with the Buddha, in that it is under such a tree that he attained enlightenment; and the eldest member of the *saṅgha*, "*saṅghattheram*," is almost by definition worthy of veneration and respect. This leaves the image, then, the "*paṭimaṃ*." Rahula has remarked that in Buddhism, "An image was considered important only if relics were enshrined in it. Without them it was a thing of little or no religious value."[104] Here,

---

Other terms can also refere to images, although in a more general sense, such as *vesa* (i.e. dress, disguise, appearance), and *obhāsa*, which as we have already seen has a broad semantic range.

[102] *Samantapāsādikā*, p. 627.

[103] Walpola Rahula, *History of Buddhism in Ceylon* (Colombo: M.D. Gunasena and Co., Ltd., 1956), p. 126.

[104] Ibid., p. 126.

however, we have only the word "image," not "image with relics," or an image that is "*sadhātuka.*"

Apparently, not all early Buddhists would have agreed with Rahula's analysis of images. But why would an image, without relics, be considered worthy of respect and veneration on its own? Part of this has to do with the degree to which the image truly is a *patimam*, truly is an "accurate measure" of the Buddha, is also significant. In other words, the degree to which the image is able to re*present* the physically absent Buddha. Thus, elsewhere in the *Samantapāsādikā* we encounter a similar passage in which an image (here containing relics) not only represents, but actually "sits in" for the absent Buddha:

> Formerly, they gave gifts to both sides of the Saṅgha [i.e. male and female], headed by the Buddha; the Blessed One sat in the middle, the *bhikkhu*s sat on the right, the *bhikkuni*s sat on the left, [and] the Blessed One was the Saṅghathera of both; then the Blessed One himself received the gifts and also enjoyed them himself; then he had them given to the *bhikkhu*s. Now, however, learned people, having [first] set up either a reliquary or an image enclosing relics, give gifts to both Saṅghas, headed by the Buddha. Having set a bowl on a stand in front of the image or reliquary, and having given water as an offering, they say, "We will give to the Buddhas."[105]

[105] *Samantapāsādikā*, vol. 3, p. 32; *pubbe 'pi buddhappamukhassa ubhatosaṅghassa dānam denti, bhagavā majjhe nisīdati, dakkhiṇato bhikkhū vāmato bhikkuniyo nisīdanti, bhagavā ubhinnaṃ saṅghatthero, tadā bhagavā attanā laddhapaccaye attanāpi paribhuñjati, bhikkhūnam pi dāpeti. etarahi pana paṇḍitamanussā sadhātukam paṭimaṃ vā cetiyaṃ vā ṭhapetvā buddhappamukhassa ubatosaṅghassa dānam denti. paṭimāya vā cetiyassa vā purato ādhārake pattam ṭhapetvā dakkhiṇodakam datvā buddhānaṃ demā 'ti....* Steven Collins writes about a remarkably similar passage that occurs at *Samantapāsādikā*, vol. 5, p. 73; see his "*Nirvāna*, Time, and Narrative," p. 237.

There are many points of interest here,[106] the most relevant of which is the temporal dimension, the emphasis on before (*pubbe*) and now (*etarahi*). Before, in the past, while the Buddha was alive, he was the leader of the Saṅgha, the one who sat at the head of the assembly, the one who first received gifts from the laity. Now, however, when the Buddha is absent, gone to *nibbāna*, a kind of *ersatz* Buddha is used to replace him, to mediate his presence: offerings are thus made to the Buddha via the medium of the statue (or *cetiya*).

Although Collins is certainly warranted in his reservations about the use of the language of "presence" with regard to Buddhism, the language in this passage comes very close, indeed, to just the sort of *presence* we see in early Christianity, even if we encounter no *emic* terms in the Buddhist materials. Peter Brown, in his *The Cult of the Saints*, describes the milieu in which the early Christian cult of the saints arose as being one in which Mediterranean men and women, beginning in the fourth century, "turned with increasing explicitness for friendship, inspiration and protection in this life and beyond the grave, to invisible beings who were fellow humans and whom they could invest with the precise and palpable features of beloved and powerful figures in their own society."[107] Thus, in venerating the bodily relics, early Christians were able to make present those who were dead. As in the early Christian context, relics were perhaps the primary means by which Buddhists brought the absent "invisible being" - the Buddha - into the visible present; as the passage from Buddhaghosa's *Samantapāsādikā* demonstrates, though, visual images such as sculptures could also serve this function. And also as in the Christian context, this presence was always in dialectical tension with absence. As Brown puts it, "The carefully maintained tension

---

[106]One of the more interesting, and puzzling, aspects of this passage is the plural *buddhānaṃ*. It is difficult to know what to make of this, but as Collins has pointed out, reference to multiple Buddhas is not terribly unusual in Theravāda texts; see his "*Nirvāna*, Time, and Narrative," p. 238. In this passage from *Sp*, however, it is not clear how more than one Buddha fits into the context.

[107]Peter Brown, *The Cult of the Saints: Its Rise and Function in Latin Christianity* (Chicago: University of Chicago Press, 1981), p. 50; see also Hans Belting, *Likeness and Presence: A History of the Image Before the Era of Art*, Edmund Jephcott, trans., (Chicago: University of Chicago Press, 1994), who points out: "The likeness is not honored in the name of the image but in the name of the person represented, the image being only a means to an end," p. 153.

between distance and proximity ensured one thing: *praesentia*...the *prasentia* on which such heady enthusiasm focused was the presence of the invisible person."[108]

We see this basic idea expressed in the many versions of the Prasenajit story, one of the clearest, and perhaps also one of the earliest, expressions of a reason for making images of the Buddha.[109] The story, as recorded by the Chinese pilgrim, Faxian, goes as follows:

> When the Buddha went up to heaven for ninety days to preach the Faith to his mother, king Prasenajit, longing to see him, caused to be carved in sandalwood from the Bull's head mountain an image of Buddha and placed it where Buddha usually sat. Later on, when Buddha returned to the shrine, the image straightaway quitted the seat and came forth to receive him. Buddha cried out, "Return to your seat: after my disappearance you shall be the model for the four classes in search of spiritual truth." At this, the image went back to the seat. It was the very first of all such images, and is that which later ages have copied.[110]

The degree to which the image *mediates* the absence of the Buddha here is obvious. Whether this is in fact a very early story that was still popular in Faxian's time, or whether it is in fact a much later

[108]Ibid., p. 88; Brown here is specifically discussing pilgrimage, a topic to which I will turn in the next chapter.

[109]A. Waley notes that there is a version in the *Ekottarāgama*, as well as various Mahāyāna and Hīnayāna texts translated into Tibetan and Chinese; see "Did the Buddha Die of Eating Pork," pp. 353-54. See also Richard Gombrich's interesting discussion of the *Kosala-Bimba-Vannanā*, a medieval Sri Lankan text in Pāli (the text as well as Gombrich's translation are printed in the article), "Kosala-Bimba-Vannanā," in Heinz Bechert, ed. *Buddhism in Ceylon and Studies on Religious Syncretism in Buddhist Countries*, Symposien zur Buddhismusforschung, I, Akademie der Wissenschaften, Göttingen, Philogisch-Historische Klasse, Dritte Folge, no. 108 (Göttingen: Vandenhoeck and Ruprecht, 1978), pp. 281-303.

[110]H.A. Giles, trans., *The Travels of Fa hsien* (Cambridge: Cambridge University Press, 1923), pp. 30-31.

"explanation" for the existence of Buddha images, the image clearly is intended to "fill in" for the Buddha in his absence, just as we have just seen in the commentary on the *Vinaya*. Xuanzang records an almost identical story, although in it King Udāyana replaces Prasenajit. In this version of the story, *the Buddha himself* explicitly expresses the function of the image. Upon his return from the Trāyastrimśati heaven, where he has been preaching the *dharma* to his mother for three months, he encounters a sandal-wood image of himself, carved by King Udāyana in his absence. The Buddha tells the image, in what amounts to a kind of prescriptive commentary on the proper place of images in the future: "The work expected from you is to toil in the conversion of heretics, and to lead the way of religion in future ages."[111] This history of scattered examples is certainly not intended to be exhaustive. Rather, I have considered these few passages here in an attempt to illustrate that Buddhists did not begin making images of the Buddha as a result of some sudden and overwhelmingly powerful "wave of visual theism" that swept across Buddhist culture with the rise of Mahāyāna.[112] There is, as we shall see in the following chapters, a much greater emphasis on visual images in the Mahāyāna, both in terms of the number of images produced as well as textual discourses that discuss these images. This emphasis did not simply burst on to the scene; it was instead the result of a gradually developed and multi-layered *habitus*, a *habitus*

---

[111]Samuel Beal, *Si-Yu-Ki: Buddhist Records of the Western World Translated from the Chinese of Hiuen Tsiang (A.D. 629)*, vol. 1 (London: Trubner, 1884), pp. 236. In a footnote, Beal gives the somewhat less hyperbolic: "To teach and convert with diligence the unbelieving, to open the way for guiding future generations, this is your work." There are numerous references to the Udāyana image in the Chinese materials; see Alexander Soper, *Literary Evidence for Early Buddhist Art in China* (Ascona, Switzerland: Artibus Asiae Publishers, 1959); for a more recent, and more thorough, discussion of these references, see Robert Campany, "'Aśokan Stūpas,' Images, and the Cult of Relics in Early Medieval China," unpublished paper presented to the 1995 session of the AAR Seminar on Buddhist Relic Veneration. See also Padmandabh S. Jaini, "On the Buddha Image," in A.K. Narain, ed., *Studies in Pali and Buddhism: A Homage Volume to the Memory of Bhikkhu Jagdish Kashyap* (Delhi: , 1979), pp 183-88; here Jaini discusses a Thai story in a Burmese manuscript of the Prasenajit story, contained within the Burmese Jātaka collection as the *Vattaṅgulirāja-Jātaka* (no. 37); and see also G. Roth's excellent article, "The Physical Presence of the Buddha and its Representation in Buddhist Literature."
[112]I borrow this phrase, out of context, from Stephan Beyer; see his "Notes on the Vision Quest in Early Mahāyāna," in Lewis Lancaster, ed., *Prajñāpāramitā and Related Systems*, pp. 329-40.

constituted by a range of overlapping and inter-connected strategies intended to respond to the *absence* of the Buddha and to contemplate - and I mean this on both the level of the individual Buddhist practitioner and of the institution of medieval Indian Buddhism - the gap between this absence and the desire, and perhaps also the need, for his *presence*.

III. Image Thought

> Therefore in the presence of an image
> Or reliquary or something else
> Say these twenty stanzas
> Three times a day.
>
> Nāgārjuna[113]

> If they can maintain mindfulness of the Buddha without interruption from moment to moment, then they will be able to see all the Buddhas of the past, present, and future right in each moment.
>
> Mahāratnakūta Sūtra[114]

An important strategy to negotiate the absence of the Buddha as a teacher and guide, and one directly relevant to the issue of visual images, is the practice of *buddhānusmṛti* (Pāli, *buddhānussati*), "recollection of the Buddha." Although this is typically portrayed as a meditational practice, *buddhānusmṛti* is also a *mediating* practice, in that it can *make present* the absent Buddha. Recollection of the Buddha also often explicitly involves the use of physical images in addition to the creation of a mental image of the Buddha - what we might call "iconographic thought" about the Buddha.

---

[113]See Jeffrey Hopkins and Lati Rinpoche, trans., *The Precious Garland and the Song of the Four Mindfulnesses* (London: George Allen and Unwin, 1971), p.87.

[114]Quoted in Garma C.C. Chang, ed., *A Treasury of Mahāyāna Sūtras: Selections from the Mahāratnakūṭa Sūtra* (University Park: Pennsylvania State University Press, 1983), p. 110.

In the Pāli materials, *anussati* tends to be rather low on the scale of things, a preliminary step in the more complex systems of meditation. Winston King, for instance, calls the different forms of *anussati* "preliminary low-level" techniques "in which one's mood is set favorably toward the meditative process but that produce no recognized level of higher awareness....this type of meditation never reaches that deep inner isolation of consciousness, completely cut off from outer stimuli, that takes place in the jhānas...."[115] In this light, *buddhānussati* is a kind of meditational warm-up, a rather simple exercise intended to "clear the slate" for the higher levels of jhānic attainment. Edward Conze notes that the descriptions of the recollections are "rather sober and restrained, without great emotional fervour."[116] *Anussati*, according to Paul Harrison, is "a kind of exercise in the power of positive thinking, but of the most abstract kind."[117]

Buddhānussati is the first item in a larger list of either six or ten things to which one should devote one's thoughts; it is "a name for mindfulness with the Buddha's virtues as object."[118] Buddhaghosa, in his long exposition of the different forms of *anussati*, opens his description of *buddhānussati* in this way:

> Now a meditator with absolute confidence who wants to develop firstly the recollection of the Enlightened One among these then should go into solitary retreat in a favourable abode and recollect the special qualities of the Enlightened One, the Blessed One, as

[115]Winston King, *Theravāda Meditation: The Buddhist Transformation of Yoga* (University Park, PA: Pennsylvania State University Press, 1980), p. 33 and p. 38.

[116]Edward Conze, *Buddhist Meditation* (London: George Allen and Unwin Ltd., 1956), p. 28. Conze here is following in a long line of "rationalizers" of Buddhism - those who wish to portray as "pure Buddhism" that which has no taint of what Conze, later in the same volume, calls practices "which offered salvation at a cheap price," p. 61. See Philip Almond, *The British Discovery of Buddhism*, for a particularly good discussion of this "rationalizing" construction of Buddhism.

[117]Paul Harrison, "Commemoration and Identification in *Buddhānusmṛti*," in Janet Gyatso, ed., *In the Mirror of Memory*, pp. 216-17.

[118]See *Anguttara Nikāya*, vol. 5, Richard Morris and E. Hardy, eds. (London: Pali Text Society, 1955-61), pp. 328-32 for the six-fold list, and *Anguttara Nikāya*, vol 1, p. 30 for the ten-fold.

> follows: "That Blessed One is such since he is accomplished, fully enlightened, endowed with (clear) vision and (virtuous) conduct, sublime, the knower of worlds, the incomparable leader of men to be tamed, the teacher of gods and men, enlightened and blessed."[119]

The effect of this practice is the greater concentration of the mind that then enables one to move on to the cultivation of the higher *jhānas*. "As he continues to exercise applied thought and sustained thought upon the Enlightened One's special qualities," says Buddhaghosa, "happiness arises in him."[120] This leads to tranquility and bliss: "When he is blissful, his mind, with the Enlightened One's special qualities for its object, becomes concentrated, and so the jhana factors eventually arise in a single moment."[121] There is thus a sort of mimetic rationale for the development of *buddhānussati* in the Pāli texts; one is to concentrate on the qualities of the Buddha in order to emulate him and, in the process, to develop those virtues he exemplifies.

Mimesis is not, however, the only rational for recollecting the Buddha.[122] At the end of the section in the *Visuddhimagga* enumerating the various qualities of the Buddha, Buddhaghosa states: "When a bhikkhu is devoted to this recollection of the Buddha, he is respectful and deferential towards the Master. He attains fullness of faith, mindfulness, understanding and merit. He has much happiness and gladness. He conquers fear and dread. He is able to endure pain. *He comes to feel as if he were living in the Master's presence*."[123]

---

[119]Ñāṇamoli Bhikkhu, *Visuddhimagga*, p. 206. Buddhaghosa's commentary is on the standard formula for *buddhānussati*: *Iti pi bhagavā arahaṃ sammāsambuddho vijjācaraṇa-sampanno sugato lokavidū anuttaro purisadammasārathi satthā devamanussānam buddho bhagavā ti*, *Dīgha Nikāya*, vol. 1, p. 49, and *Anguttara Nikāya*, vol. 3, p. 285.

[120]Ñāṇamoli Bhikkhu, *Visuddhimagga*, p. 229.

[121]Ibid., pp. 229-30.

[122]Harrison has noted that there is an apotropaic function to *anussati*; at *Saṃyutta Nikāya*, vol. 1, p. 218, for instance, the Buddha is said to have prescribed the first three *anussati* as a method to ward off fear while meditating in solitary places. See Paul Harrison, "Commemoration and Identification in *Buddhānusmṛti*," p. 218.

[123]This is Ñāṇamoli's translation, *Visuddhimagga*, p. 230, emphasis added.

Thus, by recollecting and concentrating on the Buddha's many virtues, the meditator creates a mental picture so vivid and lifelike that the absent Buddha is made present.

It is not, perhaps, immediately clear what these recollections - these mental images - have to do with visual images made of stone and wood. Buddhaghosa does not introduce any specifically *visual* language here, although his long elaboration of the special qualities of the Buddha does, in a way, create a visual image of the Buddha, such that: "When he encounters an opportunity for transgression, he has awareness of conscience and shame as vivid as though he were face to face with the Master."[124] In the *Vimuttimagga*,[125] however, this *visual* aspect is made explicit: "If a man wishes to meditate on the Buddha, he should worship Buddha images and such other objects."[126] The text does not mention meditation on the Buddha's physical form anywhere, but as Harrison has noted, this reference in the *Vimuttimagga* is "a tantalizing clue."[127]

Harrison sees a gradual movement in terms of the conception of the Buddha. At first, the Buddha was a teacher and exemplary religious figure, and the emphasis was, as we have seen, on hearing the *dhamma* directly from him and, later, conforming to the model he had established while alive. However, as Harrison points out:

> As much as the corpus of his teachings (the Dharma) was preserved, transmitted, and inexorably enlarged, his followers must still have felt keenly how

---

[124]Ibid., p.230.

[125]The relationship between these two texts is, to say the least, ambiguous, and is not really relevant here. See P.V. Bapat, *Vimuttimagga and Visuddhimagga: A Comparative Study* (Calcutta: J.C. Sarkhel, 1937).

[126]N.R.M Ehara, Soma Thera, and Kheminda Thera, trans., *The Path of Freedom (Vimuttimagga)* (Colombo: Roland D. Weerasuria, 1961), p. 141.

[127]Harrison has pointed out that in the Chinese translations of the Sanskrit Āgamas, in particular the *Ekottarāgama* III, *buddhānusmrti* is propounded "as the one practice for realizing all spiritual goals and [it] recommends that practitioners contemplate the image of the Buddha without taking their eyes off it, that they call to mind the body and the countenance of the Buddha and then his moral and mental qualities, arranged under the traditional rubrics of morality, mediation, wisdom, liberation, and the cognition and vision of liberation...," see Paul Harrison, "Commemoration and Identification in *Buddhānusmrti*," p. 220.

> unfortunate it was to be deprived of his actual presence.... It is not too difficult to conceive how *buddhānusmṛti* was pressed into service in such circumstances, until practices were evolved that entailed not merely a reminiscence of the Buddha, *but an imaginative evocation of his presence* by means of structured meditative procedures.[128]

In other words, the paradigmatic quality of the Buddha, and the concomitant emphasis on mimesis, is replaced; the Buddha becomes not so much a figure to be emulated, but one to be venerated.

Harrison has written extensively on an early Mahāyāna text that represents a developed form of *buddhānusmṛti*, a text that includes both a more standard discussion of meditation on the physical body of the Buddha,[129] as well as a detailed treatment of the importance of images in devotional practice. The text is appropriately entitled the *Pratyutpanna-buddha-saṃmukhāvasthita-samādhi-sūtra*,[130] or as Harrison translates it, the "*Sūtra* on the direct encounter with the Buddhas of the present." The main point of this *sūtra* is to "provide practitioners with the means to translate themselves into the presence of this or that particular manifestation of the Buddha-principle for the purpose of hearing the *dharma*, which they subsequently remember and propagate to others."[131] The Buddhas discussed in this text are not the historical Buddha Śākyamuni, but figures such as Amitābha. However, Harrison notes, somewhat

---

[128]Paul Harrison, "Buddhānusmrti in the Pratyutpanna-Buddha-Sammukhāvasthita-Samādhi-Sūtra," *Journal of Indian Philosophy* 6 (1978): 35-57, p. 37, emphasis added. Harrison produces a translation here of a particularly relevant passage in the *Ekottarāgama* (extant only in the Chinese translations of the Sanskrit) in which *buddhānusmrti* is discussed: "Without entertaining any other thought he earnestly calls to mind (*anusmr-*) the Buddha. He contemplates the image of the Tathāgata without taking his eyes off it...," p. 38. "Image" here is denoted by the Chinese *hsing*, and Harrison notes that it is unclear whether it refers to a *mental* image or a *physical* one, or both.

[129]I say "more standard" here because this attention to the magnificent qualities of the Buddha's body are common in the Pāli materials as well as the early Mahāyāna texts.

[130]See Paul Harrison's edited version, along with a translation, *The Samādhi of Direct Encounter with the Buddhas of the Present* (Tokyo: The International Institute for Buddhist Studies, 1990).

[131]Ibid., p. xx.

problematically, that these Buddhas are "simply idealized clones of Śākyamuni transposed to different world systems."[132]

Although the "*Sūtra* on the direct encounter with the Buddhas of the present" is largely concerned with meditational techniques (hence the *samādhi* in the title), there are several very relevant discussions of the use of images in the cultivation of this *samādhi*. For instance, the *samādhi* itself is attained through an extremely detailed visualization of the Buddha, in much the same way as we have seen in the Pāli texts, but with an even greater attention to the iconographic qualities of the Buddha's physical body. As Harrison puts it, "To aid this detailed iconographical visualization, practitioners are encouraged to imagine the Buddha's body *as resembling an image....*"[133] In the *Pratyutpanna-buddha-sammukhāvasthita-samādhi-sūtra*, images act as a kind of *visual cue*: "If you desire this most excellent of *samādhi*s / Paint pictures well, and construct images of the Incomparable One, / Which have the marks complete, resemble the colour of gold, / Are large, and flawless."[134] In other words, by gazing at the artistically created *physical* image, the practitioner is able to conjure up a detailed mental image of the Buddha; in turn, it is via this "mental visualization" that one is fully able to recollect the Buddha, a process that, if perfected, effectively brings the Buddha into the present. Significantly, even this "direct encounter" with the Buddha is described in the text in specifically iconographic terms: "In that way those bodhisattvas will see the Tathāgata (like) a beautifully set up beryl image."[135]

This idea that the Buddha's physical body resembles an image is seen elsewhere in early Mahāyāna texts. In what may be the earliest Mahāyāna *sūtra* composed in India, the *Tao-hsing Ching* of Lokaksema (compiled in 179 C.E.), we encounter this passage:

> The Buddha's body is like the images which men make after the Nirvāna of the Buddha. When they

[132]Paul Harrison, "Commemoration and Identification in *Buddhānusmrti*," p. 220.
[133]Ibid., p. 222.
[134]Harrison, *Direct Encounter*, p. 47.
[135]Ibid., p. 40.

> see these images, there is not one of them who does not bow down and make offering. These images are upright and handsome; they perfectly resemble the Buddha and when men see them they all rejoice and take flowers and incense to revere them.[136]

The context of this passage is a conversation between the Bodhisattvas Sadāprarudita, who is in search of the *Prajñāpāramitā* teachings, and Dharmodgata, who guides and instructs Sadāprarudita.[137] I will return to this story below, but what is relevant at this point is the close interplay between the present (inanimate) image and the absent (formerly animate) Buddha. As we have already seen in the Pāli texts, with the creation of the sandalwood image in the Prasenajit story, and the substitution of the image for the dead Buddha in the midst of the assembled Saṅgha as described in the *Samantapāsādikā*, the rationale for making and venerating Buddha images passes fluidly between a commemorative sort of representation of the absent Teacher, and a more ambiguous sort of recollection, one that explicitly *makes present* the Buddha. Again, what we see is metapractical reflection in action here. Indeed, as I hope has been clear from my discussion, the concepts of absence and presence in the Buddhist context always come as a set, a pair of oppositions held in a dynamic sort of tension. It is only with the positing of absence that presence becomes important, and thus the significance of the Buddha's presence is always caught up in the ultimate reality of his absence.

---

[136]Lewis R. Lancaster, "An Early Mahayana Sermon about the Body of the Buddha and the Making of images," *Artibus Asiae* 36 (1974): 287-91, p. 289.

[137]This part of the story is not contained in the Sanskrit recension of the *Astasāhasrikāprajñāpāramitā Sūtra*, the text upon which Lokaksema's *Tao-hsing Ching* is based.

Chapter Four

THE IMAGE OF WISDOM

> Indeed, those of trifling comprehension will not understand that the perfection of wisdom is the nourishment of the knowledge of the omniscient one.
>
> *Aṣṭasāhasrikāprajñāpāramitā*[1]

> Wisdom is the jewel of human beings.
>
> *Saṃyutta Nikāya*[2]

Thus far I have examined a variety of reasons for constructing Buddha images. I have discussed the great importance placed on being in the physical *presence* of the Buddha, on hearing the *dharma* directly from him, and on seeing his physical form. I have also examined some of the problems posed by the physical *absence* of the Buddha, as well as the various strategies Buddhists have employed to cope with this absence. In particular, I have argued that the construction of visual images serves to mediate, in a metapractical manner, between the wish for a *present* Buddha and the reality of his *absence*. In this chapter, I now turn to the specific dynamics of, wisdom, *prajñā*, as it relates to these issues.

First, I discuss the overall importance of *prajñā* in Buddhism: briefly in the early Nikāya, or Pāli context; and then more extensively in what I have referred to as "mainstream Mahāyāna," by which I mean primarily the *Prajñāpāramitā*, or "Perfection of Wisdom," genre, along with the work of one of the most important medieval Buddhists to write on the subject, Śāntideva. Once I have laid this more textual, and more philosophical, foundation, I shall then turn to the ways in which this most important, and most abstract, of concepts is visually represented in the two most prominent forms of Pāla-period sculptural

---

[1] *Aṣṭasāhasrikāprajñāpāramitā*, edited by P.L. Vaidya, Buddhist Sanskrit Texts, no. 4 (Darbhanga: Mithila Institute, 1960), p. 116; *na hi te 'lpabuddhayo jñāsyanti prajñāpāramitā āhārikā sarvajñajñānasyeti.*

[2] *Saṃyutta Nikāya*, vol. 1, pp. 36-37; *paññā narānaṃ ratanaṃ.*

representation of the Buddha, the *bhūmisparśamudrā* (or "earth-touching gesture") and the *dharmacakrapravartanamudrā* (or "turning-the-wheel-of-*dharma* gesture") forms.

At the heart of my discussion is my argument that these sculptures do not simply *illustrate* or *narrate* significant events in the Buddha's life. Certainly, on one level they do serve this function. But on another, perhaps more religiously significant level, such sculptures also *make available* the Buddha's *prajñā*. Furthermore, such sculptures were located in, and constituted by, what we might call a broader visual and intellectual *habitus* that was dominated by wisdom, a *habitus* that stretches all the way back to the Buddha's own lifetime, and which becomes the central concern of Pāla-period Buddhists. Thus, in seeing the Buddha - either in the flesh, or in a stone sculpture, or in a mental vision - one beholds and, perhaps more importantly, one gains an opportunity to partake of the Buddha's salvific wisdom.

I. What is *Prajñā*?[3]

> It must be admitted...the precise meaning of *prajñā* itself remains obscure. One sometimes feels that nothing definite can be said beyond the statement that *prajñā* is something which was attained by the Buddha and is attainable by the bodhisattvas.
>
> Padmanabh Jaini[4]

---

[3]Throughout this study, I have chosen to translate *prajñā* and *paññā* as "wisdom." Virtually every scholar who has written on this concept has, in one way or another, remarked on the inadequacy of English translations of *prajñā*. Some have opted for the Greek "*gnosis*", others for "understanding," still others for "insight." Since, in my opinion, none of these terms quite captures *prajñā*, I have chosen the more prosaic, and perhaps more ambiguous, "wisdom" out of lexical convenience, since it is as "wisdom" that *prajñā* is most often translated.
[4]Padmanabh S. Jaini, "*Prajñā* and *drsti* in the Vaibhāsika Abhidharma," in Lewis Lancaster, ed., *Prajñāpāramitā and Related Systems*, pp. 403.

I.A. The Pāli Context.

> Concerning things that had not been heard before, monks, there then arose in me vision, knowledge, wisdom....
>
> *Dhammacakkapavatana Sutta*[5]

Although it is with the *Prajñāpāramitā* genre that *prajñā* becomes the preeminent motif in Buddhism, *prajñā* (or *paññā*, in Pāli) plays an important - indeed, an essential - role in earlier Buddhism as well. Furthermore, I want to argue, in order to understand the visual motif of *prajñā* in the Pāla period, it is necessary to situate this motif in a much broader discursive (*and* visual) *habitus* that includes the Pāli context; in other words, it is this earlier discourse that explicitly and implicitly - or we might say consciously and unconsciously - informs and constitutes the context in which Pāla-period Buddhists beheld and responded to visual representations that involve *prajñā*.

In the *Nikāyas*, *paññā* is the third of the three-fold training (*tisikkha*), or three-fold teaching (*tividhasikkhā*), one of the most basic divisions of the *dhamma*, composed of *sīla*, *samādhi*, and *paññā*.[6] Although the three are necessarily interrelated, there is also a kind of progressive hierarchy in their relationship, in that *sīla* enables the practice of *samādhi*, which in turn enables the cultivation of *paññā*, which then opens the way to *nibbāna*. Indeed, it is precisely *paññā* that is the insight into the nature of things and which leads directly to enlightenment; thus although it must be accompanied by *sīla* and *samādhi*, it is the cultivation of *paññā* that leads to the conquering of the *āsavas*, and, ideally, which leads to *nibbāna*.[7] As one of the

[5]*Samyutta Nikāya*, vol. 5, pp. 420-31; *me bhikkhave pubbe ananassutesu dhammesu cakkhuṃ udapādi ñāṇam udapādi paññā udapādi....* As we shall see shortly, this is an extremely important passage in that it establishes Bodhgāya as the seat of wisdom, the place where true wisdom, *paññā*, first arose in the Buddha.

[6]In the eight-fold path, *paññā* consists of *sammādiṭṭhi*, correct view, and *sammāsaṅkappa*, correct intention.

[7]The Pāli is: *puna ca paraṃ bhikkhave bhikkhu sabbaso nevasaññānāsaññāyatanaṃ samtikkamma saññāvedayitanirodhaṃ upasapajja viharati, paññāya c'assa disvā āsavā parikkīṇa honti.* This somewhat formulaic passage is found in several places in the Canon: *Majjhima Nikāya*, vol. 1, V. Treckner and Robert Chalmers, eds. (London: Pali Text Society,

commentaries on Buddhaghosa's *Visuddhimagga* puts it: "It was through understanding [*paññā*] that the Blessed One reached the kingdom of the Law.... It was through understanding that he was brought face to face with nibbana...."[8]

This sense of *paññā* as insight, as what enables one to truly *see*, is found throughout the Pāli Canon, most saliently in the formulaic phrase, "Through (or with) proper wisdom one sees reality."[9] *Paññā*, then, is no ordinary form of knowledge; it is a direct, incisive kind of epistemological faculty that goes right to the heart of the nature of things. As Lamotte puts it, stressing the soteriological efficacy of the development of *paññā*,

> It is this direct, supramundane wisdom which gives rise to holiness and by means of which the ascetic, raised to the level of holy one or Arhat, can solemnly affirm: "I have understood the noble truths, destroyed rebirth, lived the pure life, done what had to be done; henceforth, there will be no further rebirths for me."[10]

Paññā, then, allows one to go beyond ordinary knowing, as suggested by the prefix of the word itself. "It is active as suggested by the 'forward' connotations of the *pa-/pra-* and not merely reflective or passive, and it goes beyond ordinary forms of knowledge."[11]

Although Pāli literature contains a somewhat boggling array of epistemological attainments - boggling in the sense that it is frequently very difficult to discern precisely how one form of

---

1960-64), p. 160, p. 204, p. 209, and p. 477; *Majjhima Nikāya*, vol. 3, p. 85; *Anguttara Nikāya*, vol. 5, p. 209, etc.

[8]This is from the *Paramattha-mañjūsā*, as quoted in Ñānamoli Bhikkhu, *Visuddhimagga*, p.215, n.9.

[9]*Anguttara Nikāya*, vol. 2, p. 171 and p. 202; *yathābhūtam sammappaññāya passati*.

[10]E. Lamotte, *History of Indian Buddhism*, p. 46; the reference here is to *Vinaya Pitaka*, vol. 1, Hermann Oldenberg, ed. (London: Pali Text Society, 1964), pp. 14, 35, 183; *Dīgha Nikāya*, vol. 1, p. 84, p. 177, p. 203; *Majjhima Nikāya*, vol. 1, p. 139; *Samyutta Nikāya*, vol. 1, p. 140; and *Anguttara Nikāya*, vol. 1, p. 165.

[11]Frederic B. Underwood, "Buddhist Insight: The Nature and Function of *Paññā* in the Pali Nikāyas," Ph.D. Dissertation, Columbia University, 1973, p. 32.

knowledge differs from another - Buddhaghosa is fairly clear in marking *paññā* as distinct.[12] *Saññā*, or perception, is "only the mere perceiving of an object, say, 'blue' or 'yellow,' it cannot bring about the penetration of its characteristics as impermanent, painful, and not-self. Consciousness [*viññāṇa*] knows the object as blue or yellow, and it brings about the penetration of its characteristics, but it cannot bring about, by endeavoring, the manifestation of the path."[13] *Paññā*, however, penetrates into the nature of *dhamma*s, cuts into the heart of reality, and leads to the dispersal of the darkness of delusion"[14]

This cutting, incisive sense of *paññā* is metaphorically expressed in several places in the Pāli Canon. In the *Vammīka Sutta*,[15] for example, there is a story about a puzzling anthill, one that blazes in the day and smokes in the night. A young man named Kumārakassapa is advised, rather cryptically, by a brahmin to dig up the anthill; in it he finds all manner of strange objects - a bolt, a frog, a strainer, etc. The brahmin instructs him to discard each of the objects (except for the snake, which is to be honored). The young man, puzzled, goes to the Tathāgata for an explanation, and he is told the metaphorical significance of each object; the digging, and the things dug up, as well as the anthill itself, are all metaphors for emotions and efforts; and finally, the tool used to dig is known as the sword of wisdom.[16] The Buddha repeats the advice to throw away the objects found in the anthill; they are, after all, material objects,

---

[12]For a useful discussion of some of these issues, see Underwood, ibid., pp. 29-32, and the sources cited there.

[13]This is Ñānamoli Bhikkhu's translation, *Visuddhimagga*, p. 480; see also the *Mahāvedalla Sutta*, *Majjhima Nikāya*, vol. 1, p. 293 ff, for a canonical treatment of this topic. C.W. Huntington notes that this division of epistemological categories is a mark of the later Abhidharmika scholastics; "In this literature, prajñā is distinguished from these two [*samjñā* and *vijñāna*] as a particular innate faculty of the mind which reveals the nature of everyday experience as it is, divorced from any preconceived notions about its reality or value," *The Emptiness of Emptiness: An Introduction to Early Indian Mādhyamika* (Honolulu: University of Hawaii Press, 1989), p. 85.

[14]See Ñānamoli Bhikkhu, *Visuddhimagga*, p. 438; the Pāli reads, in part, *Ettha pana dhammasabhāva-paṭivedhalakkhanā paññā; dhammānaṃ sabhāvapaṭicchādakmohandha-kāraviddhamsanarasā; asammohapaccupaṭṭhānā*...."

[15]*Majjhima Nikāya*, vol. 1, pp. 142-45.

[16]Ibid., p. 144; the Pāli here reads: *satthan-ti kho bhikkhu ariyāy' etam paññāya adhivacanam*.

desires, *āsavas*.[17] It is only through the effort, *viriya*, of digging with the ultimate tool, the sword (*satthan*, although in this context it might be better to use the less poetic "shovel") of *paññā* that the desire for these objects is overcome.[18]

A similar metaphor is found in the *Sunakkhatta Sutta*,[19] in which a man is struck by an arrow, and a surgeon is called to extract it. Again, the metaphors all concern cravings, emotions, etc.. The context of this story is the Buddha's reproachment of *bhikkhus* who believe that they have reached the end of the Path before they have conquered their desires, before their *āsavas* are extinguished. The arrow signifies the most obvious of the *āsavas*, *tanhā* (craving), however, although the arrow itself may be removed, there still might be poison left in the wound (that is, the residual effects of *tanhā* might still remain). It takes a skilled surgeon, and a sharp scalpel, to remove not only the arrow, but also to remove the poison left in the wound, and finally to prescribe the correct healing regiment, including the correct foods and the correct method for keeping the wound clean. The surgeon here is the Buddha himself, of course, and his scalpel is *paññā*. Although anyone can cultivate *paññā*, it is the Buddha who is the one who most skillfully wields the scalpel of *paññā* to heal the wounds of his patients; in other words, it is the Buddha who is the paradigmatic embodiment of wisdom. As we shall see, this metaphor of the sword, or scalpel, becomes iconographically linked most clearly to Mañjuśrī, who in many ways embodies *prajñā*, in the sculpture of the later Pāla period.

The link between these textual accounts of the Buddha as the paradigmatic possessor and purveyor of *paññā*, and the physical representation of this quality is, I must admit, neither obvious nor direct. Part of this, I think, has to do with the emphasis in early Buddhist representation on the life story of Śākyamuni and on the

---

[17]The snake, which the young man is told not to discard, is the ideal monk (i.e. one whose *āsavas* are destroyed, *bhikkhu khīnāsavasso*).

[18]There are many other places in the Pāli literature that this metaphor occurs; a particularly good example is found in *Milindapañha*, where wisdom is described as *chedanalakkhanā*, or "having the characteristic of cutting." See *Milindapañha*, V. Treckner, ed. (London: Pali Text Society, 1962), p. 33 for the further development of this metaphor.

[19]*Majjhima Nikāya*, vol. 2, pp. 252-62.

narration of the *Jātaka* stories, as well, as Susan Huntington has argued, on their subsequent commemoration.[20] In the so-called aniconic art of what seems to be the earliest period,[21] however, one can certainly see suggestions of the visual representation of *paññā*. For instance, one of the earliest and most common of these motifs is the *dhammacakka*; it most obviously represents and refers to the Buddha's teaching, his "turning of the wheel of *dhamma*." However, the wheel also resonates with both the event of the Buddha's first sermon at Sārnāth, the point at which he first makes his teaching known to the world, and also with the process by which he came to realize the *dharma*. At the heart of this process is the wisdom that gives the Buddha-to-be the insight into the nature of reality that enables him to become enlightened.

In the same way, the other major motifs in early Buddhist art - the *bodhi* tree, for instance, or the throne - also signify the centrality of *paññā*. I am not suggesting that these early motifs directly represent *paññā*; clearly they do not, and *paññā* is not the paramount concern, textual or visual, of this period of early Buddhism. Rather, I am suggesting that part of what these early, so-called aniconic,

---

[20]Huntington makes the very important point that in our interpretations of early Buddhist art, we frequently miss what is perhaps the most obvious level of signification; namely, that the scene depicted *is in fact the subject*. Thus, for instance, in her discussion of the so-called "Prasenajit Pillar" form Bhārhut, she argues that the subject is not the absent Buddha, but rather, the celebrators who are in fact depicted on the pillar. "I suggest that these subjects do not serve emblematic roles in these scenes: they are major 'actors' in the narratives and, therefore represent themselves and not something else," "Aniconism and the Multivalence of Emblems: Another Look," p. 124.

[21]See Vidya Dehejia, "On Modes of Visual Narration in Early Buddhist Art," *Art Bulletin* 72 (1990): 374-92; see also Dehejia, "Aniconism and the Multivalence of Emblems," as well as Susan Huntington's response to Dehejia, "Aniconism and the Multivalence of Emblems: Another Look," and Huntington's earlier "Early Buddhist Art and the Theory of Aniconism." I think, however, that much of this debate proceeds at cross purposes, and that a more sustained and detailed analysis of what is involved in the multivalent quality of this early art is long overdue. Nonetheless, I certainly agree with Huntington when she writes, in her critique of Dehejia's critique of her work: "My position is that the theory of aniconism is not valid as an all-inclusive explanation for the early Buddhist art of India and that the vast majority of artistic compositions that have been explained as aniconic scenes are not substitutes and do not portray substitutes for anthropomorphic representations of the Buddha," "Aniconism and the Multivalence of Emblems: Another Look," p. 111. For a useful discussion of the general problems with the notion of the aniconic, see David Freedburg, *The Power of Images*, "Chapter Four: The Myth of Aniconism," pp. 54-81.

figures signify is the wisdom that Śākyamuni attained, the *paññā* that enabled him to see into the true nature of reality and to become the Buddha. In her discussion of the narrative panels at Bhārhut and Sāñcī, Dehejia has suggested that when artists employed what she calls "monoscenic narration" - through which they emphasize the general supremacy of the Buddha and deemphasize the actual presentation of a specific narrative - "artists generally present the single, culminating episode of a story and focus thematically on the *wisdom and presence* of the Buddha."[22] Although the specifics of Dehejia's discussion may be somewhat suspect, I find her "monoscenic narration" idea nonetheless useful. When sculptures, paintings, relics, and *stūpa*s of the Buddha are constructed and honored and worshipped, *paññā* is a significant and important "part of the picture" even before the rise of the *Prajñāpāramitā* and its elevation of *prajñā* to the zenith of Buddhist discourse. And it is precisely this wisdom-centered *habitus* that underlies the later visual representations of *prajñā*.

I.B. The *Prajñāpāramitā* Context.

> The Buddha articulated the collection of practices for the sake of (the development of) *prajñā*. Therefore, one should develop wisdom with the desire to remove suffering.
>
> Śāntideva[23]

---

[22]Dehejia, "On Modes of Visual Narration in Early Buddhist Art," p. 380; my emphasis. Dehejia uses an example from the Ajātaśatru pillar at Bārhut to demonstrate her point. The artist was not interested in presenting the full narrative account of the miracle at Śrāvastī; rather, it "is the divine power of the Buddha that is highlighted in this narrative, in which action is totally absent."

[23]P.L. Vaidya, ed., *Bodhicaryāvatāra of Śāntideva* (Darbhanga: Mithila Institute), p. 167; *imam parikaram sarvam prajñārtham hi munirjagau \ tasmādutpādayetprajñām dukhanivrtti-kāṅksayā* \\. I have translated *imam parikaram sarvam* here as "collection of practices," although *parikara* more literally means "helper." Conze gives "(necessary) preparation" in his *Materials for a Dictionary of the Prajñāpāramitā Literature* (Tokyo: Suzuki Research Foundation, 1973). In the context in which it occurs, this phrase clearly refers to the other perfections - *dhyāna*, *kśanti*, etc. - that Śāntideva discusses in the chapters that proceed this one, faculties that are only developed, according to the author, as aids in the development of the

I begin this section not with a *Prajñāpāramitā* text proper, but with a short passage from the start of the ninth chapter of Śāntideva's *Bodhicaryāvatāra*, for this chapter is devoted to the explication of the perfection and practice of *prajñā*, the cultivation of which enables one to realize the truth of *śunyatā* and thereby to escape the grips of illusion and the *dukkha* such illusion engenders. Śāntideva is roughly a Pāla-period author - he lived and wrote in the environs of Nālandā in the first half of the eighth century - and his works, particularly the *Bodhicaryāvatāra* and his collection of doctrinal positions and sayings, the *Śiksāsamuccaya*, represent precisely what I refer to above as "mainstream Mahāyāna." Śāntideva was, certainly, firmly situated in the center of the Mādhyamaka tradition, and much of the *Bodhicaryāvatāra* consists of a pointed attack on other schools; he was also a strikingly synthetic thinker, however, combining and elucidating a wide range of central, and centrist, Mahāyāna positions.[24] Although I would not want to claim that Śāntideva is the most important or the most influential Pāla-period figure, he was clearly one of the giants - Tāranātha mentions him numerous times, and several commentaries on his works were composed during the Pāla period - and, more significantly, he is an important contemporary source for the Pāla-period conception of *prajñā* and its relevance to sculptural representations.[25]

The ninth chapter of the *Bodhicaryāvatāra* is concerned with the intricacies of *prajñā*, with its many qualities and with the effects of its cultivation. As the first verse of the chapter emphasizes, the Buddha spoke (literally sang, *jagau*) the collection of practices for the sake of (the development of) *prajñā*. According to Śāntideva, then, all of the Buddha's teachings are intended to help the practitioner develop wisdom. It is this wisdom, furthermore, as the second half of this

---

paramount perfection, *prajñā*.

[24]In the *Bodhicaryāvatāra*, Śāntideva refers to and draws on such schools as the Sautrāntika, Vaibhāsika, and Yogācāra, among others, and he frequently quotes from the *Prajñāpāramitās*. The *Śiksāsamuccaya*, by its very nature as a collection of different doctrinal positions, demonstrates the synthetic nature of Śāntideva's thought.

[25]See Chimpa and Chattopadhyaya, *History of Buddhism in India*, pp. 257-315, and A.K. Warder *Indian Buddhism*, p. 481. One of the most important commentaries is the *Pañjikā* by the Pāla-period author Prajñākaramati, who, according to Vaidya, "may have lived either in Nālandā or Vikramaśīlā," see Vaidya, *Bodhicaryāvatāra*, p. x.

verse states, that enables one to overcome suffering: "Therefore, one should develop wisdom with the desire to remove suffering." Echoing what we have already seen in the Pāli context, the commentator Prajñākaramati defines *prajñā* in his extensive commentary on this first verse as that which is able to penetrate into reality, into the dependent nature of all things,[26] and he goes on to say that in the development of each of the *pāramitā*s necessary to the Bodhisattva, beginning with *dānapāramita*, the paramount quality for attaining perfect enlightenment is *prajñā* alone. Indeed, without *prajñā*, the other perfections are of no use; they are helpers or supporters (*parikara*s or *sambhāra*s).[27]

I will return to the *Bodhicaryāvatāra* later in this chapter, but I begin this discussion of *prajñā* and the *Prajñāpāramitā* context in this somewhat anachronistic way - that is, by discussing a text and its commentary that were both written some seven centuries after the *Aṣṭasāhasrikāprajñāpāramitā* - to further emphasize the centrality of *prajñā* for the Pāla period. Indeed, there is a sense in which Śāntideva's *Bodhicaryāvatāra*, and particularly the ninth chapter, is itself an extended commentary on the *Aṣṭasāhasrikā* and the other texts of the *Prajñāpāramitā* genre,[28] in the sense that it is an elaboration on the conception of the Bodhisattva found in these texts and an elucidation of the *pāramitā*s, most importantly *prajñā*, that need to be cultivated in order to attain this exalted state. I now turn to the conception of *prajñā* as it is discussed in the *Aṣṭasāhasrikā* itself, for this is the *Ur*-text that is the foundation, the *adhiṣṭhāna*, of Pāla-period religious *praxis*.

Although the *Aṣṭasāhasrikā* is not, by any means, the longest of the *Prajñāpāramitā* texts - it is a mere 8,000 verses, as compared to, say, the 100,000 verse *Śatasāhasrikā* version - it is nonetheless a massive text, full, as Vaidya has put it, of "a queer admixture of narration, philosophical treatment, advantages of the study of the

---

[26]The Sanskrit reads: "*yathāvasthita-pratītyasamutpannavastutattvapravicayalakṣaṇā*," *Bodhicaryāvatāra*, p. 168.

[27]Again, see Prajñākaramati's commentary, ibid., p. 168.

[28]This is in keeping with the long tradition of treating the *Prajñāpāramitā* as the root text of the Mahāyāna.

work, and likely obstacles in the way of acquiring its knowledge."[29] The text is, in spite of this "queer admixture," profoundly soteriological in nature, and it is concerned most emphatically with religious *praxis*, with what Conze has aptly called, "a set of practices designed to bring about a state of complete detachment by intellectual methods."[30] This set of practices is the development of the *pāramitās*, and the state of complete detachment is the realization of *śunyatā*, of the ultimate emptiness of all things. To realize *śunyatā* is to transcend temporality, attachments, illusion, suffering, etc., and to realize, or to achieve, enlightenment.[31] The development of *prajñā*, as it is laid out in the *Aṣṭasāhasrikā*, is above all the essential means to achieve this goal.

One of the most striking features of the *Aṣṭasāhasrikā*, and indeed of the entire *Prajñāpāramitā* genre, is the self-referentiality of its discourse; throughout the text one encounters statements that elevate the study, worship, and reverence of the *Prajñāpāramitā* above all other forms of religious or intellectual practice. For instance, the text raises the question of the relative merits of reverence toward relics of the Buddha and toward the text itself. Given the existence of the physical remains of the Buddha, and the obvious benefits one gains from honoring them, why should one take up the *Aṣṭasāhasrikā* at all?

> For what reason? It is not that I have disrespect for the relics, but [people] honor them because they are *saturated with wisdom*. Just as every man who is supported by the king obtains honor, so also do the

[29]P.L. Vaidya, *Aṣṭasahāsrikāprajñāpāramitā*, p. xx. Vaidya also remarks, with a kind of bemused exhaustion, on the numerous repetitions of the text, repetitions which, obviously, add to its bulk: "The entire literature of Prajñāpāramitā is tiringly verbose, even in its shorter recensions. The Buddhist monk is never tired of using the same expressions, and never took into account wastage of time and words, not to speak of paper and ink, which commodities were not liberally available in those days," pp. xvi-xvii.

[30]Edward Conze, *The Prajñāpāramitā Literature*, pp. 14-15.

[31]See Frederick Streng, *Emptiness: A Study in Religious Meaning* (New York: Abingdon Press, 1967), for an extended discussion on the soteriological aspects of *śunyatā*.

> Buddha-relics, since they are supported by the perfection of wisdom.[32]

Indeed, in taking up the text, in worshipping, honoring, and revering it, one is also, according to the ideology expounded in the text, doing the same to relics: "Whenever one honors this very perfection of wisdom, then one also does complete honor to the relics of the Tathāgata. From what cause is this? From [the fact that] the relics of the Tathāgata have come forth from this perfection of wisdom.[33]

Gregory Schopen, among others, has argued that an important part of the devotional shift that takes place with the rise of the Mahāyāna is the development of the "cult of the book."[34] Thus in various versions of the *Prajñāpāramitā* one encounters extended discussions, if not polemics, elevating not only the doctrinal position of the text, but the actual text itself - the physical book - to the highest status of devotional objects. Again and again the text states that one will accrue more merit by honoring (doing *pūjas* to) the text: "Moreover, not only one who has learned, studied and repeated the perfection of wisdom, will have those qualities, but also one who worships a copy of it, he also, I teach, will have those advantages here and now."[35] It is important to note here, though, that the texts are frequently ambiguous about what they mean by "*prajñāpāramitā*," whether, for instance, it is the text in the physical sense of a book, or

---

[32]Akira Yuyama, ed., *Prajñā-Pāramitā-Ratna-Guṇa-Saṃcaya-Gāthā* (Cambridge: Cambridge University Press, 1976), p. 25; *kiṃ kāraṇaṃ na mi śarīri a-gauravatvaṃ api tū khu prajña-paribhāvita pūjayanti /yatha rāja-niśritu naro labhi sarvi pūjāṃ tatha prajña-pāramita-niśritu buddha-dhātuḥ //.* I have reproduced the text as it occurs in this volume, and have retained the extremely problematic word divisions printed by Yuyama.

[33]*Aṣṭasahāsrikāprajñāpāramitā*, p. 48; "*tasmāttarhi bhagavan anayaiva prajñāpāramitayā pūjitayā teṣāmapi tathāgataśarīrāṇāṃ paripūrṇā pūjā kṛtā bhavati / tatkasya hetoḥ? prajñāpāramitānirjātatvāttathāgataśarīrāṇāṃ /.*

[34]See, in particular, Schopen's "The Phrase '*sa pṛthivīpradeśaś caityabhūto bhavet*' in the *Vajracchedikā*: Notes on the Cult of the Book in Mahāyāna," *Indo-Iranian Journal* 27 (1975): 147-81.

[35]This is Conze's very condensed summary, in *The Perfection of Wisdom in Eight Thousand Lines and its Verse Summary* (Bolinas: Four Seasons, 1973), p. 112.

in the sense of the abstract faculty *prajñā* that is to be honored.[36] I shall address this ambiguity in detail below; nonetheless, what is important for the moment is this elevation of *prajñā* to the apex of the discourse.

The *leit motif* of this discourse, then, is that it is *prajñā* that underlies all efficacious Buddhist practice, and, furthermore, that without *prajñā*, all other practices are ineffective: "Without wisdom, these five perfections are eyeless; they are without a guide and are not able to touch *bodhi*."[37] *Prajñā* thus encompasses all of the perfections.[38] Indeed, it is *prajñā* that makes the Buddha the Buddha: "The Blessed One said: Therefore, oh Kauśika, the Tathāgata does not get his name from the fact that he has acquired this physical personality; rather, he gets his name from the fact that he has acquired omniscience. For the omniscience of the noble, perfectly enlightened Tathāgata, oh Kauśika, has come forth from the perfection of wisdom."[39]

The *Astasāhasrikā* goes even further than this kind of causal connection of *prajñā* and the Buddha, for it is not just that the perfection of *prajñā* is the basis for the Tathāgata's enlightenment; the Tathāgata and the perfection of wisdom are essentially *the same*. "Thus indeed, oh Śāriputra, just as the teacher is to be honored, so too is the *Prajñāpāramitā*."[40] Indeed, echoing precisely the sort of language used in the Pāli context to discuss images of the Buddha, the text states: "One might hear this deep perfection of wisdom being spoken, being taught, being explained, being pointed out, and having heard it here he might bring forth the designation 'Teacher' with

---

[36]Stcherbatsky, in his introduction to the *Abhisamayālankāra-Prajñāpāramitā-Upadeśa-Śāstra* (Tokyo: Meicho-Fukyū-Kai, 1977), notes that the term *prajñāpāramitā* is decidedly polyvalent, referring to "1) philosophic Monism, 2) Buddha's Cosmical Body, 3) the text of the p.-p. sūtras, and 4) the Path towards Salvation according to Mahāyānistic principles," p. vii.

[37]*Prajñā-Pāramitā-Ratna-Guṇa-Saṃcaya-Gāthā*, p. 35; *vina prajñā pañca imi pāramitā a-cakṣū a-vināyakā na prabhavanti spṛśetu bodhiṃ //.*

[38]See *Aṣṭasāhasrikāprajñāpāramitā*, p. 40.

[39]Ibid., p. 29; *bhagavānāha - tasmāttarhi kauśika nānenātmabhāvaśarīrapratilambhena tathāgatastathāgata iti saṃkhyāṃ gacchati / sarvajñatāyāṃ tu pratilabdhāyāṃ tathāgatas-tathāgata iti saṃkhyāṃ gacchati / yeyam kauśika sarvajñatā tathāgatasyārhataḥ samyaksam-buddhasya prajñāpāramitānirjātaiṣā /.*

[40]*Aṣṭasāhasrikāprajñāpāramitā*, p. 85; *tathaiva namaskartavyā śāriputra prajñāpāramitā yathā śāstā.*

regard to this perfection of wisdom - he thinks, 'The Teacher is face to face with me, the Teacher is seen by me.'"[41] However, whereas in the contexts I have examined in the previous chapters the discourse about the presence/absence of the Buddha has something of an ontological flavor to it, here the emphasis seems to be primarily epistemological. If one hears the text, and more importantly if one learns it and perfects the wisdom it contains, then one *knows* the teacher. Why? Because ultimately the Buddha is, like everything else, empty, and it is therefore only through the perfection of *prajñā* that one is able to realize this, that one is able truly to see the Buddha.

Towards the end of the *Aṣṭasāhasrikā* this epistemological shift is given a kind of retroactive legitimacy and validity, in that, as is so typical in the Mahāyāna *sūtras*, the redactors of the text place the discourse *back* in the context of the living Śākyamuni, conversing with Ānanda.[42] The context of this discussion is, by now, familiar, but the emphasis is markedly different from what we have seen in the Pāli context:

> In the same way in which you, Ānanda, honor me, who is now the Tathāgata...so also, Ānanda, this perfection of wisdom is to be [always] spread, praised, worshipped, venerated, respected, honored, protected, copied, recited, explained, taught, pointed out, advanced, studied, spoken, and elevated, with the same solicitude, affection, respect, and in the same virtuous spirit. That is the way for you to honor me, that is the way to show affection, serene faith, and respect for the past, future, and present Buddhas and Great Beings.... But, in short, in the same way in which I am your teacher, so is the perfection of wisdom.... If one does not want to abandon the

[41]Ibid., p.89; *sa imām gambhīrām prajñāpāramitām bhāsyamānām deśyamānāmupadiśyamānāmudrśyamānām śrnuyāt imām prajñāpāramitām śrutvā atra śāstrsamjñām prajñāpāramitāyāmutpādayet - sāstā me sammukhībhūta iti, śāstā me drsta iti cittamutpādayati /.*

[42]Here we could also say that the redactors are making *explicit* the *implicit habitus* in which this discourse is situated and in which it makes sense and has meaning.

> Tathāgata, or the *dharma*, or the *saṃgha*, if one does not want to abandon the enlightenment of the past, future and present Blessed Ones, - then let one not abandon the perfection of wisdom![43]

The final three chapters of the text contain the paradigmatic story of Sadāprarudita that illustrates the proper way in which one is to follow this advice,[44] the proper way in which one is to search for and embrace the *Prajñāpāramitā*. Furthermore, this is a story that is intimately bound up with the issue of *absence* and *presence* and with the search for the *visible* Buddha.

The story begins with Sadāprarudita off in a forest, having gone there after encountering a Buddha in his dreams who tells him to go meditate, searching for perfect wisdom without thought of his body, or his life, or fame, or glory, etc. As he meditates, he suddenly hears a voice (that of the Buddha) that tells him, "Go East! There you will hear the *Prajñāpāramitā*." The voice instructs him to search for perfect wisdom only after he has firmly resolved that all *dharma*s are empty, without signs, and wishless; furthermore, the voice tells Sadāprarudita that, among other things, he must shun false friends and honor true friends. Once this preliminary state is achieved, he will be able to learn perfect wisdom, whether from a book or from a monk versed in the *dharma* (who is also to be treated like the Teacher himself).[45]

---

[43]Ibid., p. 228; *yathā tattvamānanda etarhi me tathāgatasya tiṣṭhato...manyase....tathaiva tvayā ānanda iyaṃ prajñāpāramitā udgrahītavyā dhārayitavyā vācayitavyā paryavāptavyā pravartayitavyā deśyitavyā upadeṣṭavyā uddeṣṭavyā svādhyātavyā likhitavyā bhāvayitavyā satkartavyā gurūkartavyā mānayitavyā pūjayitavyā arcayitavyā upacāyitavyā, tayā hitaiṣitayā tena premṇā tena gauraveṇa tayā guṇvattayā / evaṃ tvayā ānanda ahaṃ pūjito bhavāmi, tena ca bodhisattvā mahāsattvāḥ....saṃkṣepeṇa ānanda yādṛśastavāhaṃ śāstā, tādṛśī te prajñāpāramitā śāstā....yasya ānanda tathāgato na parityaktaḥ, dharmo na parityaktaḥ, saṃgho na parityaktaḥ, atītānāgatapratyutpannānāṃ bhagavatāṃ bodhirna parityaktā, tasya prajñāpāramitā aparityaktā bhavatu /.*

[44]I say "paradigmatic" because the story begins, "*punaraparaṃ subhute tatheyaṃ prajñāpāramitā paryeṣṭavyā yathā sadāprarudita bodhisattvena mahāsattvena paryeṣitā...*;" ibid., p. 238.

[45]*yasya ca tvaṃ kulaputra antikātprajñāpāramitāṃ śṛṇuyāḥ śāstṛsaṃjñā tvayā tatrotpādayitavyā*, ibid., p. 238.

After seven days of austerities and concentration, however, Sadāprarudita is still in the forest, waiting to hear the *Prajñāpāramitā.* Finally, an image of the Tathāgata (*tathāgatavigrahaḥ*) comes to him and instructs him to go to the *bodhisattva* Dharmodgata in Gandhavatī; there Sadāprarudita will hear the *Prajñāpāramitā.* He is overjoyed, and, the text states, strangely (and significantly) echoing the same surgical language we have seen in the Pāli texts, that just like a man shot by an arrow who can think of nothing other than the surgeon who can remove the arrow and thereby end his suffering, Sadāprarudita could think of nothing other than hearing the *Prajñāpāramitā.*[46]

Under Dharmodgata's instruction, Sadāprarudita achieves a variety of *samādhi* states that allow him to see the Tathāgatas. When he emerges from these states, however, his vision of the Buddhas is gone, and, the slow learner that he is, he wonders where they have gone and, again, pines away for a the sight of these Buddhas.[47] This disappearance of the Tathāgatas plunges Sadāprarudita into a kind of devotional depression, and he longs to return to Dharmodgata in order to receive further instructions from him that will enable him to prolong his vision of the Buddhas. Because he has nothing to offer the *bodhisattva* out of respect and in exchange for his teaching, however, Sadāprarudita resolves to sell his body in the marketplace and offer the money to Dharmodgata. He can initially find no buyer, but Śakra, the chief of the gods, transforms himself into a young brahmin who offers to purchase Sadāprarudita's body for his father, who is in need of an object to sacrifice. Then, in one of the most bizarre episodes in all of Buddhism, Sadāprarudita cuts open his arm and sets off to crack open his bone to extract the marrow from it to be offered as sacrifice.

At this point, a merchant's daughter intercedes and, with Śakra's assistance, convinces Sadāprarudita that he is engaged in folly. They go to the woman's parents, who give them 500 carriages

---

[46] *tadyathāpi nāma puruṣaḥ saviṣena viddho nānyaṃ manasikāramutpādayati api tu kadā nāmāhaṃ śalyahartāraṃ vaidyam lapsye yo mamedam śalyamuddhariṣyati yo māmito dukkhānmocayiṣyatīti* \, ibid., p. 242.

[47] *sa ca kulaputrastebhyaḥ samādhibhyo vyudasthāt \ vyutthitasya cāsya etadabhūt kutaste tathāgatāḥ kva vā te tathāgatā iti* \, ibid., p. 244.

and 500 servant girls to offer to Dharmodgata, and then they all set out together to see the illustrious teacher. Dharmodgata then creates a magnificent tower into which the *Prajñāpāramitā* is placed, and they all honor and worship it. Finally, after all of this, and after the assembly has departed, Sadāprarudita - who still does not quite get it - asks Dharmodgata where the Tathāgatas have gone. Nowhere, he tells him. What Sadāprarudita has seen in his *samādhi* state is the form body of the Tathāgata, and the Tathāgatas are not "seeable" in terms of the *rūpakāya*.[48] This, however, is where *prajñā* comes in, for it is precisely because one has not perfected wisdom that these illusions, these mere forms, are taken as *ontologically* significant, as real. When one has perfected wisdom, one *knows* that the Tathāgatas do not, in reality, come and go; one does not become obsessed, as Sadāprarudita has, with seeing the Buddhas, but with *knowing* the true nature of the *dharma*, with training in and acting in accordance to the perfection of wisdom.[49]

It takes Sadāprarudita a long time to get this message, but when he finally does, his quest for vision is bountifully fulfilled: "In all of his births he was not deprived of the Buddha. He was reborn only where he was face to face with the blessed Buddhas; he was never without the blessed Buddhas, not even in his dreams."[50] The *Astasāhasrikā* concludes on this visual, if not visionary, note. As long as the *Prajñāpāramitā*, or the ability to perfect wisdom, is in the world the Tathāgata will remain, and people will not be deprived of the sight of the Buddha.[51]

Scholars of Buddhism have often remarked, perhaps rather unimaginatively, that there is a fundamental shift that takes place in Buddhism with the rise of the Mahāyāna, a shift from the austere, rule-bound discipline of the Theravāda (as exemplified by the *Vinaya*) to

---

[48]*na hi tathāgato rūpakāyato drasṭavyaḥ* \, ibid., p. 255.

[49]Ibid., p. 264.

[50]*sarvāsu ca jātiṣu na jāatu buddhavirahito 'bhūt \ yatra yatra buddhā bhagavantaḥ sammukhībhūtā bhavanti, tatra tatropapadyate sma \ avirahitaśca bhavati sma buddhairbhabavadhiḥ antataḥ svapnāntaragato 'pi* \ ibid., p. 260.

[51]The Sanskrit reads, *yāvadānanda iyaṃ prajñāpāramitā loke pracarisyati tāvattathāgatastisṭhatīti veditavyam....avirahitāste ānanda sattvā buddhadarśanena...ca veditavyam* \, ibid., p. 260.

the devotional thrust of the Mahāyāna, particularly as it is expressed in the *Saddharmapuṇḍarīka* and the *Prajñāpāramitā* texts. Although Sadāprarudita's quest is one that we might quite reasonably call devotional, the lesson to be found in this story of Sadāprarudita, indeed the central lesson of the *Aṣṭasāhasrikā* as a whole, is not that devotion alone will make one a *bodhisattva*. Rather, the thrust here is that knowing the text, and perfecting the *prajñā* that is its essential message, is what enables the Buddha to be seen, because it is precisely *prajñā* that is the essence of the *dharma*; it is precisely *prajñā* that gives rise to the Buddha's buddhahood.[52] There is, however, an important tension between conventional vision and wisdom evident in the *Aṣṭasāhasrikā*, as we have just seen in the story of Sadāprarudita: in order to see the true Buddha, and not just his mere form, one must develop *prajñā*; but it is also *through* the very act of seeing the Buddha that *prajñā* can be cultivated.

I have already noted this connection of *seeing* the Buddha and *prajñā* in the context of Lokaksema's version of the *Aṣṭasāhasrikā*, the *Tao-hsing Ching*. This connection is evident elsewhere as well. For instance, in the seventeenth chapter of Śāntideva's collection of teachings,[53] the *Śiksasamuccaya*, the author gathers together a wide range of verses from texts that describe and prescribe worship of the Buddhas, including worship of images. One of the eight qualities of the *bodhisattva*, for example, is to cause people to see images of the Buddha.[54] Indeed, according to the text, it is better to roast in hell than not to see the Buddha.[55] What is most important here, however, is that Śāntideva, in his compilation of the *Śikṣasamuccaya*, explicitly links seeing the Buddha, whether in the form of an image or in person, with the development of *prajñā*: To those who see the Buddha, a great

---

[52]It is rather interesting, and in my view curious, that *prajñā* is not among the standard lists of what constitutes Buddhaness, or *buddhatā*. For an extended discussion of the conception of Buddhahood in Mahāyāna texts, see Paul Griffiths *On Being Buddha: The Classical Doctrine of Buddhahood* (Albany: SUNY, 1994).

[53]The chapter is entitled, appropriately, *Vandanānuśaṃsā*, "Praises of Worship."

[54]P.L. Vaidya, ed., *Śikṣasumuccaya of Śāntideva*, Buddhist Sanskrit Texts, no. 11 (Darbhanga: Mithila Institute, 1961), p. 164; the relevant Sanskrit is *buddhabimbadarśanasattva-samādāpanatayā*.

[55]*kalpakotiṃ varaṃ pakkaṃ tryapāye bhṛśadārūṇe / na tvevādarśanaṃ śastuḥ sarvasanga-nivartinaḥ* //, ibid., p. 164.

wisdom, incalculably bright, arises.[56] Significantly, Śāntideva explicitly notes that, although it is of course best to see the Buddha in person (literally in his true form, *svarūpena*), even seeing the image of the Buddha bears infinite fruit.[57]

II. Representing the Buddha, Representing *Prajñā*

> "Bodhi, *prajñā, karuṇā*, *yoga*" - these are all ideational terms, subtle and abstract concepts which are not at all easy to transmute into concrete visual terms.
>
> Niharranjan Ray[58]

> At the point of Awakening, a buddha is wisdom concretized in a perceptible form.
>
> Gadjin Nagao[59]

II.A. Seeing Emptiness.

A central concern of mainstream Mahāyāna thought and practice is the nature of emptiness, *śunyatā*. Thus in Śāntideva's *Bodhicaryāvatāra*, we find this verse: "Forms are seen by ordinary people, and thought to be real; they do not regard them as illusions. Here lies the dispute between *yogis* and ordinary people."[60] This begins Śāntideva's long discourse on the illusory nature of all things, and on their ultimate

---

[56]Ibid., p. 164; *prajñābalamasaṃkhyeyam jāyate candrabhāsvaram*. Śāntideva takes this from the *Gaṇḍavyūha*; this same text, as quoted by Śāntideva, further links seeing in knowing by stating that to the person who sees the Buddha there will appear a circle of knowledge [*jñānamaṇḍalam*], and that for that person the sight of the Buddha will increase knowledge [*jinendrasya darśanam jñānavardhanam*].

[57]Ibid., p. 165; *api ca pratimāmātradarśanamapi tāvadaparimitaphalam tathāgatānām*.

[58]Niharranjan Ray, *Idea and Image in Indian Art* (New Delhi: Mushiram Monoharlal, 1973), p. 17.

[59]Gadjin Nagao, *The Foundational Standpoint of Mādhyamika Philosophy*, trans. by John P. Keenan (Albany: State University of New York Press, 1989), p. 24.

[60]*Bodhicaryāvatāra*, p. 168; *lokena bhāvā dṛśyate kalpyante cāpi tattvataḥ* \
na tu māyāvadityatra vivādo yogilokayoḥ \\.

emptiness. Whereas ordinary people are caught up in webs of illusion, those who know - *yogis*, that is, specifically, those who take up the *Prajñāpāramitā* and develop *prajñā* - see the world for what it is. In his commentary on this verse, Prajñākaramati explains Śāntideva's meaning by alluding to an essential distinction in Mādhyamika - and indeed in all of Mahāyāna Buddhist - thought, namely the distinction between ultimate or absolute reality, and conventional reality or truth. Thus according to Prajñākaramati, what common people see, what they mistakenly take for reality, is only *saṃvṛti*, only the conventional, mundane, and worldly, in short, only the sort of illusion as created by a magician.[61] Those who really know, though, are able to see that mere forms (*bhāvas*) are only the appearance of real existence; they are able to see beyond such object, to see that they lack any *paramārthika*, or ultimate reality.

This is not really the place to go into the intricacies of the two truth discourse, since even a cursory discussion of the subject would sidetrack us for many pages.[62] But Śāntideva's verse raises an obvious problem in the context of devotion to such things as relics and images, a problem that we have already encountered in Upagupta's veneration of an image of the Buddha: if everything is illusory, then is it not the case that honoring an image is in fact simply worshipping an illusion? Śāntideva explicitly addresses this issue in verse 36 of his chapter on *prajñāpāramitā*: "[Just as] a wish-fulfilling gem or a wish-fulfilling tree is the fulfillment of what one desires, [so] an image of the Buddha appears to those who ardently desire to be trained."[63] On

---

[61]See Prajñākaramati's commentary, ibid., p. 281.

[62]See, for instance, M.D. Eckel, *Jñānagharbha's Commentary on the Distinction Between the Two Truths* (Albany: State University of New York Press, 1987); C.W. Huntington, "The System of the Two Truths in the *Prasannapadā* and the *Madhyamakāvatāra*: A Study in Madhyamaka Soteriology," *Journal of Indian Philosophy* 11 (1983): 77-107; and Gadjin Nagao, *The Foundational Standpoint of Mādhyamika*, translated by John P. Keenan (Albany: State University of New York Press, 1989), especially Chapter 2; and also see Nagao's *Mādhyamika and Yogācāra A Study of Mahāyāna*, translated by Leslie S. Kawamura (Albany: State University of New York Press, 1991), pp. 13-22.

[63]The Sanskrit is: *cintāmaṇiḥ kalpatarurtathecchāparipūrṇaḥ / vineyapraṇidhānābhyām jinabimbam tathekṣyate /*, ibid., p. 199. I have disregarded the dual ending here, which otherwise is puzzling, but not, according to Edgerton, terribly uncommon in B.H.S. See Franklin Edgerton, *Buddhist Hybrid Sanskrit Grammar and Dictionary*, vol. one (New Haven: Yale University Press, 1953), Chapter 25.

its face, at any rate, this is a rather obscure response to the problem, but Śāntideva then goes on, in the next two verses, to illustrate his point by saying that when a ritual specialist (*gārudika*) builds a specially consecrated wooden pillar - one of a magical nature (one that among other things wards of danger and protects from things like poison), built and invested with special powers by a *gārudika*, one who is versed in various mantras and spells - the effects of that pillar do not cease with the death of the builder; on the contrary, the effects of the pillar continue long after the death of the builder.[64] Śāntideva's point goes right to the heart of the Mahāyāna conception of the Buddha and *bodhisattva*s as actively engaged in the world. That is, even after his physical disappearance, the Buddha (here called *jinastambho*, "the pillar-like conqueror"), via such physical reminders as images, continues to be available to his followers.[65]

Although these references to the availability of the Buddha in images and physical objects make up only a small portion of the *Bodhicaryāvatāra*, they are nonetheless of great importance in understanding the contemporary Pāla-period conception of images of the Buddha. Clearly, images are not what is ultimately real; or, in the language of the text, they are characterized not by *paramārthika* but by *samvṛti*. Nonetheless, images - like the magically consecrated pillar in Śāntideva's simile - are effective. On the mundane level, images fulfill one's wishes - or at least the wish to see the Buddha - and they allow the worshipper to earn merit. On a more important level, though, images make the Buddhas available, and in particular, they make available the *prajñā* that is the essential element, the paramount perfection, in attaining enlightenment. For as Prajñākaramati says in his commentary on verses 40-42 of the *Bodhicaryāvatāra*, there is no attainment of enlightenment (*bodhi*) without the realization of *śūnyatā*, and it is *prajñā* that enables one to fully realize the emptiness of all things, for it is *prajñā* that teaches

---

[64]Ibid., p. 200.

[65]*bodhicaryānurūpyena jinastambho 'pi sādhitaḥ / karoti sarvakāryāṇi bodhisatve 'pi nirvṛte* /, ibid., p. 200.

one to discriminate between what is *āropita* and what is *anāropita*, between what is the shell and what is the kernel.[66]

For Śāntideva, then, what is important in the end is not the outward appearance of the object, but the inner reality that such an object embodies. A Buddha image is merely the shell, merely the outward appearance of the Buddha, just as the Buddha's own physical body was merely his outward appearance. Hence an image, or what the image represents, is *saṃvṛti*, is hidden or covered up. *What* is covered up is, of course, the true nature of reality, what is *paramārthika*. But what is it that is *paramārthika* here? Prajñākaramati refers to the *kāya* discourse in his commentary, quoting the *Vajracchedikaprajñāpāramitā* to make his point that it is not through outward appearance that the Buddha is to be seen, that the true nature of the world is to be realized, but through the *dharma*.[67]

In the *Bodhicaryāvatāra*, Śāntideva thus uses images to illustrate the emptiness of all forms, and to demonstrate the centrality of *prajñā* in coming to the realization of this essential truth. Again, we can see how the image here functions metapractically, as a means of reflection on the relationship between proper precept and proper practice. The implication, I think, is clear: if one has perfected *prajñā*, then one sees not the mere image, but the Buddha himself. It is *prajñā* that enables one to see in the proper manner. But as we have also seen, the Buddha and *prajñā* are identical, and so to see an image of the Buddha is also to (and to attain) precisely the *prajñā* that one needs to see properly.

II.B. Images of the Buddha in *Dharmacakrapravartanamudrā*.

The *dharmacakra*, the "wheel of dharma," is one of the oldest and most common motifs in Buddhist sculpture. It is a prominent iconographic element at both Sāñcī and Bhārhut, for instance, and several of the Aśokan pillars employed the symbolism of the *dharmacakra*. Consequently, much has been written about the

---

[66]See Prajñākaramati's commentary, ibid., p. 203.

[67]See ibid., p. 200; the relevant Sanskrit reads: *dharmato buddhā draṣṭavyā dharmakāyā hi nāyakāḥ....*

importance of this symbol in early Buddhism; it has been taken to signify not just the *dharma*, but, according to some scholars, the Buddha himself in aniconic form. Hence Albert Grünwedel, at the beginning of this century, said that the *dharmacakra* "was adopted by the Buddha's disciples as the symbol of his doctrine, and combined with other symbols...stands for him."[68] By at least as early as the Kuṣāna period, Buddhists had begun to employ an iconographic extension of this most elemental of Buddhist symbols by depicting the Buddha in what is frequently referred to as the "teaching position," that is, seated cross-legged (in the *pralambapādāsana* or *vajraparyankāsana* position), his hands forming the *dharmacakra-pravartanamudrā*, the "gesture of turning the wheel of *dharma*."[69] By the Gupta period, this had become the most prevalent way of sculpturally depicting the Buddha.

I think, however, that it is important to point out that such images do not immediately seem to evoke *prajñā*. On the contrary, images of the Buddha displaying the *dharmacakrapravartanamudrā* seem most saliently to creat a kind of narrative presence of the Śākyamuni's first sermon at Sārnāth. As I shall argue, however, this narrative presence is saturated with *prajñā*, and to see such an image very much involves seeing wisdom. For as Susan Huntington has point out, these images are "indicators of the event and of Buddhist teachings in general;"[70] and as we have seen, at the heart of these teachings is *prajñā*.

One of the best known images produced in any age of Buddhist art is a fifth-century Gupta image of Śākyamuni preaching his first sermon in Sārnāth. This stele, now housed in the Sārnāth site museum, has become the hallmark of the "classical" Gupta style, what is frequently taken to be the high point of all of Indian art; Joanna Williams says of this image that it "epitomizes the 'science of beauty'

---

[68]Albert Grünwedel, *Buddhist Art in India* (London: Susil Gupta, 1901), p. 67.

[69]For a very broad and very general discussion of this and other *mudrās*, see E. Dale Saunders, *Mudrā: A Study of Symbolic Gestures in Japanese Buddhist Sculpture* (New York: Pantheon Books, 1960). Also see Deena Bandhu Pandey, *The Dharmacakrapravartana in Literature and Art* (Delhi: Oriental Publishers, 1978).

[70]See Susan Huntington, *The Art of Ancient India* (New York: Weatherhill, 1985), p. 203.

(*citravidyā*).... Spiritual perfection is translated into aesthetic terms."[71] The central image depicts the Buddha seated alone in the *dharmacakrapravartanamudrā*. Below the main image is a row of kneeling figures - the five disciples hearing the *dharma* for the first time, plus an unidentified laywoman and a child (or perhaps a dwarf). Also present at the bottom of the stele are two deer which represent, first, the locale of the first sermon in the deer park of Sārnāth,[72] and second, the power of the *dharma* to "tame" and give refuge to even these most timid of wild animals;[73] in the center of these figures is a *dharmacakra*.

It is perhaps appropriate that this single image is now so well-know, since the *dharmacakrapravartanamudrā* was the most common way of depicting the Buddha up through the Gupta period; by the Pāla period, however, the dominant form shifts to the *bhūmiśparsamudrā*, although the *dharmacakrapravartanamudrā* certainly continued to be a common way to depict not only the Buddha, but several other figures

---

[71]Joanna Gottfried Williams, *The Art of Gupta India: Empire and Province* (Princeton: Princeton University Press, 1982), p. 78. John Huntington echoes these sentiments when he writes that this image is characterized by "highly idealized realism, graceful beauty and unqualified elegance of the figure of the Buddha.... Indeed, the quietude and beatific appearance of the face has led a number of authors to indulge in speculations on the ontology of Buddhism and the image has been cited in arguments about the 'deification' of Śākyamuni," "Sowing the Seeds of the Lotus, Part II, [Rsipatana and Mrgadāva]," *Orientations* 17 (1986): 28-43, p. 40. Niharranjan Ray calls this image "the perennial fountain source of inspiration to and the sole term of reference for all such later images all over India and Southeast Asia as well as in China and Japan.... Here is indeed the fulfillment in concrete visual terms of the evolved idea of *bodhi* and its embodiment in the Buddha image," *Idea and Image in Indian Art*, p. 41.

[72]The deer and the five disciples also distinguish images of the Buddha delivering his first *dharma* talk from images of the miracle at Śrāvastī, which also have the Buddha in the *dharmacakrapravartanamudrā*.

[73]It has been further suggested by John Huntington that these deer also represent death, since, etymologically, *mrga* seems linked to the Sanskrit verbal root *mr*, to die. Thus the taming of these deers is, metaphorically, the Buddha's taming of death. Although his interpretation is intriguing and fits nicely with the Buddha's defeat of Māra and the metaphorical defeat of death (through the realization of impermanence) that I will discuss later in this chapter, Huntington is, I think, propogating a false etymology. *Mrga* (Pali *miga*) comes not from the root *mr*, but is linked with *mrg*, meaning to seek or search for (William Malandra, in a private communication, suggests that the verb was actually formed on the noun; thus the root meaning *is* deer). Thus the deer visually represent the search for the *dharma*. This, in my opinion, makes good iconographical sense as well, since the deer typically flank the *dharmacakra*, thus visually taking refuge in the *dharma*. See John Huntington, "Sowing the Seeds of the Lotus, Part II," pp. 28-29.

in the Buddhist pantheon.[74] It is, as I have remarked, neither immediately nor obviously apparent how such an image is connected to the abstract concept *prajñā*, how such an image might represent, let alone convey, the complexities and ambiguities of *prajñā*. Thus on what is perhaps the most basic level of meaning, images of the Buddha seated displaying the *dharmacakrapravartanamudrā* are what might be called narrative signifiers. By this I mean that although the image itself does not - indeed, literally cannot - "tell the story" of Śākyamuni's original *dhammavacana*, let alone deliver this first talk itself, such an image can signify the various narrative accounts of the Buddha's first sermon.[75] This is, of course, the story of the point at which the *dharma* is first made available to the world.[76] Before I consider the ways in which such an image represents and conveys

---

[74]Why such a shift took place is unclear. Susan Huntington suggests that this iconographic shift may have been symptomatic of a locative shift that took place, with the center of Buddhism in Magadha moving from Sārnāth to Bodhgayā; the first sermon took place at the former site, whereas the defeat of Māra and the attainment of enlightenment took place at the latter site. Huntington suggests, rather tentatively, that this shift "suggests that a new emphasis on the enlightenment as opposed to the preaching aspect of the religion accounts for this to some degree." See Susan L. Huntington, *The 'Pāla-Sena' Schools*, p. 96. Although Huntington's suggestion is intriguing, a close analysis of the relationship between this apparent iconographic shift and the locative, let alone ideological, shift from Sārnāth to Bodhgayā would be necessary to play out the implications of her suggestion. I shall discuss some of these issues below. For a discussion of some of the surviving *dharmacakrapravartanamudrā* images from Bodhgayā, see Janice Leoshko, "The Iconography of Buddhist Sculptures of the Pāla and Sena Periods from Bodhgayā," Ph.D.Dissertation, Ohio State University, 1987, pp. 175-82.

[75]There are many versions of this story: In the Pāli Canon, the first sermon is narrated in the *Dhammacakkapavatana Sutta* of the *Anguttara Nikāya* as well as the *Ariyapariyesana Sutta* of the *Majjhima Nikāya*; see also the *Mahāvagga*, the *Lalitavistara*, the *Mahāvastu*, the *Divyāvadāna, the Nidānakatha*, and the *Buddhacarita*, to name just a few other texts with versions of this episode.

[76]Geri Malandra has pointed out, however, that images of the Buddha in *dharmacakrapravartanamudrā* do not, necessarily, refer to Śākyamuni's first sermon. Associating all such images with Śākyamuni, she argues, "may be too narrow outside a context that includes depictions of other events in the life of the Buddha." Malandra argues that at Ellora, for instance, Śākyamuni *per se* ceased to be the all-important object of veneration and meditation; rather, as she has pointed out, a multi-tathāgata system had at least limited influence there. See Geri Malandra, *Unfolding a Mandala: The Buddhist Cave Temples at Ellora* (Albany: SUNY, 1993), p. 29, and pp. 113-14. Although I will discuss the significance of multiple Buddhas, particularly the *pañca tathatāgatas* in the Pāla period below, it is important to point out here that for Buddhists in the Pāla milieu Śākyamuni retained his preeminence in part, I would suggest, because of the locative significance of the region; that is, Magadha was no ordinary *deśa*, but the actual place where Śākyamuni himself lived and taught.

prajñā, however, I want to consider briefly what this well-known narrative itself has to do with *prajñā*.

A tentative answer might well be, quite simply, "not much." Neither the Sanskrit nor the Pāli versions of this story dwell particularly on the role of wisdom in the Buddha's preaching of the first sermon, although *paññā* is, as we have already seen, said to be one of the mental faculties connected to the Middle Path that arise to the Buddha and allow him to fully comprehend and then explain the Four Noble Truths, such as in the *Samyutta Nikāya*: *me bhikkhave pubbe ananassutesu dhammesu cakkhuṃ udapādi ñāṇaṃ udapādi paññā udapādi....*"[77] In the extended version of this episode in the *Lalitavistara*, various forms of the verb *jñā*, "to know," are used in describing the benefits and effects of the *dharma* that the newly-enlightened Buddha makes known, but even there *prajñā* is in no way what we could legitimately call prominent.

It seems quite likely that such images were in some way intended to evoke the narrative accounts of Śākyamuni's first sermon by calling to the mind of the viewer the story, or by serving as "visual props" in the oral transmission of the narrative, and we can assume that the story of the Buddha's sermon was fairly well known in medieval India; it is, however, an interpretive stretch, if not a leap, to suggest that a Pāla-period Buddhist would naturally or automatically connect his or her viewing of a sculpture of a *dharmacakrapravartanamudrā* Buddha to these very specific textual references to *paññā*. Images of the Buddha that include this *mudrā*, then, essentially employ the mode of visual narration that Dehejia calls "monoscenic": "In this mode, a single, easily identifiable scene excerpted from one of the episodes of the narrative, is presented to stimulate the viewer's recognition of the story.... Having given enough information to identify the tale, the artist leaves the viewer to narrate the story himself...."[78] This is not to say, however, that *prajñā* was entirely out of the picture. Certainly on the most obvious level a Pāla-period image of the Buddha in the *dharmacakra-pravartanamudrā* signifies Śākyamuni's first sermon at Sārnāth. But images, while they may

---

[77]*Samyutta Nikāya*, vol. 5, pp. 420-31.

[78]Dehejia, "On Modes of Visual Narration in Early Buddhist Art," p. 374.

perhaps be "mono*scenic*," are hardly "mono*semic*." Indeed, the story that the viewer self-narrates is contingent on the context in which that viewer is situated, and by the Pāla period, as I have argued, this context was saturated with *prajñā*. Thus when the Chinese pilgrims visited the major Buddhist sites in Magadha, they saw, certainly, the vestiges of Śākyamuni's activities there, the places where he had actually lived, meditated, taught, and performed miraculous feats; however, they also saw at these places vestiges of both the past and future Tathāgatas' perfected wisdom. Indeed, for these pilgrims, it would seem that *prajñā* was to be seen everywhere in this milieu.[79] So, for instance, when Faxian visited Bodhgayā in the fifth century, he was struck that this was the place "where all past Buddhas have attained, and all to come must attain, to perfect Wisdom."[80] Xuanzang, in the seventh century, also saw Bodhgayā as the place where the Buddha reached perfect wisdom, and he was moved to tears when he considered that he had not himself been present when the Buddha attained this perfect wisdom.[81]

In the Pāla period, a time when, as I have argued, *Prajñāpāramitā* ideas and practices were very much in the air, an image of the Buddha in the *dharmacakrapravartanamudrā* would quite likely have narrated something other than, or perhaps more accurately, something *in addition to*, Śākyamuni's first sermon. For medieval Buddhists, it was the perfection of *prajñā* that was seen to be at the heart of the *dharma*; it was *prajñā* that allowed the dharma to be known, that, in effect, caused the wheel of *dharma* to be turned. Thus I would posit that a crucial self-narrating possibility for a Pāla-period Buddhist viewing an image of Śākyamuni in the *dharmacakrapravartanamudrā* was, therefore, the *Prajñāpāramitā* texts' emphasis on the centrality of *prajñā* in the Tathāgata's ability

---

[79]It is, of course, impossible to *prove* that there is a correlation between what the Chinese pilgrims saw and what Indian practitioners saw; although this may be self-evident, what I offer here is an *interpretation*, an *extended inference* based on the available evidence, and not an empirically verifiable proof.

[80]James Legge, trans., *A Record of Buddhist Kingdoms* (New York: Dover Publications, 1965), p. 88.

[81]Samuel Beal, *The Life of Hiuen-tsiang* (London: Kegan Paul, Trench, Trübner and Co., 1914), p. 105.

to make known the *dharma*; without *prajñā* there could have been no Buddha in the past and no Buddhas in the future, and without the Buddhas, there could be no *dharma*.[82]

Logically, of course, this does not translate into an easy equation: the Buddha=*prajñā*, and therefore, representations of the Buddha=representations of *prajñā*. Something fairly close to this equation does, however, occur in the *Astasāhasrikā*, where the Buddha tells Ānanda that the *Prajñāpāramitā* should be honored and revered in the same way as the present Buddha.[83] Although a Pāla-period image of the Buddha in the *dharmacakrapravartanamudrā* could not possibly "tell the whole story," we must acknowledge, I think, that such an image would have communicated something more polysemic, and more complex, than simply "Śākyamuni preaching his first sermon." Nearly one hundred years ago, James Burgess said of this *mudrā* that it "typifies 'the unity of wisdom with matter,'...or the assuming of the material forms by the Buddha and Bodhisattva for the purpose of spreading the right understanding among animate beings."[84] Despite his vague and elusive "unity of wisdom with matter" language, Burgess' remarks strikes me as being quite close to the mark, in that it felicitously states the way an abstract faculty such as wisdom can be concretely represented, and further the way such a representation can convey this faculty. Indeed, it is not insignificant that the *dharmacakrapravartanamudrā*, as we shall shortly see, becomes the standard gesture for images directly related to *prajñā* and to the *Prajñāpāramitā*, such as with images of Mañjuśrī, as well as with images of the deity Prajñāpāramitā herself.

---

[82]We could stretch this analysis of the visual resonance of the *dharmacakrapravartanamudrā* even further, given that the Pāla kings employed this motif on their official seals - there also can be no *dharma*, and hence no *prajñā* (and hence no enlightenment), without a righteous king to maintain order in the kingdom.

[83]See *Astasāhasrikāprajñāpāramitā*, p. 228, for the full statement of this equation.

[84]James Burgess, "Buddhist Mudras," *Indian Antiquary* (Bombay) 26 (1897): 24ff.; quoted in E. Dale Saunders, *Mudrā*, p. 231.

II.C. Images of the Buddha in *Bhūmisparśamudrā*.

> Those again who are endowed with the power of the perfection of wisdom, and with the sharp sword of wisdom, they become inaccessible to the Evil Maras, unassailable by them."
>
> *Suvikrantavikrāmaparipṛcchā Prajñāpāramitā (Nirdeśa) Sūtra*[85]

> [O]ne is never satiated to behold such an image, and has no desire to go and behold another....even people of little faith when standing in front of the image felt it impossible not to shed tears.
>
> Dharmasvāmin[86]

The episode signified by the *bhūmisparśamudrā*, the "earth-touching gesture," which is also sometimes referred to as the *māravijaya*, or "victory over Māra" episode, represents the point at which Śākyamuni achieves enlightenment, the point at which he becomes the Buddha.[87] As with the *dharmacakrapravartanmudrā*, however, it is not self-evidently obvious how *bhūmisparśamudrā* images of the Buddha are involved with *prajñā*. John Huntington has called this event "the *summum bonum* of Buddhist soteriology." "It is this moment," he writes, "the moment of gaining the right to enlightenment and not the actual Enlightenment, that is the validation of the soteriological methodology taught by the Buddhists."[88] In other words, this is the culmination of the *dharma*. For such a climactic event, it is

[85]This is Conze's translation, printed in his unpublished manuscript, "Prajñāpāramitā Sūtras: Commentary on Hrdaya," p. 84.

[86]G. Roerich, *Biography of Dharmasvāmin* (Patna: K.P. Jayswal Research Institute, 1959) p. 67.

[87]See Giuseppe Tucci's somewhat extravagant remarks on this idea in his *The Theory and Practice of the Mandala* (London: Rider and Company, 1961), pp. 86-89.

[88]See John Huntington, "Pilgrimage as Image: The Cult of the *Astamahāpratihārya*," part I, *Orientations* 18 (1987): 55-63, p. 58, and John Huntington, "Sowing the Seeds of the Lotus, Part I," *Orientations* 16 (1987): 46-61, p. 61.

narratively rather straightforward, although the many recensions of the episode differ greatly in narrative detail.[89]

Just at the point at which he is about to attain *bodhi*, Śākyamuni is confronted by Māra, who realizes that he is about to be defeated by this man who has discovered the means with which to cut through all artifice. Māra, however, who is as we have already see the very embodiment of subterfuge, creates all manner of illusion and temptation to distract and defeat the Buddha-to-be. He unleashes his various armies - appropriately named desire, discontent, hunger and thirst, craving - but Śākyamuni is unmoved by Māra's attempts. Māra then uses his own daughters to tempt Śākyamuni, to stir in him lust and desire, but again to no avail. So Māra assaults him verbally, and challenges his very right to be beneath the *bodhi* tree, his right to enlightenment. Śākyamuni responds that all of the millions of offerings that he has made in his many lives have given him the right to enlightenment. Māra, however, persists; he says there is no witness to support Śākyamuni's claims. Śākyamuni's response is the exact moment depicted in *bhūmisparśamudrā* images: he reaches out his right hand and touches the earth. The *bhūdevī*, the goddess of the earth (who is sometimes depicted in the images),[90] is impartial and free from malice, and thus she serves as the ideal witness. The *bhūdevī* bears witness to Śākyamuni's enlightenment by creating a tremendous earthquake, rendering open the earth - a response reminiscent of the effect the first sermon creates.

As with the narrative accounts of the Buddha's first sermon, the narrative accounts of the defeat of Māra do not particularly focus on the role of *prajñā* in this event, but as with the *dharmacakra* episode, *prajñā* is very much part of the picture. First, as we have already seen, Bodhgayā, the site of this confrontation, has a special association with *prajñā*; as Faxian puts it, Bodhgayā is the place where

---

[89]There are various accounts of this event in Pāli and Sanskrit texts; see for instance the *Ariyapariyesana Sutta* of the *Majjhima Nikāya*; see also versions of this episode in the *Mahāvastu*, the *Nidānakatha*, the *Buddhacarita*, and the *Lalitavistara*. For a particularly useful account of the various versions of this event, see Janice Leoshko, "The Iconography of Buddhist Sculpture," pp. 76-91; see also John Huntington, "Sowing the Seeds, part I."

[90]See Janice Leoshko, "The Case of the Two Witnesses to the Buddha's Enlightenment," *Marg* 39 (1988): 39-52.

all Tathāgatas achieve perfect wisdom. Furthermore, implicit in the narrative is the conception of *prajñā* as cutting through illusion and delusion, as the scalpel that cuts out the *āsava*s, the sword that hacks through Māra's treachery. Thus it is his *prajñā* that enables the Buddha to defeat Māra, just as it is *prajñā* that enables the Buddha to see through the transitory nature of the world, to see through the emptiness of all *dharma*s, and, ultimately, to see through and conquer "death," of which Māra is the embodiment.[91]

The earliest known images of the Buddha in the *bhūmisparśamudrā* date to the Kuṣāṇa period, but it is in the Pāla period that they become the most prevalent sculptural depiction of Śākyamuni throughout northeastern India. That an iconographic shift, a move from the *dharmacakrapravartanamudrā* to the *bhūmisparśamudrā*, took place seems relatively clear, based on extant sculptural remains from Bodhgayā and other contemporary sites in India and Southeast Asia. *Why* this apparent iconographic shift took place, however, is a matter of considerably more speculation.

Susan Huntington, for instance, has suggested that this iconographic shift paralleled a locative shift, a shift away from Sārnāth to Bodhgayā as the preeminent place in the Buddhist world: "Just as the prevalence of the *dharmacakra mudrā* and the preeminence of Sārnāth (where Śākyamuni Buddha first preached) during the Gupta period are undoubtedly correlated, a relationship seems to exist between the popularity of the *bhūmisparśa mudrā* and the importance of Bodh Gayā...."[92] Janice Leoshko, in her study of the art of Bodhgayā during the Pāla and Sena periods, has written: "A seeming rise in the production of imagery in eastern India, the increased popularity of Bodhgayā as a site to visit, and changes in doctrine and practice may have been some the contributing factors for the popularity of the form."[93] Geri Malandra, in her recent book on the iconography at Ellora, has noted this iconographic move at this site as well, and further noted that this shift in the mode of representing

---

[91]For a useful discussion of this correlation, see Alex Wayman, "Studies in Yama and Māra," *Indo-Iranian Journal* 3 (1959): 44-73, 112-31, particularly pp. 112-25.
[92]Susan Huntington, *The Art of Ancient India*, p. 96.
[93]Janice Leoshko, "The Iconography of Buddhist Sculptures," p. 77.

the Buddha suggests that "a new doctrine was being propounded by a new sect."[94] The evidence for such a concomitant, and correlative, doctrinal shift is rather less clear.

The question can still be asked, however: What sort of doctrinal shift might have gone along with this iconographic shift? One obvious answer would be the rise of the *tantra*s and, especially, of the Vajrayāna, and the increased emphasis on Buddhas other than Śākyamuni's, in particular Aksobhya, whose characteristic hand gesture is the *bhūmisparśamudrā.* This was possibly the case at Ellora and Aurangabad in Maharashtra, and also at Ratnagiri in Orissa.[95] These sites, however, are much better preserved than most of those within the Pāla sphere. Furthermore, they are what might be called "periphery locales," in that they are away from the center, and what I have called centrist, Buddhist milieu of Magadha. A certain caution should be exercised, I think, in equating all Buddhism of this period with the rise of *tantra*, as I have earlier argued.[96] Indeed, even at such doctrinally innovative sites as Ellora and Ratnagiri, images of the Buddha displaying the *bhūmisparśamudrā* cannot easily be separated from the historical Buddha Śākyamuni.[97] As Malandra points out, at these sites "these images seem to refer explicitly to the enlightenment episode and, thus, indicate that the image as a whole should be

---

[94]Geri Malandra, *Unfolding a Mandala*, p. 62.

[95]For Ellora, see Malandra, *Unfolding a Mandala*; for Aurangabad, see J. Huntington's article, "Cave Six at Aurangabad: A Tantrayāna Monument?" in J. Williams, ed., *Kalādarśana: American Studies in the Art of India* (New Delhi: Oxford and IBH Publishers, Co. with A.I.I.S., 1981): 47-55; see also Nancy Hock, "Buddhist Ideology and the Sculpture of Ratnagiri, Seventh through Thirteenth Centuries." Ph.D. Dissertation, University of California, Berkeley, 1987, particularly pp. 2-35.

[96]See my "Reevaluating the Eight-Ninth Century Pāla Milieu: Icono-Conservatism and the Persistence of Śākyamuni" *Journal of the International Association of Buddhist Studies* 19.2 (1996): 281-300 .

[97]Snellgrove states this point nicely: "Thus it would seem, despite the philosophical changes described above, that a majority of Indian Buddhists remained faithful to the earlier traditions concerning Śākyamuni, his former births as Bodhisattva, and the original traditions concerning the Buddhas who had preceded him," *Image of the Buddha* (Paris: UNESCO, 1978), p. 89.. Oddly, however, Snellgrove all but ignores his own thesis, instead consistently pushing the dominance of tantra and Vajrayāna in the Pāla period; for instance, he identifies several images of Śākyamuni as Aksobhya, when in fact there is no iconographical reason for such an identification with the images in question.

viewed, on one level, as a representation of the historic figure of Śākyamuni."[98]

For the Pāla milieu, at least, this "one level" is perhaps the one to emphasize. Bodhgayā, the site of the enlightenment, lay within the Pāla realm, a fact that must not have been lost to Pāla-period patrons. Indeed, Śākyamuni most obviously figures in the icono-*logic* of these images: the *bhūmisparśamudrā*, like the *dharmacakrapravartana-mudrā*, is most obviously a visual narrative of an event in the life of Śākyamuni, and at least visually has little to do with the expanded notions of Buddhahood prevalent in the *tantra*s and in Vajrayāna sources.[99] At first glance, then, the prominence of the *bhūmisparśamudrā* would seem to be a conservative move, an emphasis on the historical Buddha's activity at Bodhgayā.

The Buddha's defeat of Māra at Bodhgayā does not, of course, lead to his ultimate destruction; Māra does not shrivel up and "die," but is, on the contrary, a constant presence in Buddhist discourse. In the *Astasāhasrikāprajñāpāramitā*, Māra is said to be an obstacle to practitioners, a constant threat to distract one from studying, copying, and understanding the *Prajñāpāramitā*.[100] However, to this, the Buddha adds that Māra cannot really hinder the Bodhisattva who truly

---

[98]Malandra, *Unfolding a Mandala*, p. 70; see also Hock, "Buddhist Ideology and the Sculpture of Ratnagiri, p. 29.

[99]The *bhūmisparśamudrā* does, however, figure in the non-mainstream representation of some of the Buddhas besides Śākyamuni; see Janice Leoshko's discussion in her "The Iconography of Buddhist Sculptures," pp. 117-230; also see Nancy Hock, "Buddhist Ideology and the Sculpture of Ratnagiri," pp. 37-56. Geri Malandra has further pointed out that interpreting images of the Buddha in the *bhūmisparśamudrā* to representing Śākyamuni also fits the context in which these images were situated at Ellora. Malandra argues that such images were explicitly intended to equate Ellora and Bodhgayā; see Malandra, *Unfolding a Mandala*, particularly pp. 70-71. For the Pāla materials, however, there is very little evidence to suggest that such images fit into larger Mandalas, and based on the prevalence of the *Astamahāpratihārya* images I have discussed in the previous chapter, I would suggest that here we are dealing with a much more conservative ritual milieu. For more on this topic, see Janice Leoshko, "Pilgrimage and the Evidence of Bodhgays's Images," in K.R. van Kooij and H. van der Veere, *Function and Meaning in Buddhist Art* (Groningen, 1995), pp. 45-57. Leoshko notes that based on the surviving sculpture, Bodhgayā was not perhaps as conservative as some have thought, although she also points out that "at Bodhgaya itself perhaps of greatest importance was the idea of the event of enlightenment," p. 53. See also my, "Reevaluating the Eight-Ninth Century Pāla Milieu: Icono-Conservatism and the Persistence of Śākyamuni."

[100]See *Astasahāsrikāprajñāpāramitā*, p. 110.

applies his or herself. Thus Śāriputra asks the Buddha how one can take up the *Prajñāpāramitā* if Māra is determined to cause obstacles, and the Buddha replies that the Tathāgatas are there to help, to use their powers, and that, perhaps more importantly, the *Prajñāpāramitā* itself is there to aid in the defeat of Māra: "Thus the *Prajñāpāramitā*, which expresses the ultimate truth, is set up for all beings for the sake of understanding all *dharma*s as they really are."[101] Not just for comprehending reality, but for cutting through Māra's illusion and getting at the truth of *śunyatā*.

Again, this is not to say that for medieval Indian Buddhists this was the self-evident significance of sculptures of the Buddha in the *bhūmisparśamudrā*. Such images are, rather, decidedly polyvalent, and involve a kind of scale of meanings, a variety of devotional and hermeneutical possibilities: on the narrative level, such an image visually tells the story, or acts as a visual cue for telling the story, of Śākyamuni's defeat of Māra and his concomitant enlightenment,[102] the point at which the Buddha becomes the Buddha; this narrative, in turn, represents the supreme triumph of the *dharma*, the soteriological efficacy of the Buddha's teaching (it defeats death!); furthermore, these images signify the centrality of Bodhgayā as a pilgrimage place and center of Buddhism.

What a medieval Indian Buddhist would have seen in such an image, what sorts of connections he or she would have made, and what sorts of reactions such vision would have entailed and provoked, would have very much been an open-ended issue and, again, very much context bound. Thus depending on his or her particular grounding in the shifting *habitus*, one might have seen here a present Śākyamuni, an absent Tathāgata, an object intended to remember the Buddha, a representation of his enlightenment, a signification of the possibility of this enlightenment for all beings, and so on.

---

[101]Ibid., pp. 111-12; *tathā hi prajñāpāramitā paramārthopasamhitā sarvadharmānām yathābhūtaprativedhāya pratyupasthitā sarvasattvānām* \. Mitra's 1888 version of the text has *pratibodhāya*, instead of *prativedhāya*, which seems to me to make more sense.

[102]Māra, in fact, is frequently depicted on Pāla-period *bhūmisparśamudrā* images, usually as a small figure off to the side, a visual reminder to the viewer/participant of the many impediments that must be overcome, and thus also a reminder of the real need for *prajñā*. See J. Leoshko, "The Case of the Two Witnesses."

All of these possibilities, however, are resonant with *prajñā*. Behind all of these possibilities, hovering over and under such possible interpretations and associations, is *prajñā*, is the wisdom that leads to enlightenment, that cuts through all illusion and reveals the true nature of reality. The image, as I have suggested, serves as a metapractical object that gives rise to reflection on these various levels of significance. And as I shall discuss in the next two chapters, this implicitly represented *prajñā* becomes significantly more explicit when we shift our gaze from representations of the Buddha to representations of such figures as Mañjuśrī, Avalokiteśvara, Cundā, and Prajñāpāramitā herself.

Chapter Five

REPRESENTING PRAJÑĀPĀRAMITĀ

> A person will indeed know this: When the noble, perfectly enlightened Tathāgata was training in the way of the *bodhisattva*, he learned this *Prajñāpāramitā*, [and so] we too should learn it, thinking, "This is our teacher."
>
> *Aṣṭasāhasrikāprajñāpāramitā*[1]

I have argued in the last chapter that Śākyamuni is from the very beginning intimately associated with *prajñā*, and that this association, furthermore, was also at play in even the earliest images of the Buddha. It is wisdom that ultimately enables him to attain enlightenment, that enables Gautama to triumph over Māra and to become the Buddha. And it is wisdom that is at the heart of the *dharma* that he first makes known at Sārnāth. With the rise of the Mahāyāna, *prajñā* moves to the center of Buddhist discursive and ritual practice as the perfection *par excellence*. I have also explored in the last chapter the ways in which - through the use of what I shall call "resonant iconography" - this abstract cognitive faculty is *indirectly* visually expressed, represented, and presented when the Buddha is sculpturally represented. I have thus argued that during the Pāla period, when *prajñā* is very much at the center of Buddhist discourse and practice, to see an image of the Buddha was to see wisdom, since the essential quality of the Buddha is this *prajñā* that leads him (and, ideally, the viewer of, or participant in, such an image) to enlightenment.

---

[1]*Astasāhasrikāprajñāpāramitā*, p. 31; *tathā hi sa evaṃ jñāsyati - atra prajñāpāramitāyāṃ tathāgato 'rhan samyaksambuddhaḥ pūrvaṃ bodhisattvacaryāṃ caran śiksitaḥ \ asmābhirapyatra śiksitavyam \ eṣo 'smākam śāsteti \ tiṣṭhato vā kauśika parinirvṛtasya vā tathāgatsyārhataḥ samyaksambuddhasya bodhisattvairmahāsattvaih prajñāpāramitaiva pratisartavyā \.*

REPRESENTING PRAJÑĀPĀRAMITĀ

In this chapter, I explore the *direct* representation of *prajñā* itself, specifically in the form of the deity Prajñāpāramitā, who first emerges in India sometime around the eighth century. I pay close attention here to the textual discourse on *prajñāpāramitā*, particularly that contained within the *Aṣṭasāhasrikāprajñāpāramitā* and related texts, since it is this discourse, I argue, that underlies and leads to the sculptural representation of what is frequently called in Western scholarship the "Goddess of Wisdom," the "Mother of the Buddhas," even "Mother Wisdom."

I have divided the present chapter into three main parts. First, I examine the textual discourse on the supremacy of the *Prajñāpāramitā* as an object of veneration. An important component in this discourse is the ideological shift away from the veneration of the physical remains of the Buddha to the veneration of the *Prajñāpāramitā* text itself. An essential component in this shift, in turn, is an amalgamation of the received conceptions of the *rūpa* and *dharmakāya*s; both become contained in a single object, the *Prajñāpāramitā* book.

Second, I will examine the essential rationale for this shift, a topic I have touched on in the last chapter: namely, the conception of the *Prajñāpāramitā* as the source and origin of the Buddha's enlightenment, as the teacher of the Tathāgatas, as their "mother". Western scholars have frequently taken this discourse literally, and discussed Prajñāpāramitā as some sort of a mother goddess. I will, in this regard, examine in detail the specific passages that employ such "mother language," and I will argue that in fact such interpretations - Prajñāpāramitā as Mother Wisdom, the Mother of All Buddhas, etc. - is often misguided and overdetermined, and, among other things, skews our understanding of the sculptural representation of Prajñāpāramitā and the relation such representation has with the textual discourse.

In the third section of this chapter I discuss some specific examples, and some specific iconographic features, of the sculptural representations of what we might call the major "*prajñā* females" of the Pāla period: Prajñāpāramitā, Tārā, and Cundā.

I. Relics, Books, and the Field of Veneration

> Indeed, Kauśika, this *Prajñāpāramitā* makes for beings this spot of earth a *caitya* to be honored, thought of, worshipped, adored, revered, venerated, and respected.
>
> *Aṣṭasāhasrikāprajñāpāramitā*[2]

> Therefore, Blessed One, when a *pūja* is done to the *Prajñāpāramitā*, it is a *pūja* to the venerable past, present, and future Buddhas.
>
> *Aṣṭasāhasrikāprajñāpāramitā*[3]

One of the most striking aspects of the *Prajñāpāramitā* genre is, as I have already noted, the degree of self-referentiality in the texts. In any given *Prajñāpāramitā* text, a vast portion of that text will be devoted to praising the text itself, to describing in detail the advantages of reciting, writing, and most of all, venerating the actual physical book. As a rhetorical device - and indeed as part of a larger polemic - such self-referentiality is not particularly surprising, since these texts were clearly composed and redacted in a milieu of competing Buddhist discourses. Among many other things, the redactors of the texts were engaged in an attempt to shift the locus of non-discursive practice, that is of ritual veneration, away from the physical relics of the Buddha and toward the written form of the *Prajñāpāramitā*. This was no small matter, for as Schopen has noted, the redactors of the *Prajñāpāramitā* genre "were attempting to introduce a radical innovation in the face of an established cult form of central importance," and they thus "had to contend at every step with the historical priority and dominance of the

---

[2]Ibid., p. 18; *anayaiva hi kauśika prajñāpāramitayā pṛthivīpradeśaḥ sattvānāṃ caityabhūtaḥ kṛto vandanlyo mānanīyoḥ pūjanīyo 'rcanīyo 'pacāyanīyaḥ satkaraṇīyo gurukaraṇīyaḥ.*

[3]Ibid., p. 50; *tasmāttarhi bhagavan prajñāpāramitāyāṃ pūjitāyāmatītānāgatapratyutpannānāṃ buddhānāṃ bhagavatāṃ pūjā kṛtā bhavati /.* I have intentionally omitted the article preceding "Prajñāpāramitā" here, preserving the amibiguity, about which I will have more to say shortly, that is inherent in the line as to the exact identity of the object of veneration (i.e. book or deity).

stūpa/relic cult of early Buddhism in the milieu in which it was attempting to establish itself."[4]

We see the expression of this "radical innovation," for instance, in the fourth chapter of the *Aṣṭasāhasrikā*, a short section that focuses on the devotional merits of the *Prajñāpāramitā* in relation to the merits of the relics of the Buddha, the question is explicitly raised as to whether it is in fact better to venerate the relics of the Tathāgata or to venerate the text. The Buddha poses the question: "If, Kauśika, this Jambūdvīpa filled to the very top with relics of the Tathāgata were offered to you, and if a written *Prajñāpāramitā* were offered to you; being restricted to one of these two pieces of good fortune, which would you choose?"[5] Kauśika does not hesitate with his answer: he would take the *Prajñāpāramitā* book.

As we have already seen, however, this is *not* because the relics of the Buddha are themselves not valuable and not worthy of veneration. On the contrary, the redactors of the text are careful to state that the relics of the Buddha *are* highly respected, and worthy of veneration. They simply are not *as good* as the text. Śakra thus answers the Tathāgata's question:

> Certainly, Blessed One, it is not that there is in me disrespect for the relics of the Tathāgata. There is in me, Blessed One, respect for the relics of the Tathāgata. But, indeed, Blessed One, the relics of the Tathāgata obtain honor because they originate from this *Prajñāpāramitā*. Therefore, Blessed One, when worship is done to this very *Prajñāpāramitā*, then the Tathāgata's relics are fully worshipped. Why is this?

[4]Gregory Schopen, "The Phrase '*sa pṛthivīpradeśaś caityabhūto bhavet*'," pp. 169 and 168.

[5]*Aṣṭasāhasrikāprajñāpāramitā*, p. 48; *sacetkausika ayaṃ te jambūdvīpaḥ paripūrṇaś-cūlikābaddhastathāgataśarīrāṇāṃ dīyet iyam ca prajñāpāramitā likhitvopanāmyet tata ekatareṇa bhogena parivāryamāno 'nayordvayorbhāgayoḥ sthāpitayoḥ katam tvaṃ kausika bhāgaṃ gṛhṇīyāḥ*\\.

> Because the relics of the Tathāgata originate from the *Prajñāpāramitā*.[6]

Indeed, according to the redactors of the *Aṣṭasāhasrikā*, when one worships the relics, one is really worshipping the *Prajñāpāramitā*, because the relics are merely the receptacles (*āśrayabhūtāni*) of the Tathāgata's knowledge and wisdom, not its origin, nor its cause, nor what brings it forth (*na tāni pratyayabhūtāni, na kāraṇabhūtāni, na jñānasyotpādāya*). It is the *Prajñāpāramitā* that is the true origin and cause of the Buddha's knowledge and wisdom, and "as the cause of the knowledge of the omniscient one, the *Prajñāpāramitā* is worshipped in worshipping the Tathāgata's relics."[7]

It is, therefore, naturally more efficacious to go directly to the source and to venerate and to honor the *Prajñāpāramitā* than it is to worship the Buddha's physical remains, because really the relics come from (*nirjāta*) the *Prajñāpāramitā*. It is striking, and perhaps surprising, though, that this "going to the source" does not refer simply to reading and to learning the *content* of the texts; rather, it is the *container* that assumes a significant importance here. The book itself becomes a cult object.[8]

The context of this "cult of the book" discourse is central to the Pāla period representation of *prajñā*, for it is precisely this apparent shift in the object of veneration, I would argue, that leads to - or constitutes the underlying field of, as Bourdieu would have it - the development of Prajñāpāramitā as a deity and that, perhaps more importantly, elevates her to the same, if not actually a higher, plane as that of the Buddhas. Furthermore, this devotional shift leads to important developments in the visual representation of *prajñā*, in particular the practice of sculpturally representing books that becomes

---

[6]Ibid., p. 48; *na khalu punarme bhagavaṃsteṣu tathāgata-śarīreṣvagauravam / gauravameva me bhagavaṃsteṣu tathāgataśarīreṣu / api tu khalu punarbhagavan itaḥ prajñāpāramitāto nirjātāni tathāgataśarīrāṇi pūjāṃ labhante / tasmāttarhi bhagavan anayaiva prajñāpāramitayā pūjitayā teṣāmapi tathāgata-śarīrāṇāṃ paripūrṇā pūjā kṛtā bhavati / tatkasya hetoḥ? prajñāpāramitānirjātatvāt-tathāgataśarīrāṇāṃ /.*

[7]Ibid., p. 48; *evameva bhagavan sarvajñajñānahetukā tathāgataśarīreṣu pūjā kṛtā bhavati.*

[8]I use this phrase, "cult object," with a certain reluctance, given the tremendous amount of ideological baggage such language carries.

increasingly prominent in the Pāla milieu from the tenth century onward.[9]

In an article on issues directly germane to this subject, Gregory Schopen has argued that such passages as those from the *Astasāhasrikāprajñāpāramitā* that I have just quoted - and in particular the key phrase "*sa prthivīpradeśaś caityabhūto bhavet*" that occurs in the *Astasāhasrikā*, *Vajracchedikā*, and other texts in the *Prajñāpāramitā* genre - are both reflective and constitutive of a broad ideological shift within the early Mahāyāna, a shift away from the veneration of *stūpa*s and relics and toward the veneration of texts. "The emphasis in the *AsP*," writes Schopen, "is clearly on the presence of the *dharmaparyāya* in written, book form."[10]

Schopen poses a very basic question: what, exactly, does the phrase "*sa prthivīpradeśaś caityabhūto bhavet*" mean? Specifically, how are we to understand the compound "*caityabhūta*"? Does it mean, as Conze translates it, that the spot of earth where the *Prajñāpāramitā* is spoken, revealed, or placed will become "*like* a shrine"? Or, more simply, does the phrase mean that the spot of earth will become an actual *caitya*? Or, does the phrase mean that the spot of earth will become a particular sort of *caitya*, a "true, a real, a fit *caitya*"? Schopen's characteristically prolix discussion need not concern us in great detail here; the important point he makes for this context is that the *Astasāhasrikā* is explicitly concerned with the superior value of the *written* form of the book as an object of veneration in terms of the relative value of the veneration of *stūpa*s and relics. Relics and *stūpa*s are certainly worthy of veneration according to the discourse of the *Astasāhasrikā*, as we have already seen, but the book is more valuable and more valued, because the book is the source of the Tathāgata's wisdom, and consequently the source of his attainment of enlightenment, and thus the source of the value of the relics.

The place where the book is located *is* a *caitya*, therefore, and, as Schopen suggests, it is not just any *caitya*. As Schopen puts it, "Our contexts," and here he means the *Astasāhasrikā*, as well as the

---

[9]See the next chapter for an extended discussion of this practice.

[10]Schopen, "The Phrase '*sa prthivīpradeśaś caityabhūto bhavet*'," p. 155.

Vajracchedikā, the *Saddharmapuṇḍarīka*, and several other early Mahāyāna texts, "leave no doubt as to how the tradition understood the term *caityabhūta*: the *pṛthivīpradeśa* was not *like* a *caitya*, nor was it just a *caitya*...;"[11] rather, according to Schopen, the book is explicitly equated with the *bodhimaṇḍa*, literally the *essence* of enlightenment, the very seat under the Bodhi tree at Bodhgayā where Gautama attained enlightenment. Lamotte has called the *bodhimaṇḍa* the "présence toute spirituelle de la Loi ou du *dharmakāya* des Bouddha."[12] Thus in the third chapter of the *Aṣṭasāhasrikā* we are told that just as those men or ghosts who have gone to the actual *bodhimaṇḍa*, that is to Bodhgayā, or to its vicinity, cannot be harmed (except as a result of their own former deeds), so also anyone who sets up, or venerates, the *Prajñāpāramitā* book cannot be harmed.[13]

I think that it is entirely reasonable to ask as this point: What does all of this have to do with the visual representation of *prajñā*, and particularly with the representation of the deity Prajñāpāramitā? These passages, after all, are concerned with the presence of the book, not with the presence of a deity or a sculpture of a deity. A related question that must be addressed in this regard, then, is: What exactly is involved in the physical presence of the book? Is the discourse about the significance of the book as a locus, and thus conveyor, of *dharmaparyāya*, that is the oral and written discourse on the *dharma*? Or is the focus on the significance of the book as, for lack of a better term, a *sacred object*?

One way to address this issue is to focus on what I see as a subtle but essential shift in the conception of the *dharmakāya* here. In this same section of the *Aṣṭasāhasrikā* with which I have just been concerned, there is an overt equation of the book, the relics/body of the Buddha, and the *dharmakāya*: "This is the real body of the Tathāgatas. Why is this? As the Blessed One has said: 'The Blessed

---

[11]Ibid., p. 177.

[12]Étienne Lamotte, *La Concentration de la Marche Héroïque (Śūrangamasamādhisūtra)*, Mélange Chinois Bouddhique, vol. xiii (Bruxelles, 1965), p. 221.

[13]See *Aṣṭasāhasrikāprajñāpāramitā*, p. 28, for the full Sanskrit.

Buddhas have *dharma* as their bodies'."[14] This can, of course, be taken to imply the presence of the Buddha at that spot of earth where the text is, or where it is recited, and so on, because it is the *dharma* that constitutes the true presence of the Buddha. This would then be a restatement of the basic formula about the equivalence of the Buddha and the *dharma* that we have already encountered in the earlier Pāli context: *yo kho Vakkali dhammaṃ passati so maṃ passati, yo maṃ passati so dhammaṃ passati.*[15] Thus the *Prajñāpāramitā* book is equated with the *dharmakāya* - indeed it is the *real dharmakāya*, the true body of the teachings - since the genre conceives of itself as the supreme expression of the *dharma.*

I am not sure, however, that what we see here is simply continuity, or at least not a simple continuity; rather, what we see here is precisely the sort of *malleable*, *ad hoc* nature of *habitus* that enables and encourages what Kasulis calls metapraxis. This passage, and the context in which it is embedded, is not primarily concerned with the doctrinal content of the *sūtra*, in other words with the traditional (or at least the expected) conception of the *dharmakāya;* rather, it is the physical book - what would seem to be more properly a *rūpakāya* - that is here equated with the *dharmakāya*. This is an equation that puts a significant spin, I think, on the logic of the *ye dhammaṃ passati* formula. The Pāli formula conveys the notion that one is able to see the physically absent Buddha (i.e. the *rūpakāya*) by hearing or learning - and not simply *seeing* in a strictly literal sense - the *dharma* (i.e. the *dharmakāya*); in other words, the focus is on the *contents* of the texts, on the teachings and the discourse on those teachings, on *dharmaparyāya*.

In the *Aṣṭasāhasrikā* passages, however, the focus is as much on the *container* as on the contents. So, for instance, in the third

---

[14]Ibid., p. 48; *etaddhi tathāgatānāṃ bhūtārthikaṃ śarīraṃ / tatkasya hetoḥ uktaṃ hyetadbhagavatā dharmakāyā buddhā bhagavantaḥ /*. It is ambiguous whether the "*etad*" here refers to the *Prajñāpāramitā* discourse or the physical book or both; there is no mention of "*pustaka*" (book) here, although "*likkhitvā*" (having written or copied) occurs earlier in the same passage, indicating, I think, that the physical book is the referent. For more on this passage, and in particular the whole issue of what is meant by the phrase *dharmakāyā buddhā bhagavantaḥ iti*, see Paul Harrison, "Is the *Dharma-kāya* the Real 'Phantom Body' of the Buddha?" *Journal of the International Association of Buddhist Studies* 15 (1992): 44-94.

[15]*Samyutta Nikāya*, vol. 3, p. 120.

chapter of the text, appropriately entitled *Aprameyagunadhārana-pāramitāstūpasatkāraparivartah* ("The chapter on the reverence for the container of perfections, which holds immeasurable virtues"),[16] one encounters a passage in which the Buddha tells Kauśika that those gods and humans who seek enlightenment will come to the place where someone has set up the *Prajñāpāramitā* text, and "having come there, they will look at this *Prajñāpāramitā* in the form of a book, and they will salute it respectfully, honor it, support it, learn it, remember it, offer to it, explain it, show it, recite it, reveal it, and repeat it."[17]

Clearly we are dealing here with a *written* book (*likhitvā pustakagatām kṛtvā*);[18] and, equally clearly, we are dealing with a written book that is intended to be looked at (*preksisyati*) and worshipped (*namaskarisyanti, pravartayisyanti*). In this regard, the book functions in the same way as, or in an analogous way to, the way that a relic or an image would function; that is, as a highly valued and respected *object*, the mere sight of which is efficacious. The book here, then, seems to be analogous to the Tathāgata's *rūpakāya*. However, the book here also functions as a text to be learned (*udgrahīsyanti*), read aloud (*vācayisyanti*), and explained (*deśayisyanti*); or put another way, as something *more than an object*, more than a *rūpa*. Thus the book in this regard is not just significant as a *container*, but also for its *contents*, the supremely stated *dharma* that it contains. Thus the book is *also* functioning as, or analogous to, the Tathāgata's *dharmakāya*.

From this specific passage, and from dozens of similar passages in the *Astasāhasrikā* and related texts, it is impossible to know precisely how the physical book fit in to a ritual and discursive context.[19] It is unclear, for instance, whether *dharmaparyāya*, oral or

---

[16]It is worth noting that the word I have here translated as "container" is in fact "*stūpa*," a further expression of the kind of "cult of the book" ideology I have been discussing.

[17]*Astasāhasrikāprajñāpāramitā*, p. 42; *te 'pi tatrāgatya enām prajñāpāramitām pustakagatām preksisyante vandisyante namaskarisyantyudgrahīsyanti dhārayisyanti vācayisyanti paryavāpsyanti pravartayisyanti deśayisyantyupadeksyantyuddeksyanti svādhyāsyanti.*

[18]This phrase occurs just prior to the passage I have just quoted, ibid., p. 42.

[19]One thing that is unclear, for instance, is the exact sense of what I have here translated as "set up" - established, in the sense of a discourse, or physically set up in the sense of a physical text to be treated as an object of veneration. See the next chapter for a more detailed discussion of this.

written, was a contingent part of devotion to the text, or whether dual emphasis was placed on the contents and the container. Certainly from the passage I have been discussing, it would seem that in some way the text *as a book*, an object *to be seen*, allowed the practitioner to partake of its contents. In other words, *to see* the book, and to honor and worship it, allowed the devotee to partake of the *prajñā* that is its essential content.

There would seem, then, to be an amalgamation of the *dharmakāya* (the contents) and the *rūpakāya* (the container) in the air; or, to put it more boldly, it would seem that what we might call devotional vision (*preksisyante vandisyante namsakarisyanti*...) begins here to take precedence over learning and recitation. Admittedly, this is all only inferentially gleaned from the discursive position of texts such as the *Aṣṭasāhasrikā*, but when we add to this textual discourse the sculptural evidence from the later Pāla period - as I shall do later in this chapter and in the chapter that follows - what we see is not only a shift from the relics to the book, but a shift from the conception of the book *as simply a container* of the *dharma* (that is, as *rūpakāya*), to the book *as the dharma* (that is, *dharmakāya*). In short, as the Pāla period progresses, increasingly *the book is the thing*, and Prajñā-pāramitā becomes the embodiment of the book.

II. Buddha Mother, Mother Wisdom

> Homage to that mother of the multitude of Bodhisattvas, Śrāvakas, and the Buddha.
>
> *Abhisamayālaṃkāranāmaprajñāpāramitopadeśaśāstram* [20]

> If the Buddha died about 480 B.C., it would have taken about four hundred years until he was provided with a spiritual "mother" in the shape of the *Prajñāpāramitā*.... If,

[20] *Abhisamayālamkāra-Prajñāpāramitā-Upadeśa-Śāstra*, p. 1; *tasyai śrāvakabodhisattvaganino buddhasya mātre namah.*

> as I believe, the *Prajñāpāramitā* originated in the South of India, it would represent an irruption into Buddhism of the devotion to the Mother-Goddess current in the more matriarchal Dravidian society in which it originated.
>
> Edward Conze [21]

We have already seen that the *Prajñāpāramitā* is said, in the *Astasāhasrikā* and other texts of the genre, to be the source of the Tathāgatas, past, present, and future. An important element in this discourse is the elevation of the physical book, so that it occupies a venerational plane equal to, if not actually higher than, the Buddha. Another important element in this discourse, one that goes directly to the heart of the representation of Prajñāpāramitā, is descriptions of Prajñāpāramitā as the "mother" of the Buddhas. The issue I wish to address first in this section, then, is what exactly these texts mean by "mother." What language and rhetoric do the redactors of the texts employ? and can we tell, from the discursive context, the intent of this language and rhetoric? As should be clear from the above quotation from Edward Conze, scholars have frequently interpreted this "mother" language literally, and seen in it evidence that a "Cult of the Mother Goddess" had taken root in the earliest strata of the Mahāyāna. Are they justified? This examination of the textual discourse on Prajñāpāramitā as a purported mother goddess is important for two reasons: First, the degree to which scholars have freely interpreted such passages in the *Prajñāpāramitā* has, as I will demonstrate, skewed our understanding of the conception and development of Prajñāpāramitā as a deity; second, and perhaps more important, is the way in which the textual discourse on the *Prajñāpāramitā* text as the source of the Tathāgatas underlies, informs, and leads to the eventual sculptural depiction of Prajñāpāramitā. Indeed, as I shall demonstrate, Buddhists during the Pāla period did not seem to emphasize the maternal nature of Prajñāpāramitā at all; that is, they did not take the mother language literally, but *figuratively*, representing her

---

[21]Edward Conze,"The Development of Prajñāpāramitā Thought," in Conze, *Thirty Years of Buddhist Studies*, p. 125.

iconographically as she is described textually, as the true source of the *dharma*.

II.A. Wishing for a Mother.

One of the first Western scholars to introduce the "Buddha Mother" interpretation was Samuel Beal, in his *A Catena of Buddhist Scriptures from the Chinese*, first published in 1871. Beal actually uses "mother" to describe Cundā, a deity closely related to, and often confused with, Prajñāpāramitā.[22] According to Beal's translation of the Chinese, Cundā is the "Mother of the Seven Koṭis of Buddhas," the "Holy Mother of all the Buddhas."[23] The Chinese terms Beal translates - *fo-mu*, *neang-neang*, *shing-moo* - are themselves translations of several Sanskrit terms, *bhagavatī*, *devī*, and *mātṛkā* that occur in the *Sādhanamālā* and other iconographic texts that describe Cundā. As S.D. Singhal has put it recently, Beal's overly literal translation, innocuous as it seems, "has remained a source of misapprehension and confusion," transforming Cundā - and, by extension, Prajñāpāramitā - from a highly regarded female figure (even a goddess) into a divine mother.[24]

Beal's extrapolated translation has been repeated with a striking consistency over the years. In her 1928 *Gods of Northern Buddhism*, Alice Getty, for instance, directly refers to Beal's translation, and says, without further comment, that Cundā "is sometimes called the 'Mother of Buddha'."[25] Conze, for his part, nearly always refers to Prajñāpāramitā as a mother; for instance, in his 1949 study of the iconography of Prajñāpāramitā, he posits that the

---

[22]This confusion is entirely understandable, since Prajñāpāramitā and Cundā share nearly identical iconographies; see below for more on this.

[23]Samuel Beal, *A Catena of Buddhist Scriptures from the Chinese* (London: Trübner & Co., 1871), p. 413.

[24]Sudarshan Devi Singhal, "Iconography of Cundā," in Lokesh Chandra, ed., *The Art and Culture of South-East Asia* (New Delhi: Academy of Indian Culture and Aditya Prakashan, 1991), p. 399.

[25]Alice Getty, *The Gods of Northern Buddhism: Their History and Iconography* (New York: Dover Publications, 1928), p. 129. Getty also uses the "Mother of the Buddhas" epithet in her description of Prajñāpāramitā, noting that she is called this in the "exoteric doctrine," p. 131.

"mythological consciousness" (whatever that may be) led the early Mahāyānists to create a mother goddess, and that, therefore, a discussion of Prajñāpāramitā contributes to the "history of the Mother-goddess who, from the Palaeolithic onwards, has occupied so great a place in human affection."[26] In the same article, he further emphasizes Prajñāpāramitā's maternal character: "The femininity of Prajñā-pāramitā is usually fairly obvious. She is normally bare to the waist. As she is essentially a mother-goddess, her full breasts are conspicuous."[27] As we shall see, however, these are hardly the most notable iconographic features of Prajñāpāramitā images.

Again demonstrating the *paramparā* of the Academy, scholars continue to rely on just these interpretations, frequently questioning the context of neither the indigenous discourse (and thus the intent of the language used) nor the secondary interpretation of this primary discourse. For instance, Joanna Rogers Macy, in an article heavily indebted to David Snellgrove's interpretation of female Buddhist deities,[28] itself heavily indebted to Conze, concludes her discussion of Prajñāpāramitā with this remarkable interpretation: "Imaged as light and space, pregnant zero and matrix of dimension, this clear-eyed, compassionate Mama was, at a key point in the Dharma's history, its channel and its symbol."[29] An even more recent example of the persistence of Beal's original misstep is a rather bizarre volume entitled, *Mother of the Buddhas: Meditation on the Prajnaparamita Sutra*, which intends, with a highly devotional spin, to present "a picture of the universe as seen through the eyes of Mother Prajnaparamita, the wisdom Goddess...."[30] The problem with such interpretations, however, is that they simply are not warranted by what the texts themselves actually say. Indeed, such interpretations are

---

[26]Edward Conze, "The Iconography of the Prajñāpāramitā," Parts I and II. *Oriental Art* 2 (1949-50): 46-52; and 3 (1950-51): 104-09, p. 47.

[27]Ibid., "Part II," p. 104.

[28]See for instance David Snellgrove, *Buddhist Himālaya* (Oxford: Bruno Cassirer, 1957), particularly pp. 80ff.

[29]J. R. Macy, "Perfection of Wisdom: Mother of all Buddhas," in Rita M. Gross, ed, *Beyond Androcentrism: New Essays on Women and Religion* (Missoula: Scholars Press, 1977), p. 330.

[30]Lex Hixon, *Mother of the Buddhas: Meditation on the Prajnaparamita Sutra* (Wheaton, IL: Quest Books, 1992), p. 12. This volume is clearly intended to be devotional, and not schlolarly, and it is little more than an ammended, popularization of Conze's translation.

more clearly a reflection of these authors' own agendas - if not fancies - than the indigenous discourse of the texts.[31]

Let me first return briefly to Beal, who set this particular wheel in motion. The words in question here are *bhagavatī*, *devī*, and *mātṛkā*. The first two terms can certainly both be translated as "mother," but this is not their primary sense; "blessed" or "respected" woman would have been more standard, or even "goddess." *Mātṛ* (or *mātṛkā*) is more ambiguous, since its primary meaning is, in fact, "mother," although as with *bhagavatī* and *devī*, it has considerable semantic range. One immediate problem with relying on Beal's translation/interpretation and incorporating it into the *Prajñāpāramitā* discourse is that he is translating from the Chinese recension of the *Sādhanamāla*, which itself reflects a variety of interpretations - some of them quite late, i.e. post eleventh century - of this very discourse. Thus if we wish to understand the discursive context of this mother language, we must look to the source, the *Prajñāpāramitā* texts themselves.

II.B. Mother Talk in the *Prajñāpāramitā*.

The *Prajñāpāramitā* texts do indeed employ mother language in their praise of the *Prajñāpāramitā* and in their enumerations of the text's many benefits. For instance, in the *Aṣṭasāhasrikā*, *mātā* is first encountered in a list of praise and epithets for the *Prajñāpāramitā*: "The blessed [*Prajñāpāramitā*] gives light...the blessed *Prajñāpāramitā* is the remover of the darkness of ignorance and delusion...the blessed *Prajñāpāramitā* is the *mother* of the *bodhisattva*s and the great beings, on the basis of the emptiness of her own marks.[32] However, the precise meaning of the word "*mātā*" here - the word translated as "mother" - is not at all clear, nor, for that matter, is the referent of the

---

[31]Such agendas range from Conze's attempt to equate Buddhism and Greek philosophy - see his review, "Prajñā and Sophia," *Oriental Art* 1 (1948): 196-97 - to Macy's feminist reading of the Mahāyāna, to Hixon's New Age Spiritualism.

[32]*Aṣṭasāhasrikāprajñāpāramitā*, p. 86; the Sanskrit is, "*avabhāsakarī bhagavan... mohatamastimiravikariṇī bhagavan prajñāpāramitā... svalakṣaṇaśūnyatāmupādāya mātā bhagavan bodhisattvānāṃ mahāsattvānām prajñāpāramitā....*

epithets, and here, in my opinion, lies the problem. Let me first address the question of the referent.

The text simply says "*prajñāpāramitā*." It does not say "the *Prajñāpāramitā* book," or "the *Prajñāpāramitā* teachings," or "Prajñāpāramitā the deity." Until this point in the *Aṣṭasāhasrikā*, *prajñāpāramitā* has referred either to the larger set of doctrines and practices that make up what we would call the "*Prajñāpāramitā* discourse," or, as we have just seen, to the physical text. It is usually clear by the context which of the two the redactors intended, or, as can also be the case, when they seem to have meant both the discourse and the physical book. In the passage from the *Aṣṭasāhasrikā* that I quoted at the start of this section, it seems on the surface that the redactors are referring to the *Prajñāpāramitā* discourse; there is, for instance, no mention of books or writing (as there is in the passages I have just discussed in the last section). Indeed, just prior to this line, in the same passage, Śāriputra describes the *Prajñāpāramitā* as "the accomplishment of the cognition of the omniscient one," and "the condition of omniscience."[33] However one translates it, "*prajñāpāramitā*" in this context seems to signify something like the *dharma* in its fully realized form, the epitome of wisdom, as well as the state one attains through mastering this discourse. Until the occurrence of "*mātā*" well in to this passage, the redactors give no indication that they intend to signify anything other than the discourse.

The question here, then, is are we bound to take the "*mātā*" literally? Conze certainly thought so: he glosses over any ambiguity in the passage, and translates "*svalakṣaṇaśūnyatāmupādāya mātā bhagavan bodhisattvānāṃ mahāsattvānāṃ prajñāpāramitā*" as, "She is the Mother of the Bodhisattvas...,"[34] and, consequently, construes all other occurrences of "*prajñāpāramitā*" as "she." In other words, in a few sentences Conze has transformed a discourse and, perhaps, a physical text into a full-blown Mother Goddess; and what is more, he

[33]Ibid., p. 86; *sarvajñajñānaparinispattirbhagavan prajñāpāramitā sarvajñatvam bhagavan prajñāpāramitā.* The *tvam* is difficult to render into English. Literally, one might say that the *Prajñāpāramitā* is "knowledge-*ness*," although that seems rather cumbersome. Conze translates it as the "state of all-knowing."

[34]See Edward Conze, trans., *Aṣṭasāhasrikā Prajñāpāramitā*, Bibliotheca Indica, no. 284 (Calcutta: The Asian Society, 1958), p. 54.

has done so, it seems, purely on the basis of a single word, "*mātā*." But what, exactly, does and can *mātā* mean? Does it have to mean "mother" in a literal sense, or at all, for that matter?[35] Elsewhere in the *Astasāhasrikā*, after all, the discourse and the book are referred to as the true *source* of the Buddhas; it is the *Prajñāpāramitā* that gives *rise* to the Buddhas.

To put the question differently, is it not at least possible that we are dealing here with metaphorical talk, and that this *mātā* rhetoric is precisely that, *rhetoric*? Indeed, in the last line of this passage - an extremely important line that I will return to below when I discuss the iconography of Prajñāpāramitā - we get another version of this same rhetoric. The *Prajñāpāramitā* is said to be the "turner of the wheel of *dharma*, the fulfillment of the twelve aspects of the three turnings."[36] Here, again, the redactors are celebrating the *Prajñāpāramitā* discourse - and not, I think, the mother or the goddess - as the true source of the *dharma*, and therefore as the true source of the Buddhas.

The mother metaphor occurs elsewhere in the *Astasāhasrikā*, and again the rhetorical nature of the usage becomes clear. Chapter Twelve, for instance, opens with a simile: "Subhūte, it is just as when there is a mother with sons."[37] In such a case, if the mother were to fall sick, the sons would care for her, would, among other things, protect her and give her what she needs, keep mosquitoes and crawling insects away from her, and so on. And why, the *Bhagavan* asks, would this be the case? Because the sons would be aware that they owe their very existence to their mother, that she brought them into existence with great pain and that she instructed them in the ways of the world.[38] The text then states that *in the same way* the Tathāgatas should regard the *Prajñāpāramitā*.[39] Clearly, the redactors are not saying, quite suddenly, that the *Prajñāpāramitā* should be regard as a

---

[35]A full investigation of this question would, of course, require a rather sweeping philological effort far beyond my scope here.

[36]*Astasāhasrikāprajnāpāramitā*, p. 86; *paripūrnatripariartadvādaśākāradharmacakrapravartanī bhagavan buddhānāṃ bhagavatāṃ prajñāpāramitā*.

[37]Ibid., p. 125; *tadyathāpi nāma subhūte striyā bahavaḥ putrā bhaveyuh*.

[38]The relevant Sanskrit reads: etayā hi vayam janitāh/*duskarakārikaisā asmākāṃ jīvitasya dātrī lokasya ca saṃdarśayitrī*, ibid., p. 125.

[39]Ibid., p. 125; *evameva subhūte tathāgatā arhantaḥ samyaksambuddhā imāṃ prajñāpāramitāṃ samanvāharanti*..

mother, or a mother goddess, but rather, that *it* (and not, as Conze has it, *she)* - the text and the discourse - should be treated with the same sort of respect and veneration shown to a mother by her sons. And again, the reason for this is clear; just as a mother is the source of her sons, so is the *Prajñāpāramitā* the source of the Tathāgatas, the *janayitrī* (creator) and the *darśayitrī* (guide).[40]

There is no question that this is both a potent and an intentional metaphor. As José Cabezón has pointed out, there was a range of terms available to Buddhists, and the use of feminine nouns for *Prajñāpāramitā*, particularly "mother," must be seen as intentional.[41] Still, this is just a metaphor, used to assert the supremacy of the *Prajñāpāramitā* teachings, which, as the source of the wisdom of the past, present, and future Buddhas, is the ultimate expression of the *dharma*.

In short, then, I think Beal and Conze and virtually all of those who follow are simply wrong in seeing in the various *Prajñāpāramitā* texts a cult of the Mother Goddess, and I would agree with Singhal that such carelessly extrapolated translations have been the "source of misapprehension and confusion." This, however, is in my opinion where things get most interesting. For once we have cleared up this issue of Prajñāpāramitā as Mother Wisdom or a Mother Goddess, we can then look at the development of sculptural representations of her - which clearly derive from these and other textual discourses, although, as I shall show in a moment, *not* with an emphasis on the maternal character of Prajñāpāramitā - with a new clarity.

---

[40] *Prajñāpāramitā* is also elswhere called *jananī* (producer) and *āhārikā* (nurse); ibid., p. 228.

[41] See José Ignacio Cabezón, "Mother Wisdom, Father Love: Gender-based Imagery in Mahāyāna Buddhist Thought," in Cabezón, ed., *Buddhism, Sexuality, and Gender* (Albany: SUNY, 1992), pp. 181-99, particularly pp. 184-85. Cabezón writes: "Just as the mother is one of the two principal causes of a child, so too is wisdom one of the two chief causes of enlightenment. The other, of course, is method. To stress this fact, namely that wisdom is what nurtures the adept on the path, it is characterized as their 'mother.' Just as a mother must bear the child in her womb for ten (lunar) months, the traditional gestation period, so too does wisdom nurture the adept along the way through the ten bhūmis, the stages of the bodhisattva path. Hence, it is gestation in mother wisdom's womb that brings about the birth of enlightened beings."

III. Representing *Prajñāpāramitā* in Sculpture

> Prajñāpāramitā is a lovely yellow. In her left hand, she holds the *Prajñāpāramitā* book on a lotus; her two principle hands display the *dharmacakramudrā.*
>
> *Niṣpannayogāvalī* [42]

> The venerable *Prajñāpāramitā* is the turner of the wheel of *dharma*, the fulfillment of the twelve aspects of the three turnings of the blessed Buddhas.
>
> *Aṣṭasāhasrikāprajñāpāramitā* [43]

III.A. Searching for a Source.

One of the most common methodological problems facing art historians - or any historian, for that matter - is the source of inspiration behind a particular piece of art. What gave rise to such an image? what were the precedents? what was in the artist's mind when he or she conceived of such a work? Often the answer to such questions, in art history, becomes a matter of *influence*, and, in particular, a matter of *who* was influenced *by whom*: In order to understand the work of David Hockney, say, one must understand how Hockney was influenced by Picasso, who was influence by Cezanne, who was influenced by Manet, who was influence by Ingres, and so on. As Brendan Cassidy has pointed out, however, this emphasis in art history on influence has had a tendency to suffocate the discipline methodologically: "One style begets another style, artists influence other artists, but the impact of extra-artistic factors rarely enters the discussion. A token nod in the direction of social context with a

---

[42] B. Bhattacharyya, ed., *The Niṣpannayogāvalī of Abhayākaragupta*, Gaekwad's Oriental Series, 59 (Baroda: Oriental Institute, 1949), p. 65; *prajñāpāramitā kamanīyakanakakāntiḥ padmastha prajñāpāramitāpustakadharā karadvayena dhṛtadharmacakramudrā.*

[43] *Astasāhasrikāprajñāpāramitā*, p. 86; *paripūrṇatriparivartadvādaśākāradharmacakrapra-vartanī bhagavan buddhānām bhagavatām prajñāpāramitā.*.

reference, say, to the patron of an altar-piece, is considered all that is required to acknowledge that art indeed is part of the larger cultural, economic, religious, and social experience of humankind."[44]

The other extreme in art historical discourse is to turn to the methodology formulated by Panofsky and Warburg - iconology. Here, the issue is still essentially *influence*, but the attempt is made to uncover the broader cultural forces that produce an artist and a particular work of art. Certainly, as I have already noted in Chapter One, there are problems with Panofsky's methodology, particularly in the context of Indian Buddhism. If, for instance, we hope to find *the* text that will explain the development of Prajñāpāramitā as a sculpturally representable deity, we shall look in vain. There is no single text, no single source, but rather, as I have been attempting to argue in the preceding chapters, a whole field of texts and practices and ideas that make up the Pāla context. Furthermore, if we pay too much attention to the "symbolic value" or the "disguised symbolism" - to use two of Panofsky's own terms - of a particular image, hoping to demonstrate that behind such symbolism lies the "basic attitude of a nation, a period, a class, a religious or philosophical persuasion,"[45] we run the risk of seriously overdetermining a given work. As the painter Frederick Turner said of the critic John Ruskin on this subject: "He knows a great deal more about my paintings than I do, he puts things into my head and points out meanings I never intended."[46]

Despite the problems with Panofsky's methodology - or at least with the way it has been employed - there is something fundamentally sound in it: the emphasis on context, on the complex of ideas that go into the production and reception of any given work of art. What I have been attempting in the previous chapters has very much been in the spirit of Panofsky; I have attempted to construct a complex field of practice, a thick convergence of ideas and practices which constitute and in which is situated the visual representation of *prajñā*. At this point, however, I must move somewhat in the opposite direction; I must move from an image *back* to a text.

---

[44]Brendan Cassidy, *Iconography at the Crossroads*, p. 4.
[45]Erwin Panofsky, *Studies in Iconology*, p. 7.
[46]Quoted in Cassidy, *Iconography at the Crossroads*, p. 7.

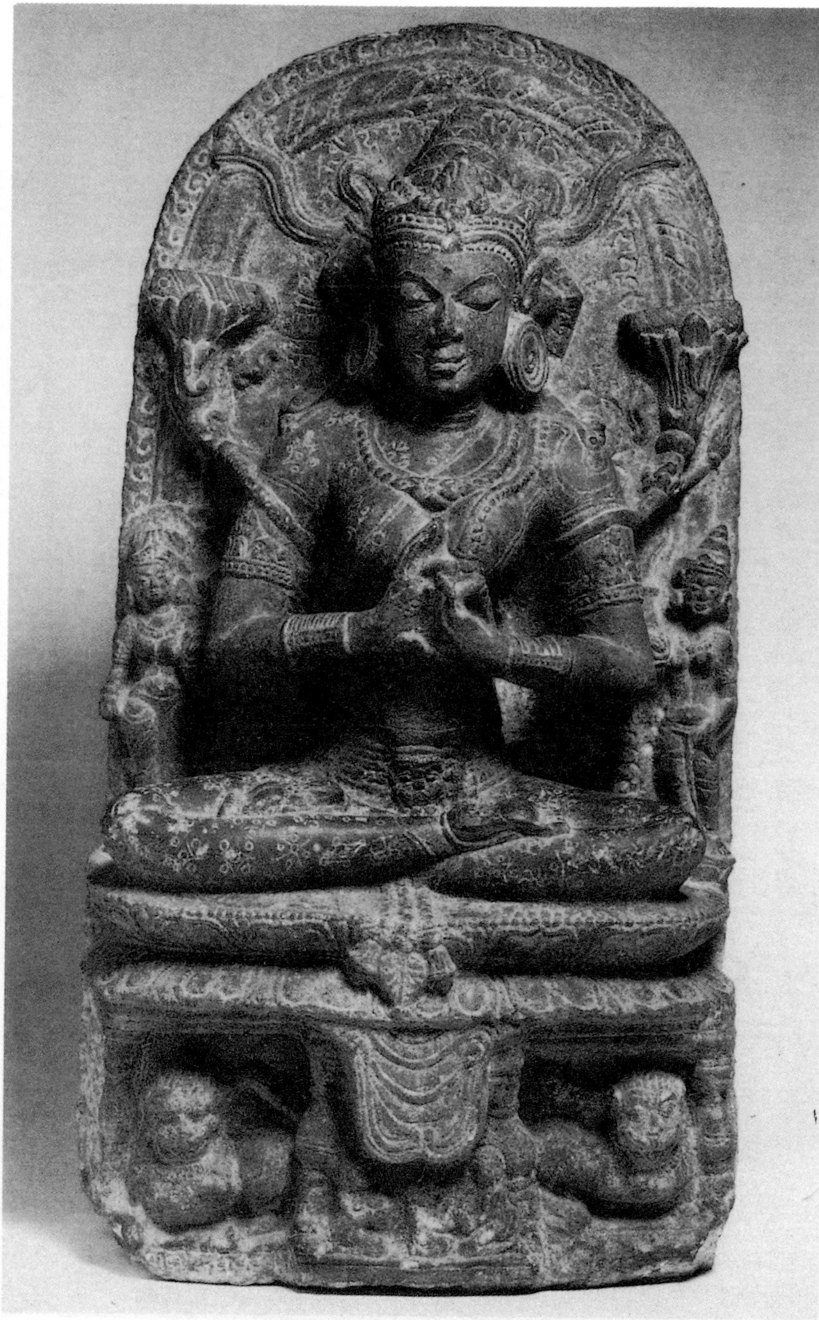

Fig. 1. Stone Prajñāpāramitā, 9th century, Bihar, Avery Brundage Collection, photo courtesy of the Museum of Asian Art, San Francisco

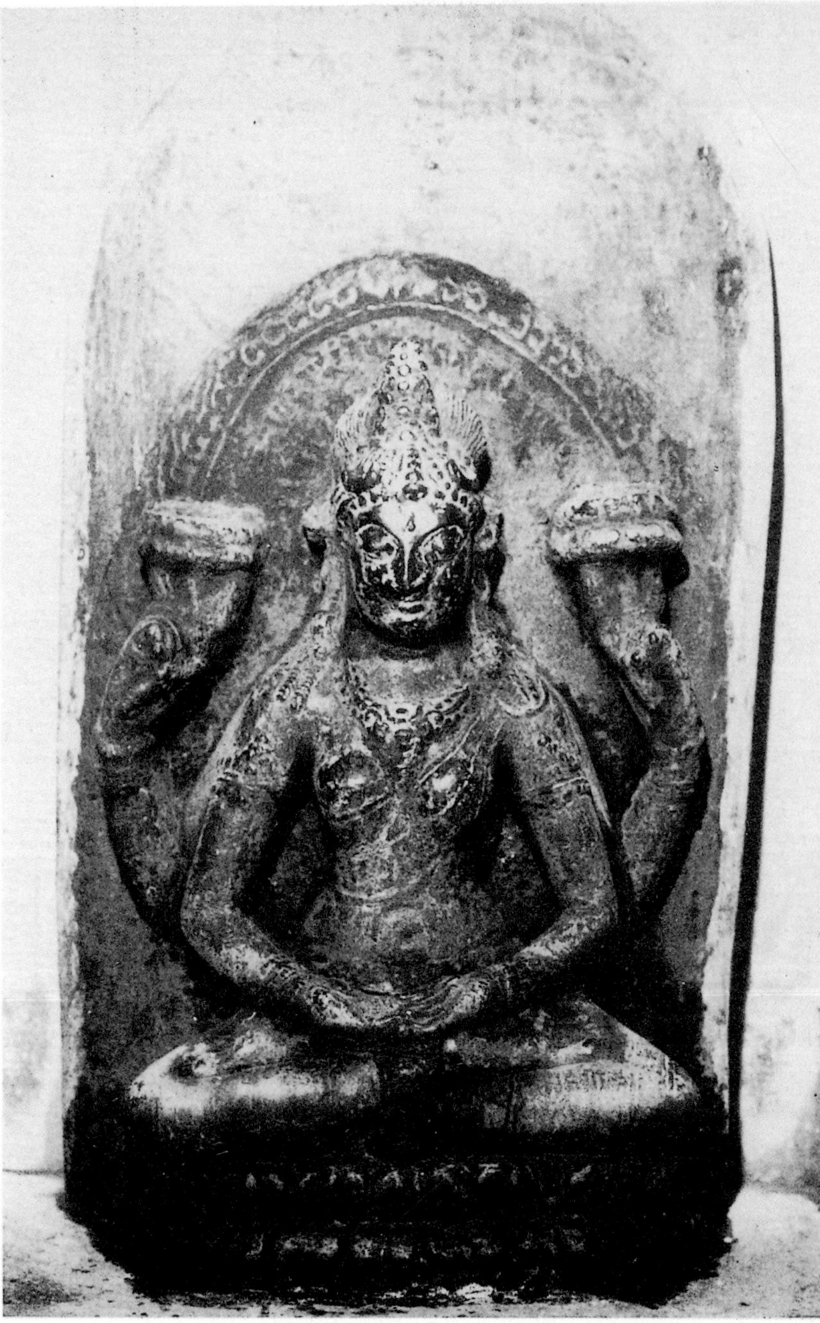

Fig. 2. Stone Prajñāpāramitā, 9th century, Bodhgayā, photo courtesy of Janice Leoshko

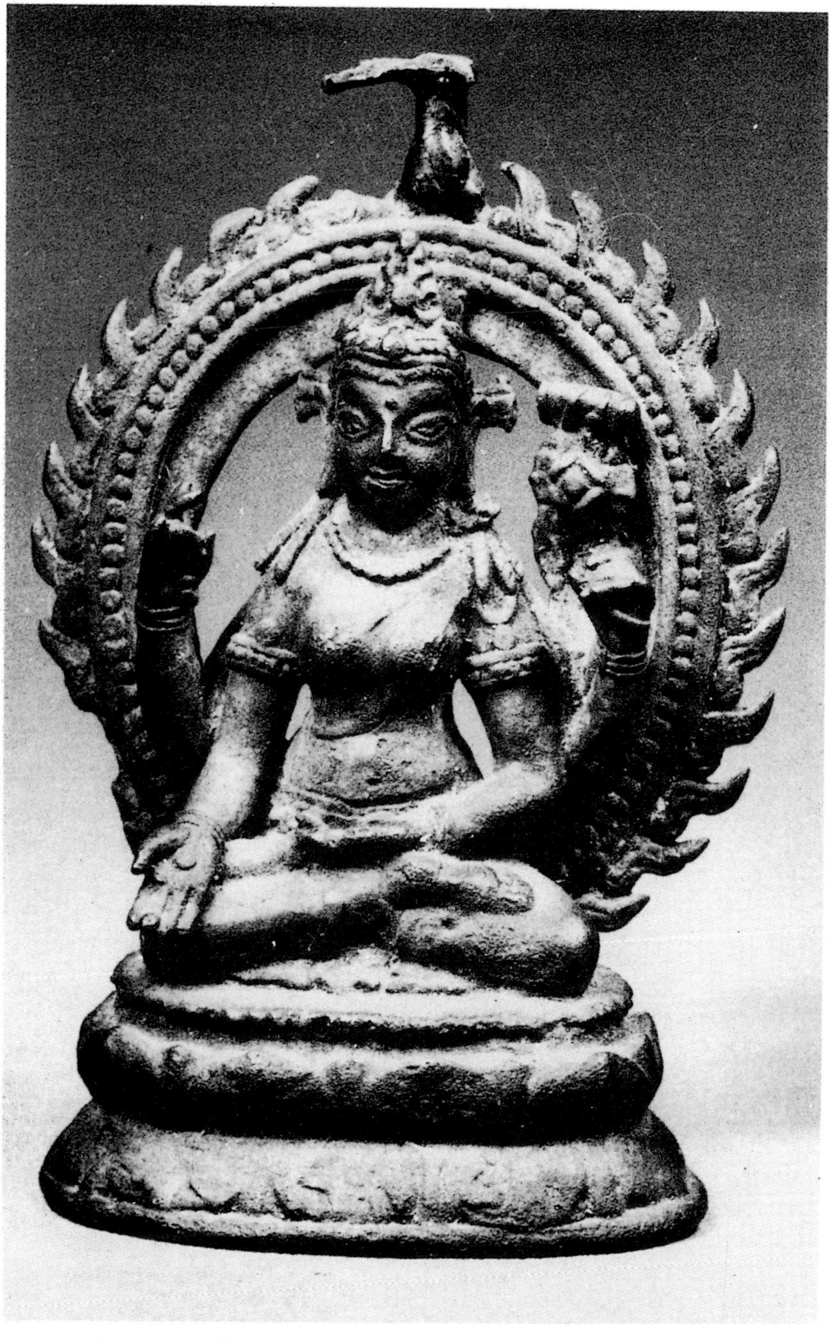

Fig. 3. Bronze Prajñāpāramitā, 9th century, Nālandā, Nālandā Museum, photo courtesy of the American Institute of Indian Studies

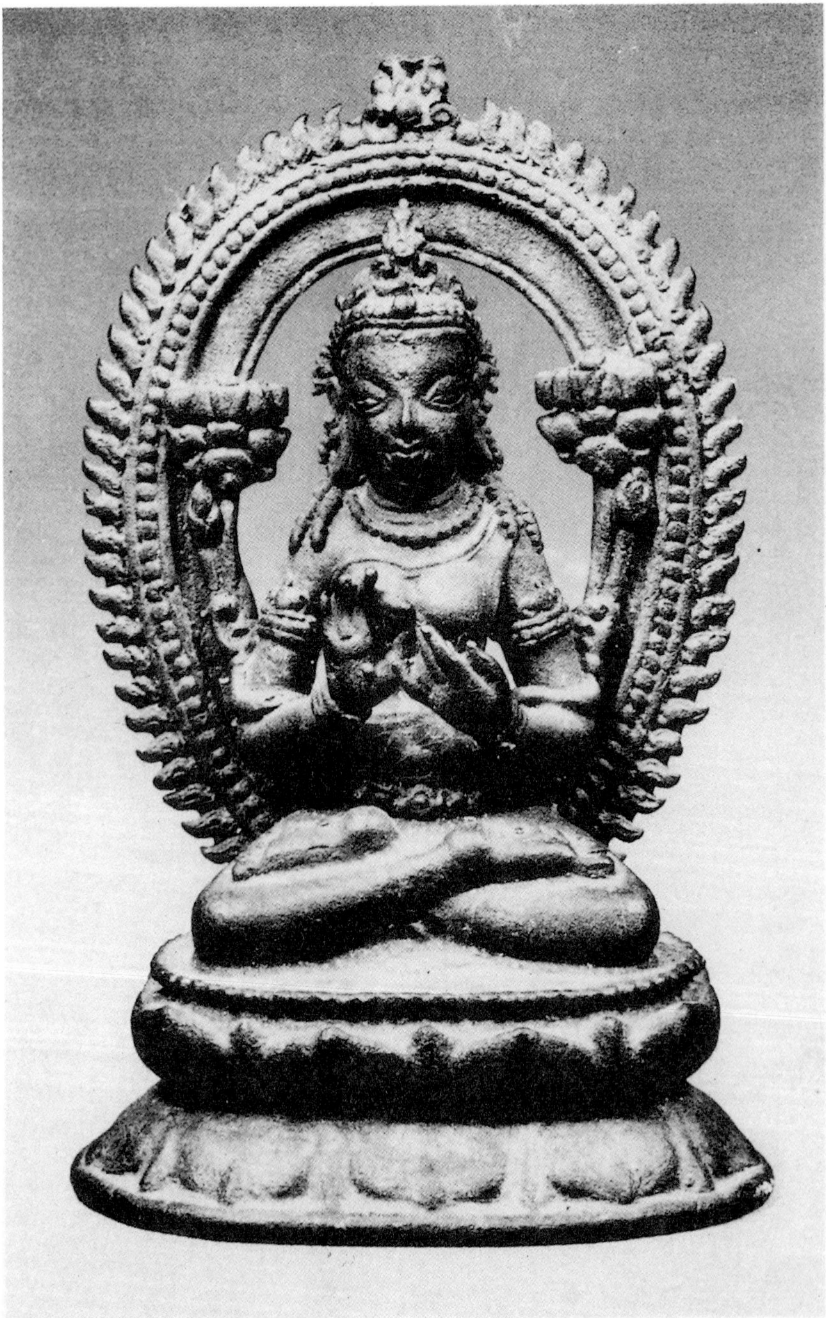

Fig. 4. Bronze Prajñāpāramitā, 9th century, Nālandā, Nālandā Museum, photo courtesy of the American Institute of Indian Studies

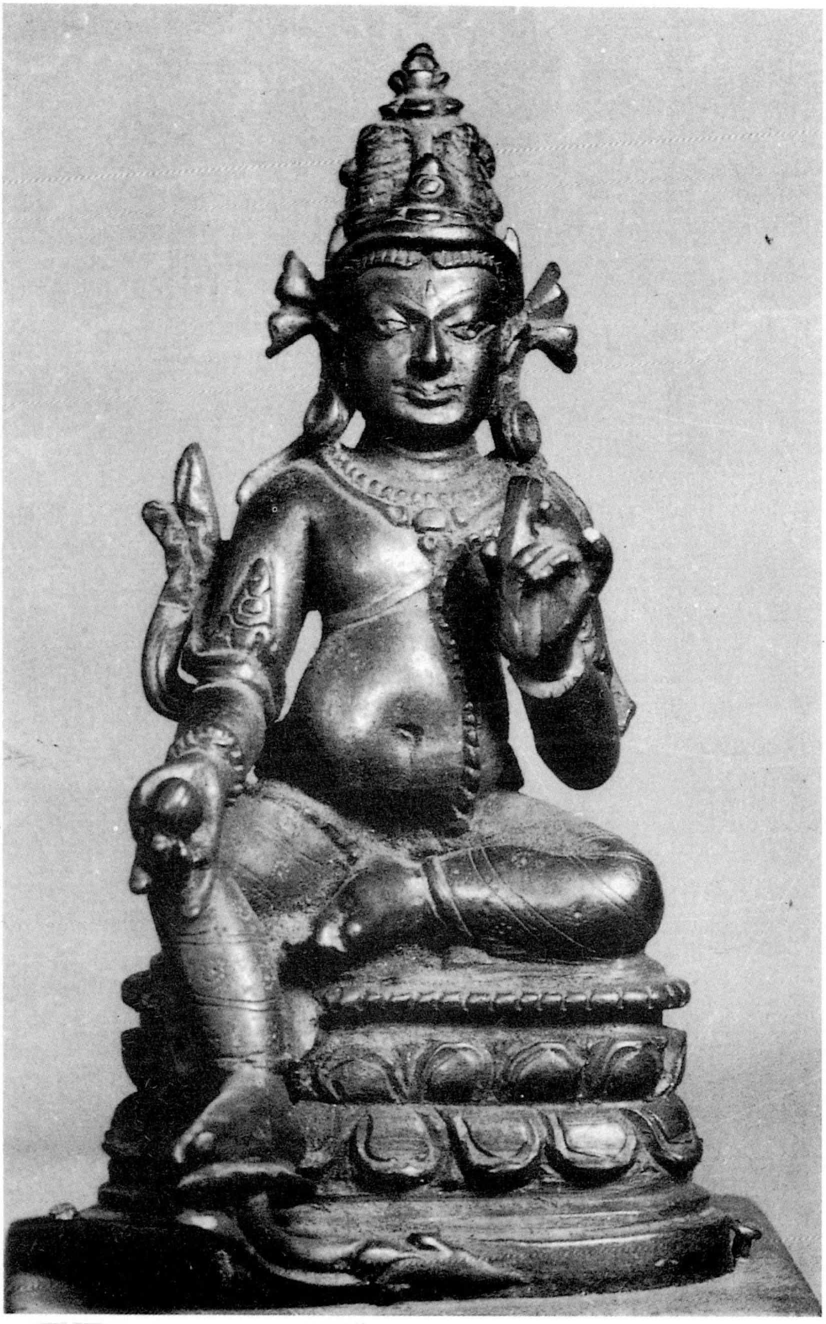

Fig. 5. Bronze Mañjuśrī, 10th century, Bihar, National Museum, New Delhi, photo courtesy of the American Institute of Indian Studies

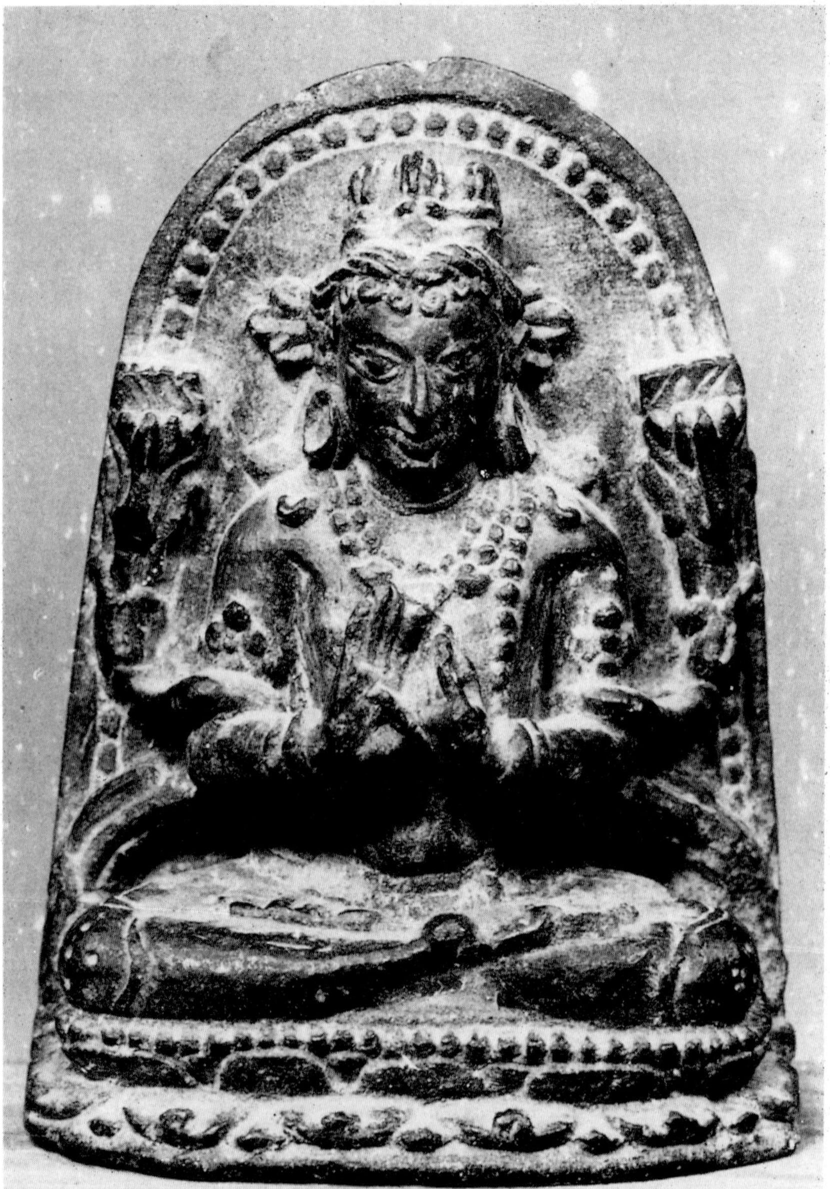

Fig. 6. Stone Mañjuśrī, Nālandā, 10th century, Nālandā Museum photo courtesy of the American Institute of Indian Studies

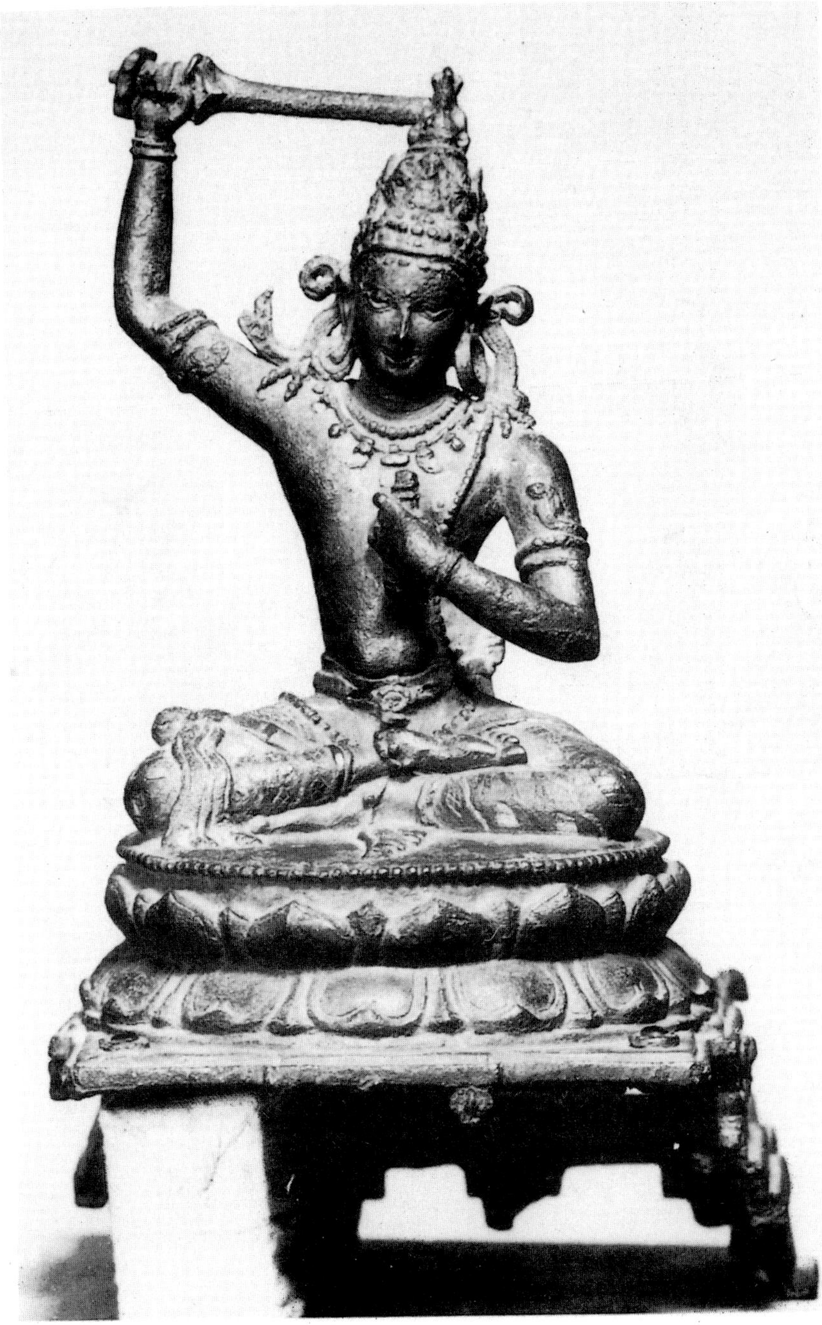

Fig. 7. Bronze Mañjuśrī, 9th century, Nālandā National Museum, New Delhi, photo courtesy of the American Institute of Indian Studies

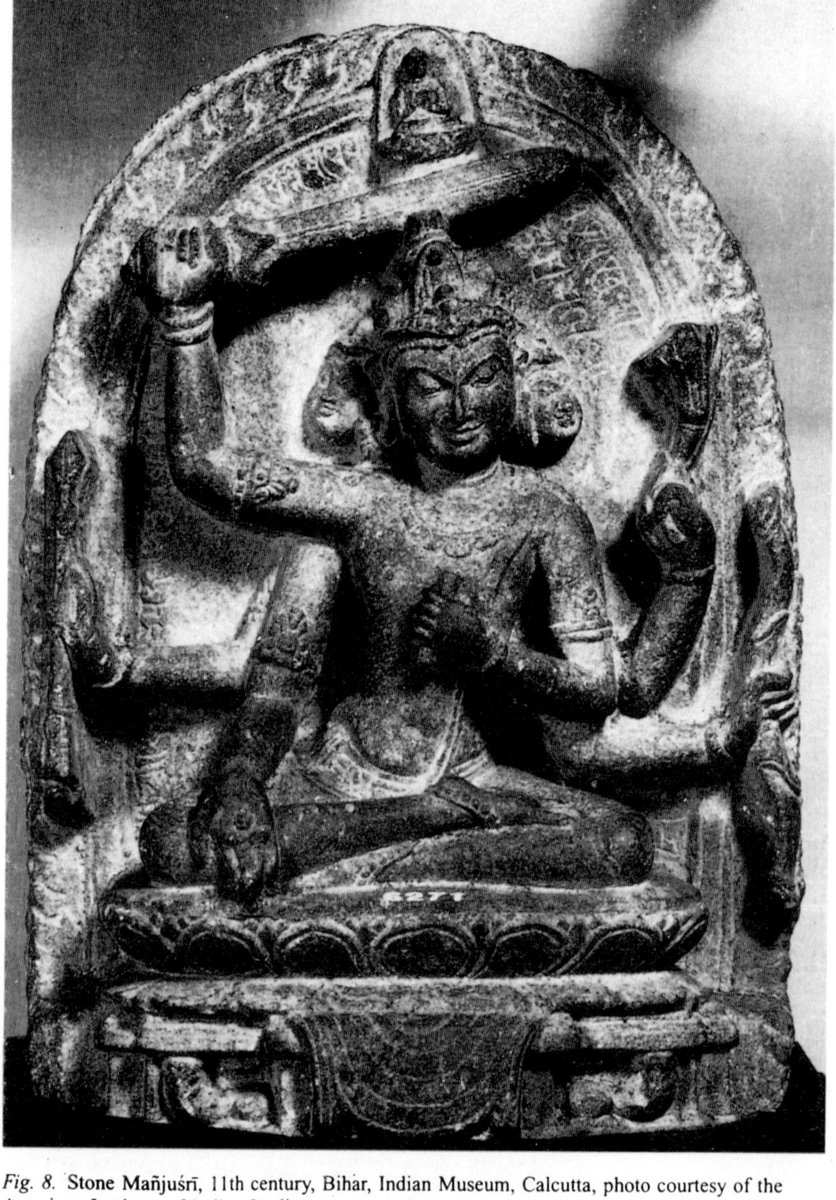

Fig. 8. Stone Mañjuśrī, 11th century, Bihār, Indian Museum, Calcutta, photo courtesy of the American Institute of Indian Studies

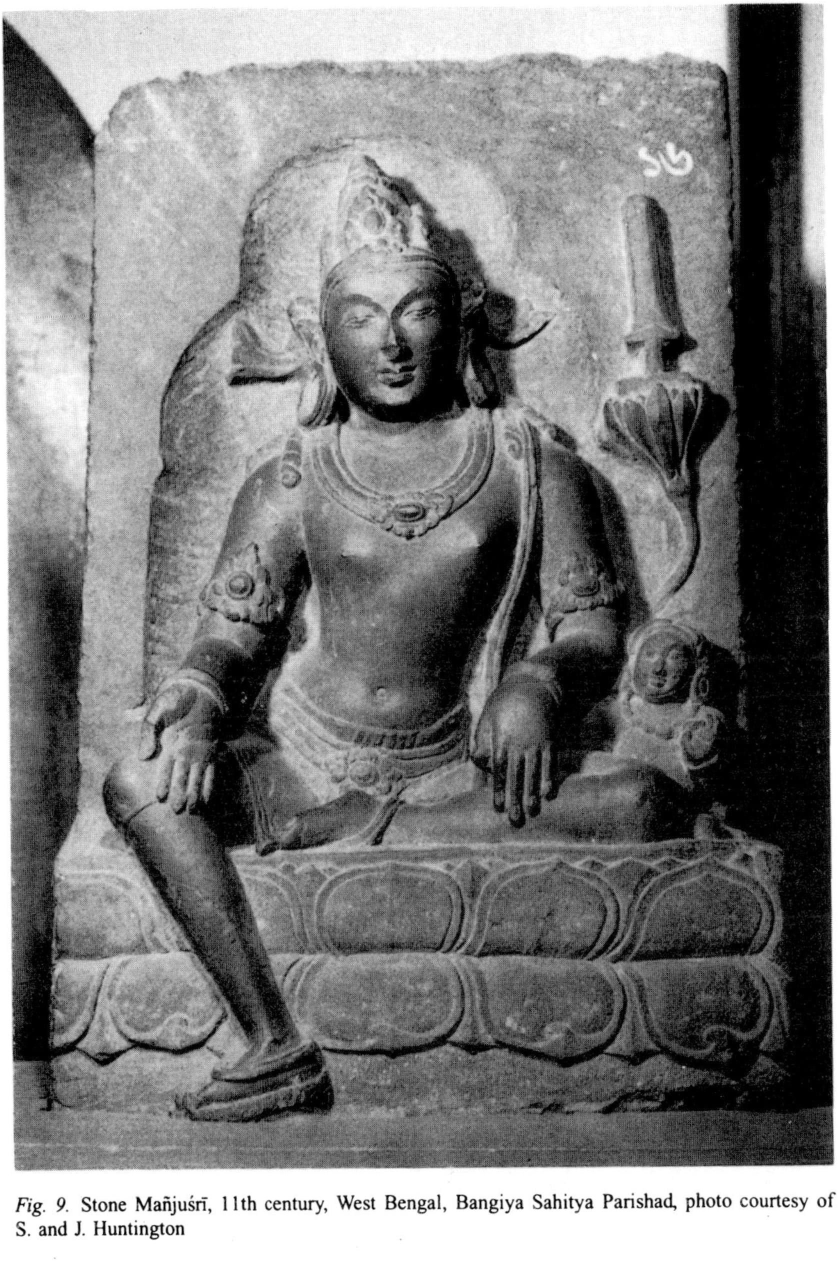

Fig. 9. Stone Mañjuśrī, 11th century, West Bengal, Bangiya Sahitya Parishad, photo courtesy of S. and J. Huntington

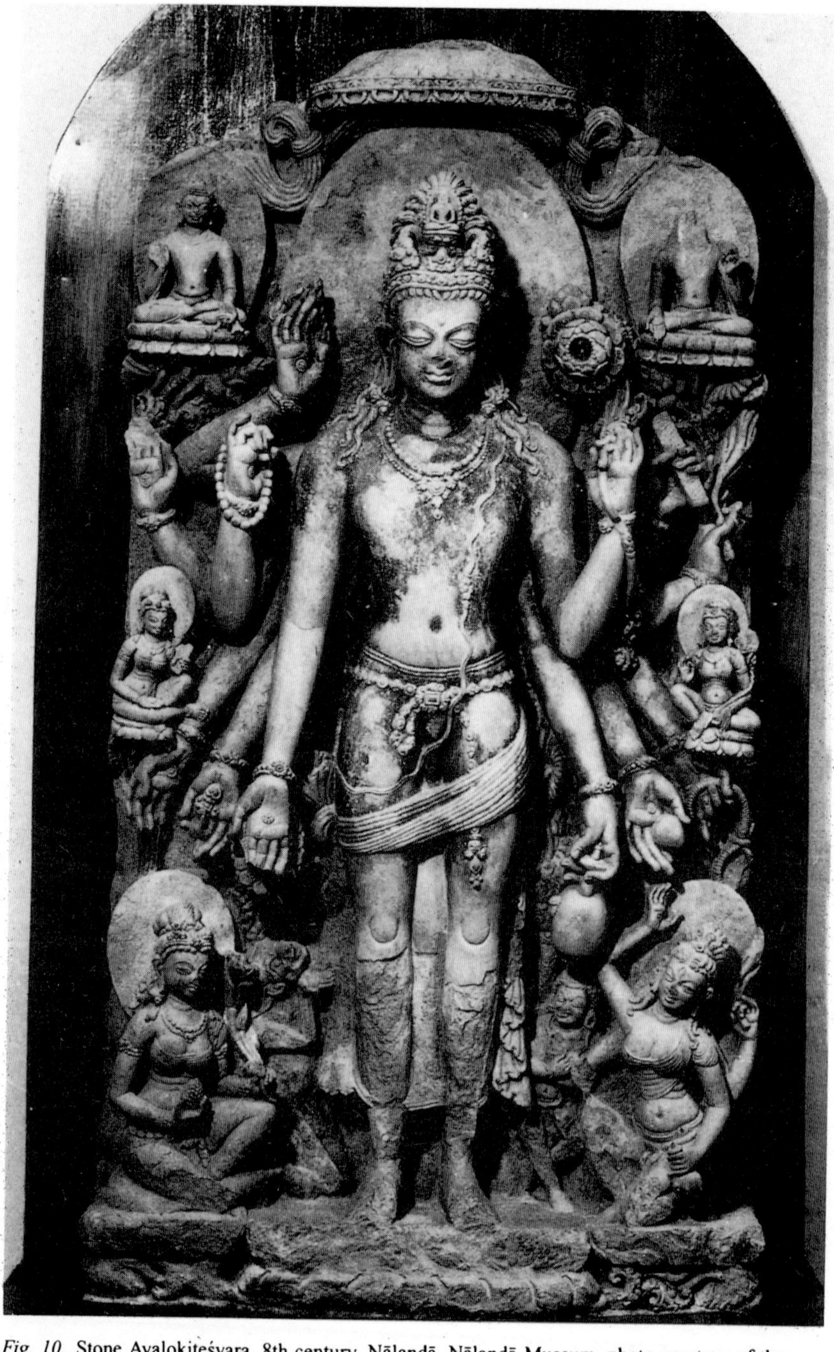

Fig. 10. Stone Avalokiteśvara, 8th century, Nālandā, Nālandā Museum, photo courtesy of the American Institute of Indian Studies

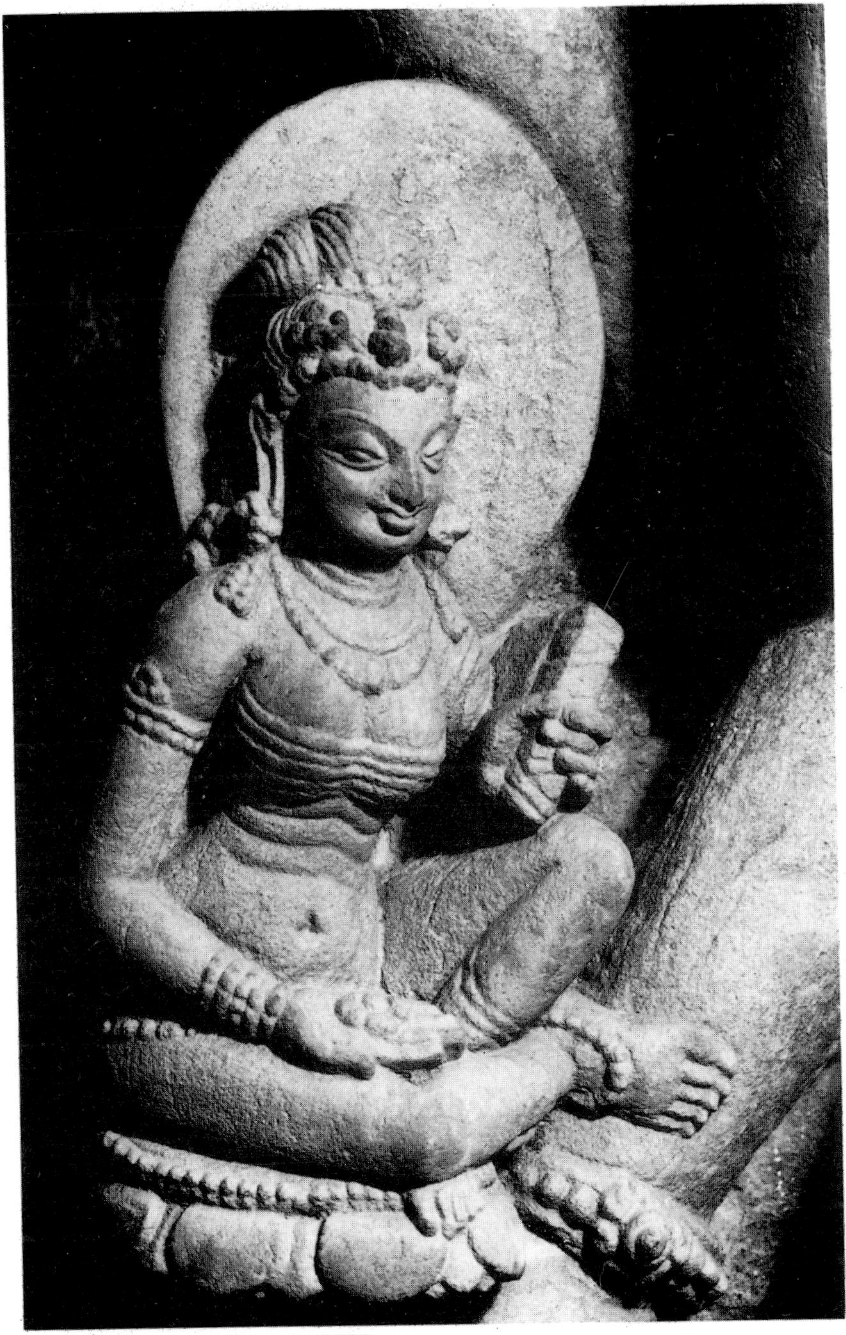

Fig. 11. Detail of stone Avalokiteśvara, 8th century, Nālandā, Nālandā Museum, photo courtesy of the American Institute of Indian Studies

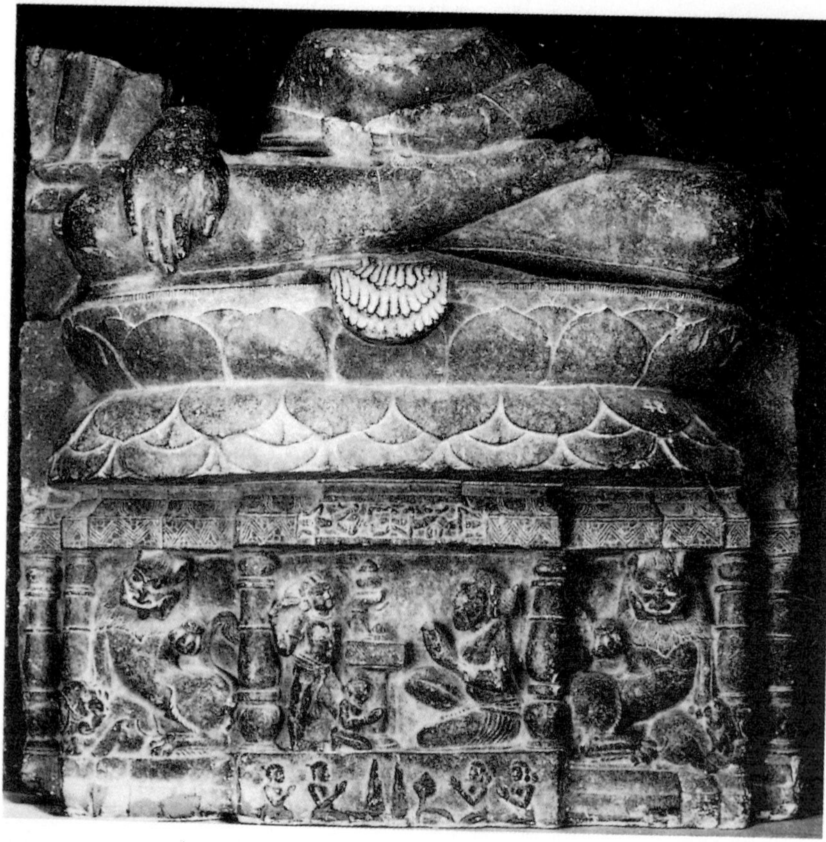

Fig. 12. Stone *bhūmisparśamudrā* Buddha fragment, 9th century, Orissa, Kiching Site Museum, photo courtesy of the American Institute of Indian Studies

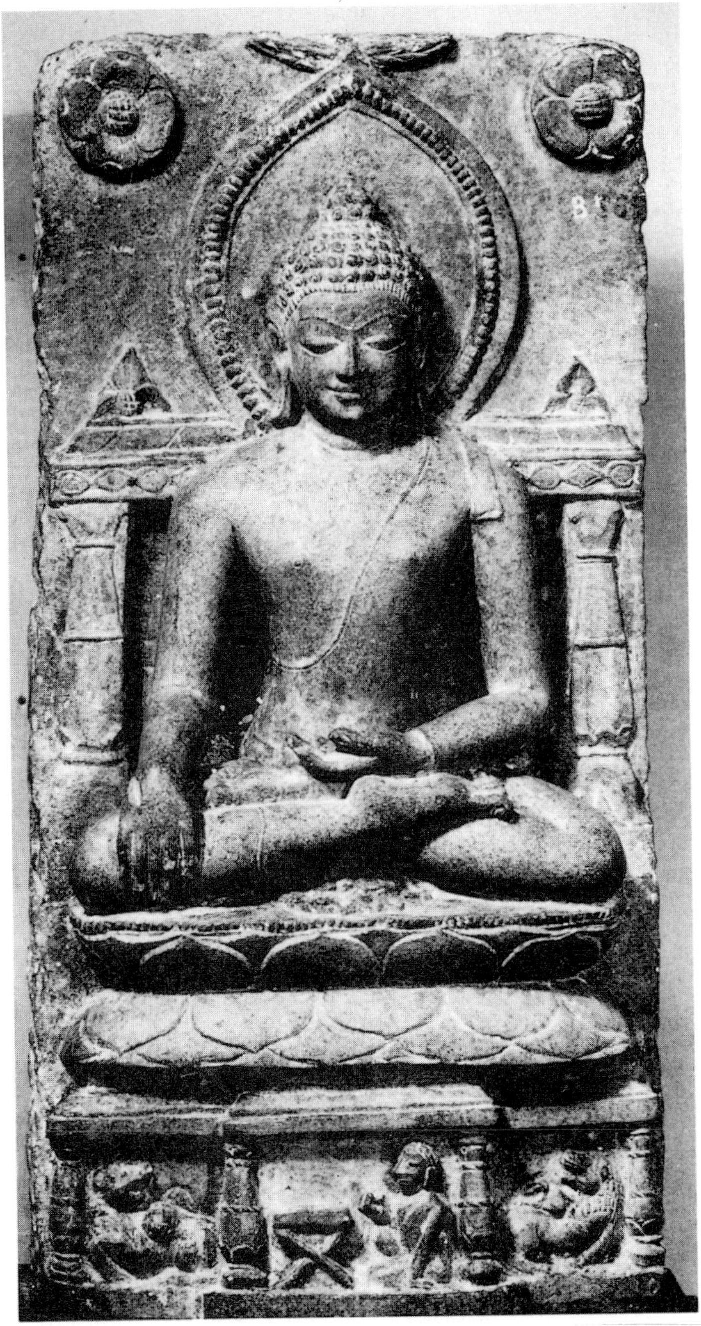

Fig. 13. Stone *bhūmisparśamudrā* Buddha, 11th century, Orissa, Indian Museum, Calcutta, photo courtesy of the American Institute of Indian Studies

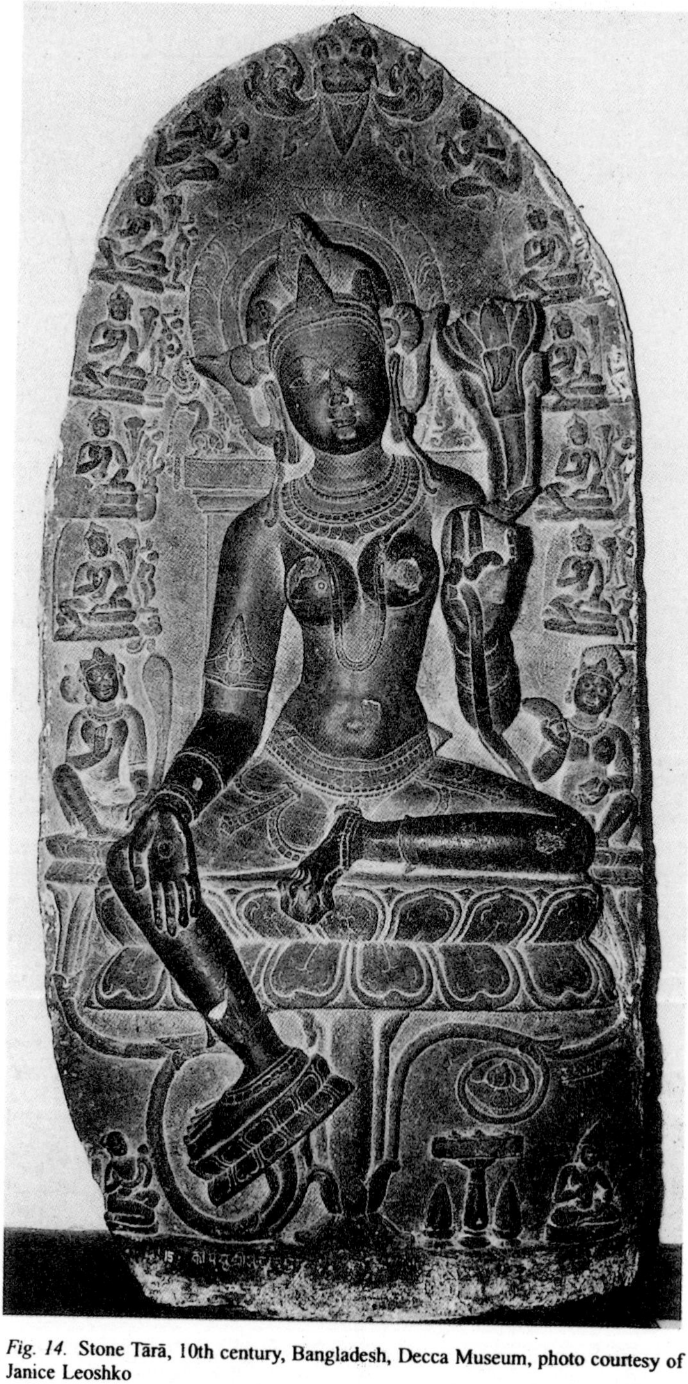

Fig. 14. Stone Tārā, 10th century, Bangladesh, Decca Museum, photo courtesy of Janice Leoshko

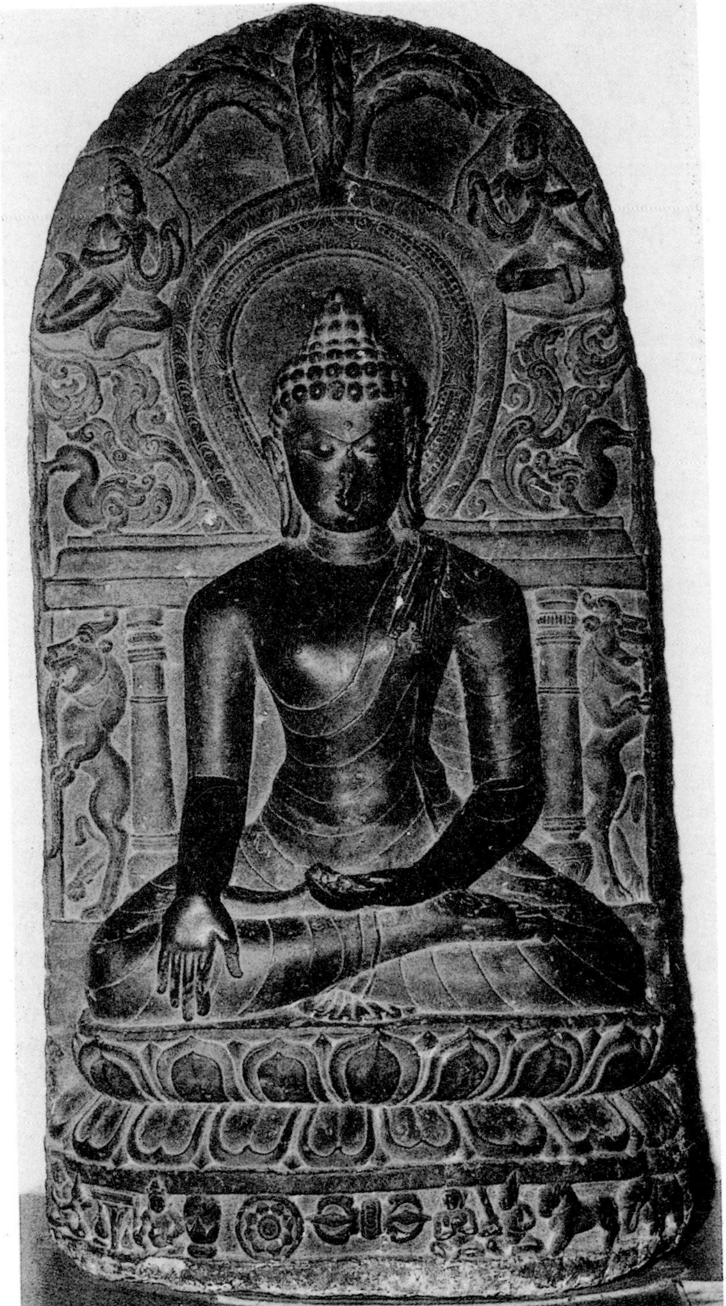

Fig. 15. Stone *bhūmisparśamudrā* Buddha, 10th century, Bangladesh, Decca Museum, photo courtesy of Janice Leoshko

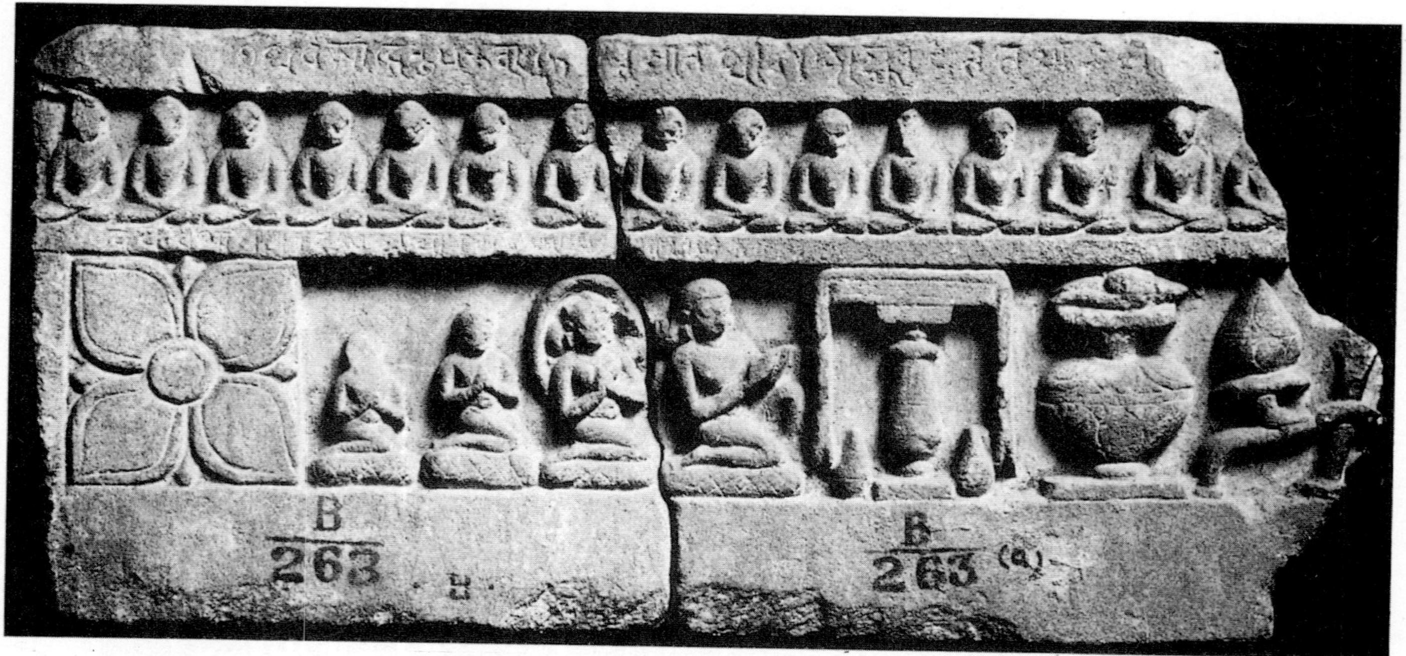

Fig. 16. Stone pedestal, Bodhgayā, 10th century, Lucknow State Museum, photo courtesy of the American Institute of Indian Studies

Although I want to avoid the kind of one-to-one correlation between an image and a text that has been justifiably critiqued in art history, I do want to posit that the *Prajñāpāramitā* genre of texts was a tremendously important element in the context out of which images of Prajñāpāramitā emerged. Let me again emphasize, however, that this context itself is constituted, in turn, by the very conceptions of *prajñā* and visual images of the Buddha that I have been discussing; thus the methodological image I want to retain is one of layers and layers of praxis and metapraxis - layers not simply stacked one upon another, but layers which also meld and clash and create new layers in the process, something like a contested and negotiated version of Yeats' gyres.

The earliest mention of a Prajñāpāramitā image has frequently been taken to be in Faxian's account of his travels in North India, and this in turn has been taken as evidence for the emergence of Prajñāpāramitā as a deity in the fifth century. This is, for example, Conze's widely-accepted opinion.[47] It is important to note, however, that Conze makes this point in spite of the fact - by his own admission, even - that no images nor supporting texts survive from this period: "All the early representations of Prajñāpāramitā are now lost. No surviving examples seems to be older than ca A.D. 800. All the documents of the historical development which must have taken place in those four centuries between 400 A.D. and 800 are no longer available to us. We are therefore unable to say anything very definite about the historical sequence of the various types."[48] What is striking about this reference is how frequently it has been repeated. For instance, D.C. Bhattacharyya, in his otherwise thorough account of the iconography of Prajñāpāramitā, simply accepts Conze's reading of Faxian, concluding, as Conze does, "that the image concept of Prajñāpāramitā might have been established and to a certain extent systematized by the end of the fourth or the beginning of the fifth century AD."[49]

---

[47]E. Conze, "The Iconography of Prajñāpāramitā, Part I," p. 47.

[48]Ibid.

[49]D.C. Bhattacharyya, *Studies in Buddhist Iconography* (New Delhi: Monohar, 1978), p. 34.

Faxian notes that, "Students of the Mahāyāna present offerings to the Prajñā-Pāramitā, to Mañjuśrī, and to Kwan-she-yin [Avalokiteśvara]."[50] The context of this comment, however, which Conze and others completely ignore, is important. Faxian is discussing what sorts of objects various groups make offerings to: the *bhikkhunīs* to the "tope of Ānanda," the *śramaneras* to Rāhula, the *Abhidharma* masters to the *Abhidharma*, the *Vinaya* masters to the *Vinaya*, and so on. Clearly, this is not just about making offerings to images, but also making offerings to *texts*, and I would argue that in context Faxian does not mean *images* of Prajñāpāramitā at all, which of course goes with the conception of the book as an object of veneration.[51]

The other place scholars have typically begun discussions of Prajñāpāramitā is with the *Sādhanamālā* and the *Nispannayogāvalī*, two collections of *sādhanas* and *dhāranīs* of numerous deities, both of which contain iconographic descriptions of Prajñāpāramitā. Both of these texts, however, are quite late; the earliest *Sādhanamālā* manuscript, for instance, dates to Newari era 285, or 1165, while the *Nispannayogāvalī* must be no earlier than the twelfth century, since it was composed by Abhayākaragupta. Thus, although these are certainly extremely important sources - and ones that I shall consider later on - they do not help much in tracing the early iconographic development of Prajñāpāramitā. In fact, there is no Indian source that describes the iconographic representation of Prajñāpāramitā that is earlier than the twelfth century.

III.B. Images of Prajñāpāramitā.

It is extremely difficult to locate the earliest Prajñāpāramitā image, let alone anything like an *Ur*-image. As I have noted, the reference Faxian makes to offerings to the *Prajñāpāramitā* has typically been taken to mean that Prajñāpāramitā images began to be made in the

---

[50]James Legge, *A Record of Buddhistic Kingdoms*, p. 46.

[51]I do not have access to the Chinese original here, but it seems significant that Legge has used the definite article in translating the passage about offerings to Prajñāpāramitā, implying, I think, that it is the text that is venerated, and not an image.

fifth century. In addition to the various problems I have just raised with regard to such an interpretation, no Prajñāpāramitā images survive from this period. Indeed, no images of Prajñāpāramitā can be said with any certainty to predate the ninth century.[52] My goal here is not to create a catalogue or chronology of surviving images; rather, I will attempt to locate the sculptural depiction of Prajñāpāramitā in the larger context of the representation of *prajñā* that I have been discussing throughout this study.

Although the preponderance of surviving Prajñāpāramitā images are small bronzes, mostly dating to the tenth century, I wish to begin not with them but with one of the earliest Prajñāpāramitā images, a very unusual and strikingly well-preserved stone image from Bihar that, in spite of its uniqueness, I believe sheds valuable light on the general complex of motivations and meanings behind representations of Prajñāpāramitā (fig. 1). Although it is impossible to date this image with precision, since it bears no dated inscription, it is clearly one of the earliest known sculptural representations of the deity - about the middle of the ninth century, based on stylistic comparisons to dated objects.[53] Prajñāpāramitā here is seated with her

[52]The only images of Prajñāpāramitā that I know of which might contradict this are one published in F. Asher, *Art of Eastern India*, plate 250, and another by Debjani Paul, *The Art of Nālandā* (Leiden: E.J. Brill, 1987), pp. 161-62, and plate 9. The image in Asher, however, is problematic, for Asher gives no specific date - it is not dated - and, furthermore, identifies the image as Tārā. The image, however, comes from Salban Vihāra in Bangladesh, which would place it in the eighth century; and the iconography of the image, particularly the book on one of the lotuses, would seem to identify the piece as Prajñāpāramitā, although this, too, is not certain. The Nālandā image discussed by Paul is, I think, even more ambiguous. Paul says that it has generally been thought to be Vajraśāradā; she argues, though, that the figure is depicted coming out of a pot, and that the pot is guarded by a pair of snakes, and that this iconography links the figure to the legend that the *Prajñāpāramitā* was protected by *nāga*s until it manifested itself to Nāgārjuna. She sees this image as representing the "first step in the process" of transforming the *Prajñāpāramitā* into a deity, p. 169. Paul's interpretation is plausible, although it is contingent on the identification of a companion image as Nāgārjuna. Furthermore, given that the figure's left arm is broken off, it is difficult to interpret its iconography - this could, I think, just as plausibly be Cundā, who also is occasionally flanked by *nāga*s.

[53]See Huntington and Huntington, *Leaves from the Bodhi Tree*, p. 131, footnotes 1-3, for a discussion of the dating and province of this image. They base this date on a comparison with, among other images, a Tāra found in Itkhauri District in Bihar, dated to the eighth year of Mahendrapāla, or 858 C.E.; see Susan Huntington, *The 'Pāla-Sena' Schools*, fig. 40. Janice Leoshko suggests that this image may in fact have originally been located Bodhgayā; see J. Leoshko, "The Iconography of Buddhist Sculptures," p. 300.

legs folded across her lap in what is known as the *vajraparyankāsana* position. She is two-armed, her hands forming a variation of the *dharmacakramudrā* or *dharmacakrapravartanamudrā*, the *vyākhyānamudrā*. To either side of her are two *nīlotpala* (blue lotuses), and on top of each is a *pustaka*. She is flanked by two female attendants. At the base of the stele, between two lions, are two kneeling worshippers and a deer. The image is inscribed with the so-called Buddhist creed, *"y(e) dharmmā hetuprabhavā he(tun) te shā(ṃ)...,"*[54] and a short donative inscription that simply reads *kikābhap(ū)rvasya*, stating that the image was given by someone named Kikābhapurva, a name which tells us little.

The first question we must ask of such an image - a question that may seem simple, or even simple-minded - is how do we in fact know this is Prajñāpāramitā? How do we know that this is not Cundā or Tārā? *We* know this image is Prajñāpāramitā because the later iconographic texts tell us what Prajñāpāramitā should look like, how she should be sculpturally represented. So, for instance, we turn to the *Sādhanamālā*,[55] and find that this image corresponds closely to the *kanaka* (golden) Prajñāpāramitā,[56] described in *sādhana* 154.[57] Using this source for such an identification, however, entangles one in a serious methodological anachronism, one that is seldom noted: the image in question *pre-dates* the *Sādhanamālā* by a good 300 years! Furthermore, although we know rather little about the composition and actual use of texts such as the *Sādhanamālā*, it is entirely likely that it was written not as an iconographically *prescriptive* manual, but as an aid in orienting practitioners toward proper practice in light of already existing images.

---

[54]For an intersting discussion of this "creed," see Daniel Boucher, "The Pratītyasamutpādagathā and Its Role in the Medieval Cult of the Relics," *Journal of the International Association of Buddhist Studies* (1992): 1-27.

[55]This is only the most commonly cited source. Other important texts that can be used for identification are the iconographic compendiums such as the *Sādhanasamuccaya*, the *Sādhanasaṃgraha*, the *Dharmakoṣa-saṃgraha* as well as the various *maṇḍala*-oriented texts, such as the *Nispannayogāvali*, and the *Vajrāvalīnāma-mandalopāyikā*; also useful are a variety of *tantras*. Again, however, these are all late - from the twelfth century onward.

[56]See Huntington and Huntington, *Leaves from the Bodhi Tree*, p. 131.

[57]See B. Bhattacharyya, ed., *Sādhanamālā*, Gaekwad's Oriental Series, nos. 26 and 41 (Baroda: Oriental Institute, 1925 and 1928).

This raises, I think, an important larger methodological issue, for if we want to understand the *context* of an image such as this, we must attempt to use data that constituted and that reflects that context; we must, to reiterate my basic methodological point throughout this study, pay close attention to the contemporary field of praxis, to the complex range of discursive and visual practices available to ninth-century Buddhists in Bihar. Furthermore, although a text such as the *Sādhanamālā* is indispensable for the scholar attempting to sort out the complexities of the later Buddhist pantheon, it is doubtful that Buddhists *on the ground* had such texts at their ready disposal. The question, then, must not be how *we* know that this particular image is Prajñāpāramitā, but how did *Pāla period Buddhists* know this, and, more importantly, *what* did this identity mean to them?

First, let me state quite clearly that I am not at all certain that a Pāla-period Buddhist "on the ground" - as opposed, say, to the patron who commissioned it, or the *śilpins* who actually made it - would have recognized this unusual image as, specifically, Prajñāpāramitā, nor that such an exact identification would have been particularly relevant or important. This is not to say, however, that a Pāla-period Buddhist would not have recognized such an image as a representation of *prajñā*. In other words, a ninth-century Buddhist in Bihar might very well *not* have known that this was Prajñāpāramitā, but he or she would have, I want to argue, seen such an image in the more general visual and devotional context, or field, of the "*prajñā* deities" that were more commonly represented in the ninth century: Cundā, in particular, but also Tārā, other forms of Prajñāpāramitā, and even such male figures as Mañjuśrī,[58] if not also the Buddha himself. There are, however, three details included on this particular image that potentially tell us a great deal about the visual and intellectual context in which the stele was originally situated. The details are: 1) the two books atop the lotuses; 2) the hand gesture the figure makes; and 3) the two kneeling figures and the deer at the base of the *stele*.[59]

---

[58]I discuss these figures later in this chapter and also in Chapter Six.

[59]I know of no other Prajñāpāramitā images that definitely employ this particular iconography, although an eleventh-century image reproduced in D.C. Bhattacharyya, *Buddhist Iconography*, plate 12, currently in a private collection, appears to have a deer on the base.

First, there is the representation of the book, which is perhaps *the* single, incontrovertible iconographic feature of Prajñāpāramitā images; although the presence of the book does not necessarily signify Prajñāpāramitā, Prajñāpāramitā virtually always has the book - in other words, the *pustaka* is a necessary iconographic condition, but not a sufficient one.[60] The book is generally held to be the *Prajñāpāramitā*,[61] although I think potentially too much can be made of this identification. Visually, there is nothing about the books themselves that specifically signify the *Prajñāpāramitā*; however, even without the specific identification, the book would signify, at least, learning, wisdom, and teaching - in short, the *dharma*.[62] The identification of the book as the *Prajñāpāramitā*, however, of course ties in with the discourse in the *Prajñāpāramitā* itself, with the constant invocation to set the book up as an object of veneration. Here it is, set up, a physical object - or, more properly, the representation of a physical object - to be honored. Although it is impossible to reconstruct the consciousness of a ninth-century Buddhist in Bihar, it is, I think, clear that this image is strikingly resonant with the textual discourse, and, furthermore, I would argue that it is thus possible to infer that the textual discourse on the supremacy of the *Prajñāpāramitā* was an important, and indeed an *essential*, component in the field of practice here.

---

[60]There is a variety of deities who are represented with the book; I shall have a great deal more to say about this topic below.

[61]Again, we must turn to texts such as the *Sādhanamālā* to provide proof of this: *sādhana* 154, for instance, contains the compound "*prajñāpāramitāpustakā*;" *Sādhanamālā*, p. 313. I know of only one instance where the book is purported to be a different text - the *Ekallavīra-Canda-Mahārosana-Tantra*, which calls the book *kāmaśāstra*; this, however, is clearly a late sectarian extrapolation. See D.C. Bhattacharyya, *Studies in Buddhist Iconography*, p.43, for a brief discussion of this point.

[62]This idea seems to have been shared in contemporary Brahmanical circles; the *Visnudharmottara Purāna*, for instance, says that Saraswatī should be represented with a book, and that her hands which hold the book are the *Veda*s, while the book itself is all of the *śāstra*s; see Priyabala Shah, ed., *Visnudharmottara-purāna*, third *Khanda*, Gaekwad's Oriental Series, no. 130 (Baroda: Oriental Institute, 1958), 64th *adhyāya*.

The variation of the *dharmacakrapravartanamudrā* here is also something of an identifying signifier,[63] although this is not the typical *mudrā* for Prajñāpāramitā images. A variety of images eventually come to display this *mudrā*; this, however, is one of the earliest non-Buddha images to employ this hand gesture.[64] As I have already discussed, this *mudrā* is one of the standard gestures of Śākyamuni, who is, of course, *the* turner of the wheel of *dharma*. Why would a *śilpin* constructing an image of Prajñāpāramitā, or a patron commissioning such an image, employ this particular *mudrā*? Recall the *Prajñāpāramitā* discussion of the true source of the Tathāgatas, in which it/she is said to be the "*dharmacakrapravartanī*."[65] In the *Prajñāpāramitā* this is a radical move, for it discursively replaces, or at least displaces, Śākyamuni as the originator of the *dharma*; it is the *Prajñāpāramitā* - the teachings and the effect of the teachings, i.e. perfected wisdom - that is here discursively represented as the true source of the teachings of all of the Buddhas. The *Prajñāpāramitā* not only conceives of itself as the supreme expression of the *dharma*, but as the true turner of the wheel of *dharma*. The text, as we have already seen, *is* the teacher.

This radical textual move, however, becomes even more radical when it is visually represented. A ninth-century Buddhist would undoubtedly have been trained to expect the Buddha here. Or, to put it more subtly, the ninth-century *habitus* of such an image - the largely unconscious "schemes of perception, thought and action....whose limits are set by the historically and socially situated conditions of its production"[66] - was the awareness of the Buddha displaying the *dharmacakrapravartanamudrā*, delivering his first sermon at Sārnāth, as well as the knowledge (both mental and physical) of the proper forms of veneration and ritual practice

---

[63]The deity actually displays the *vyākhyānamudrā*, the gesture of explanation. For a discussion of this *mudrā*, and its relation to the *dharmacakrapravartanamudrā*, see S.K. Saraswati, *A Survey of Indian Sculpture* (Calcutta: ,1958), pp. 129ff.

[64]There is, for instance, a bronze Mañjuśrī from Salban Vihāra, dated to the eighth century (now at the Maināmati Site Museum, Bangladesh), that displays the same mūdra; see F. Asher, *Art of Eastern India*, plate 249.

[65]*Astasāhasrikāprajñāpāramitā*, p. 86.

[66]Bourdieu, *The Logic of Practice*, pp. 54-55.

appropriate before such an image. The complex of agents responsible for the construction of this particular image seem to have been intentionally playing on this general conception of Śākyamuni, subtly yet decidedly moving the Buddha aside in this image, co-opting his place of preeminence by co-opting his iconography, while at the same time retaining the expectation that it is the Buddha who is being represented, with all that such a representation implies. Again we see the malleable, *ad hoc* nature of *habitus*, which enables "agents to cope with unforeseen and constantly changing situations."[67] And we also see here an example of the metapractical nature of images, the way in which they play on the relationship between various contested doctrinal positions.

This is a complex point, and again, I draw on Bourdieu's formulation of *habitus*:

> The *habitus* which, at every moment, structures new experience in accordance with the structures produced by past experiences, which are modified by the new experiences with the limits defined by their power of selection, brings about a unique integration, dominated by the earliest experiences, of the experiences statistically common to members of the same class.[68]

In other words, the representation of Prajñāpāramitā is necessarily located in the discursive and ritual context of the representation of the Buddha, and thus such a representation of Prajñāpāramitā plays on, consciously and unconsciously, all of the associations and implications involved in representations of the Buddha. Such a representation, furthermore, clearly plays on the discursive, doctrinal debate about the legitimacy of the Mahāyāna *sūtras*, i.e. their status as true *buddhavacana*.[69]

---

[67]Ibid., p. 61.
[68]Ibid., p. 60.
[69]See Graeme MacQueen, "Inspired Speech in Early Mahāyāna," Two Parts. *Religion* 11 (1981): 306-19, and *Religion* 12 (1982): 49-65; see particularly Part II.

In this particular image, this shift in the visual discourse is further emphasized, or accomplished, by the two devotees and, more importantly, by the deer at the base of the *stele*. As I have already argued in the context of images of the Buddha, this iconographic detail visually transports the viewer into the presence - or, perhaps more accurately, the pastness - of the Buddha delivering his sermon in the deer park at Sārnāth. Prajñāpāramitā has *visually* displaced the Buddha in a most pointed way here, though: she is literally seated in his place.[70] She is the originator and source of the *dharma*, not a mother goddess at all, but the teacher *par excellence*.[71] This particular sculpture, then, presents a striking correlation between image and text: the presence of the two *pustaka*s atop the lotuses emphasize, in a rather obvious way, the *Prajñāpāramitā* texts; the female figure displaying the variation of the *dharmacakrapravartanamudrā* gives the text a literal - or actually physical - sort of life, moving the viewer from the abstract to the concrete, from a rhetorical, metaphorical source to a physical teacher; and, finally, the deer and the devotees position the viewer as a *hearer* of the true *dharma*, the *Prajñāpāramitā*.

Now, let me provide a few qualifications. To say that Prajñāpāramitā *displaces*, visually or otherwise, the Buddha during the Pāla period is somewhat hyperbolic. Some of the details on this particular image are very unusual: the deer and the two devotees, for instance, are not standard details on Prajñāpāramitā images. Indeed, the specific iconographic program of this image is remarkably, and unusually, similar to several contemporary images of Śākyamuni, although this seems to me to add credence to my argument that Prajñāpāramitā usurps Śākyamuni's place in this specific image. As I have already noted, though, Śākyamuni does remain the single most prominent figure throughout the Pāla period,[72] and Prajñāpāramitā images that survive from the Pāla period make up only small minority

[70]It is perhaps necessary to note here, however, that I am not implying that images of Prajñāpāramitā became more prevalent than images of Śākyamuni - this is certainly not the case.

[71]Recall, too, that the *Prajñāpāramitā* is repeatedly referred to, in the text, as *śastā*.

[72]See my "Reevaluating the Eighth-Ninth Century Pāla Milieu: Icono-Conservatism and the Persistence of Śākyamuni."

of the extant images. Snellgrove thus seems to be correct when he says that Prajñāpāramitā attained "no great cult."[73]

However, images of Prajñāpāramitā have been discovered at virtually all of the monastic sites in northeastern India.[74] And although the majority of such images are small bronzes, a few stone images of Prajñāpāramitā have been found at Pāla monastic sites, such as a ninth-century stone image now at Bodhgayā (fig. 2). A number of small bronze images that are thought to depict Prajñāpāramitā have been found at Nālandā and Kurkihār, most slightly later than the image I have just been discussing, dating from the ninth-tenth century.[75] Most of these images are similar, seated four-armed Prajñāpāramitās (fig. 3). The lower left hand rests across the lap in a half *dhyānamudrā*, sometimes holding a bowl;[76] the lower right hand displays the *varadamudrā*; the upper left hand holds a lotus, atop which rests the book; finally, the upper right hand holds an *akṣamāla*, or rosary. The *varadamudrā*, or "gift bestowing gesture," displayed by these images is interesting, suggesting, perhaps, that the deity

---

[73]David Snellgrove, *Indo-Tibetan Buddhism* (Boston: Shambhala Publications, 1987), pp. 150-51.

[74]Conze's 1949 "inventory" is still useful, despite its date; see "The Iconography of Prajñāpāramitā, Part I," pp. 51-52. Likewise, see Benoytosh Bhattacharyya's *The Indian Buddhist Iconography* (Calcutta: Firma K.L. Mukhopadhyay, 1958), pp. 107-99. See also Marie-Thérèse de Mallmann, *Introduction a L'Iconographie du Tântrisme Bouddhique* (Paris: Libraire Adrien-Maisonneuve, 1975), pp. 305-07; for Nālandā, see Debjani Paul, *The Art of Nālandā*; for a useful discussion of such images in Orissa, see Thomas Donaldson's typographical discussion in his unpublished manuscript, "Iconography of Orissan Images of Prajñāpāramitā and other Buddhist Goddesses of Wisdom." For an especially thorough discussion of the general iconography of Prajñāpāramitā, as well as a discussion of some specific images, see D.C. Bhattacharyya, *Studies in Buddhist Iconography*, particularly pp. 29-67. Again, however, I think it is worth pointing out that with all of the images discussed in these studies, there is always a degree of ambiguity concerning their exact identification, and what is most important, in my opinion, is not whether an individual image depicts Prajñāpāramitā or Cundā or Tārā, but that such an image clearly is intended to represent and present *prajñā*.

[75]See Sisir Kumar Mitra, ed., *East Indian Bronzes* (Calcutta: Centre of Advanced Study in Ancient Indian History and Culture, Calcutta University, 1979); Debala Mitra, *Bronzes from Bangladesh: A Study of Buddhist Images from District Chittagong* (Delhi: Agam Kala Prakashan, 1982); Debala Mitra, *Bronzes from Achutrajpur, Orissa* (Delhi: Agam Kala Prakashan, 1978).

[76]The bowl is also one of Cundā's attributes, so these images may in fact not be Prajñāpāramitā.

presents the devotee with the "gift" of *prajñā*.[77] Furthermore, the presence of the *aksamāla* would seem to convey the notion of learning the texts; it is used to keep count of the verses during memorization. Another small image (fig. 4), also from Nālandā, depicts a two-armed form of Prajñāpāramitā, who displays the *dharmacakramudrā*, flanked by two books on top of two lotuses.

Again, just as it is impossible to unambiguously identify any one of these images as Prajñāpāramitā, it is also difficult to place these small images contextually. [78] It seems likely that they might have been part of a larger *mandala*.[79] It is possible that such images were used in private rituals; they were certainly cheaper to produce and easier to transport than larger stone images, making them, as Susir Mitra puts it, "highly suitable for personal possession and private worship." [80] It is also quite possible that such images were intended to be placed in niches in individual monk's cells and used in *anusmrti* exercises analogous to those I have discussed in Chapter Three.[81] Whatever the exact context of such images, however, it is at least clear that *prajñā* was a constant presence throughout the Pāla milieu.

III.C. Cundā.

Closely related to Prajñāpāramitā - indeed, as I have noted, frequently indistinguishable from her - is Cundā, a deity about whom surprisingly

---

[77]Saunders, in his *Mudrā*, p. 53, says of this mudrā: "Beginning with the idea of the charity accorded by the Buddha, this *mudrā* grants all desires and becomes, by extension, the symbol of the 'Gift of Truth' made by the Buddha, Truth of Doctrine, Truth of the means to salvation."

[78]For a good idea of the difficulties involved here, see the general discussion in Part One of Nihar Ranjan Ray and K. Khandalavala, *Eastern Indian Bronzes* (New Delhi: Lalit Kalā Akademi, 1986), pp. 1-102. See Sisir Kumar Mitra, ed., *East Indian Bronzes*, "Appendix A: Important Hoards and Finds," pp. 125-32, for a useful, though incomplete, discussion of the various find sites of these images. One problem posed by finds such as the Kurkihār hoard is that we simply do not know who gathered together the images, nor why, nor whether the images represent a particular, intentional collection, random sampling.

[79]Again, however, the texts that place Prajñāpāramitā in *mandalas* are all relatively late, and so are not terribly useful in understanding the context of such early images. See, however, Walter Clark's still useful *Two Lamaistic Pantheons*, 2 Volumes (Cambridge: Harvard University Press, 1937); see also Giuseppe Tucci, *The Theory and Practice of the Mandala*.

[80]S.K. Mitra, ed., *East Indian Bronzes*, p. 1.

[81]Indeed, the remains of the monastic cells at Nālandā frequently include small niches, which may have been used precisely to house such small images.

little is known.[82] She is, in Puspa Niyogi's words, a "popular but mysterious goddess in the Buddhist world."[83] Indeed, as Mallmann has pointed out, even "La signification du nom est controversée."[84] Conze and Getty both link her to Durgā;[85] she also, as we have seen above, is sometimes said to be a "Buddha Mother;"[86] in the *Nispannayogāvalī*, she is the embodiment of the *cundādhāranī*, a text mentioned in Śāntideva's *Śiksasamuccaya*.[87] None of these references, however, tells us much about Cundā's character. This same sort of ambiguity holds true for visual representations of Cundā as well. Geri Malandra puts it nicely when she says that there is, and perhaps also was, "a generally felt ambiguity about her iconography," and that she "is a particularly variable figure...."[88]

Is this ambiguity, however, an *etic* or an *emic* one? In other words, although *we* might have some difficulty differentiating the iconography of Prajñāpāramitā and Cundā,[89] would Pāla period Buddhists have felt the same ambiguity? Again, I think the answer is "yes," but with some qualifications. I am not suggesting, certainly, that Pāla-period Buddhists could never tell the difference between one deity and another, or, even, that such differences never mattered. Rather, I am suggesting that the ambiguity *we* see in representations of deities such as Cundā and Prajñāpāramitā may well have been intentional, so that, depending on the specific ritual context in which such images were situated, the identity of the figure depicted was

---

[82]B. Bhattacharyya notes that, at least from what the *Sādhanamālā* tells us, "it is not possible to ascertain the character of the deity or her origin," *Indian Buddhist Iconography*, p. 220. See also J.E. van Lohuizen-de Leeuw, "The Pattikerā Chundā and Variation of Her Image," in A.B.M. Habibullah, ed., *Nalini Kanta Bhattasali Commemoration Volume* (Dacca: Dacca Museum, 1966), pp. 117-43; Thomas Donaldson, "Iconography of Orissan Images of Prajñāpāramitā and other Buddhist Goddesses of Wisdom;" Puspa Niyogi, "Cundā - a Popular Buddhist Goddess," *East and West* 27 (1977): 299-310; and Sudarshan Devi Singhal, "Iconography of Cundā."

[83]Puspa Niyogi, "Cundā - a Popular Buddhist Goddess," p. 299.

[84]M. de Mallmann, *Introduction a L'Iconographie du Tântrisme Bouddhique*, p. 143.

[85]Edward Conze, *Thirty Years of Buddhist Studies*, pp. 254-55; Alice Getty, *The Gods of Northern Buddhism*, p. 93.

[86]S. Beal, *A Catena of Buddhist Scriptures*, p. 413.

[87]*Nispannayogāvalī*, pp. 249-52; *Śiksasamuccaya*, p. 173.

[88]G. Malandra, *Unfolding a Mandala*, p. 98.

[89]D.C. Bhattacharyya goes so far as to say that "it is not possible to particularize the iconographic features of *any* god or goddess, or to suggest any formula for their identification," *Studies in Buddhist Iconography*, p. 61, emphasis added.

malleable. In some contexts, it may have been crucial that a particular image represented a specific figure, such as Cundā; in other visual contexts, though, a blurring of identities could have served to underline and emphasize the essential association these figures had with *prajñā*.

Thus, despite the mystery and controversy, and the iconographic ambiguity, representations of Cundā, like the closely parallel representations of Prajñāpāramitā, are quite clearly visually resonant with *prajñā*. Indeed, many of her iconographic attributes are ones we have already encountered: Cundā frequently displays the *dharmacakrapravartanamudrā*, for instance; she nearly always holds a book; and, depending on how many arms she has, she sometimes also holds a sword.[90] "The goddess Cundā," writes S.D. Singhal, perhaps extrapolating a bit too liberally, "symbolizes the creative impulse of wisdom, the inspiring action, the vivifying animation of illumination."[91] I say that Singhal extrapolates, largely because there simply is no textual source for her characterization; however, since Cundā is, as we have already seen, textually described using the same "mother of all Buddhas" language that we see in connection with Prajñāpāramitā, Singhal is warranted, I think, to emphasize that Cundā is closely related to, and in some sense can be said to embody and convey, *prajñā*. Sculptures of Cundā support such a description as well.

As with the representations of Prajñāpāramitā, the majority of Pāla period images of Cundā seems to be small bronzes, dating to the ninth and tenth centuries,[92] although stone images are not quite as uncommon as stone Prajñāpāramitā images. For instance, there are two eighteen-armed stone images of Cundā located at Bodhgayā that both provide evidence of Cundā's iconographic link with *prajñā*: both

---

[90]See *Nispannayogāvalī*, pp. 48-57; see also *Sādhanamālā*, p. 271. For an extensive discussion of Cundā's iconographic forms, J. van Lohuizen-de Leeuw, "The Pattikera Chundā and Variations of Her Image," in A.B.N Habibullah, ed, *Nalini Kanta Bhattasali Commemoration Volume* (Dacca: Dacca Museum, 1966), pp. 119-43; see also Janice Leoshko, "Iconography of Buddhist Sculpture," pp. 303-05.

[91]Sudarshan Devi Singhal, "Iconography of Cundā," p. 386.

[92]See, for instance, the 18-armed image in D. Paul, *The Art of Nālandā*, pp.169-70, and pl. 63; see also the interesting terra cotta image in the same volume, pl. 78. Stone images of Cundā are relatively common at Ellora; see G. Malandra, *Unfolding a Mandala*, pp. 97-99.

hold, among many other things, a book, and both display the *dharmacakrapravartanamudrā*.[93]

Judging from the plethora of surviving Cundā images from Orissa, it would seem that she was more popular outside of the Pāla region proper - although still within the broader Pāla-period cultural milieu. An Orissan image, a twelve-armed Cundā now in the Patna museum, found perhaps at Udayagiri and dated to the eighth/ninth century, is particularly illustrative of Cundā's iconographic relationship with *prajñā* and also is an interesting example of how the Pāla concern with the visual representation of *prajñā* that we see in the Pāla milieu seems to have spread to neighboring regions as well. In this image, Cundā sits in the *lalitāsana* position (unusual for images of Cundā), holding a bowl in her lap, and she is surrounded by several smaller figures - a Buddha displaying the *bhūmisparśamudrā*, and two standing female figures, one of which is broken. Most significant in this context, however, is the presence of the book. Indeed, here the book sits elevated atop a lotus held in one of the deity's left hands, positioned higher than her other implements, as if *prajñā* is intended to be conspicuously prominent, raised above the other items she holds.

In virtually all of the various Pāla-period Prajñāpāramitā and Cundā images, as well as in all of the later textual descriptions of such images, one iconographic detail remains a constant: the book. The book is sometimes held aloft, sometimes held close to the chest; it is frequently placed atop one or more lotuses. It is always prominent. Thus from the larger stone images such as the one I have been discussing here, to the small metal images that were discovered in the Nālandā, Kurkihār, and elsewhere, wisdom, *prajñā*, is visually emphasized. Furthermore, not only do such images *emphasize prajñā*, but they are also part of an ongoing discourse - a metapractical discourse - about the efficacy of this *prajñā* and the dual importance of the relationship between both *vision* and *wisdom*: to *see* the book is to *know* the book, just as the *vision* of the Buddha could lead to the *understanding* of the *dharma*.

---

[93]See J. Leoshko, "Iconography of Buddhist Sculpture," pp. 303-05. and figs. 160-62; see also figures 163 and 164, for two additional Pāla-period images of Cundā.

Beginning sometime in the eighth century, and extending well into the twelfth, there is what really can be justifiably called an explosion of books in Indian Buddhist sculpture. Just as the early Mahāyāna *sūtra*s rhetorically emphasized the physical book and the *prajñā* it conveyed, extolling the virtues of the text and encouraging the practitioner to set it up and to venerate it, later Indian Mahāyāna *visually* emphasizes the book; the book thus becomes a standard iconographic motif not just associated with Prajñāpāramitā, but with Mañjuśrī, Tārā, and a whole range of female deities, all of whom, as we shall see in the next chapter, are intimately associated with *prajñā*. The book becomes *the* signifier of *prajñā*, to the point that it is quite literally placed on a pedestal.

Chapter Six

THE BOOK IS THE THING

The deification of books is not unknown in Buddhism.

Benoytosh Bhattacharyya[1]

The recurrent issue in this study has been the question of how, and why, an abstruse, recondite, and frequently very slippery philosophical concept, *prajñā*, is visually represented. I have argued that through the use of what I have called *resonant iconography*, Buddhists during the Pāla period represented, and made available, *prajñā*. That is, Buddhists during this period employed a variety of biographical episodes, hand gestures, and symbols - all of which have a range of possible associations - not only to convey the importance of *prajñā*, but also to give the participants in such images the opportunity to partake of the Buddha's wisdom. So, for instance, Pāla-period *śilpin*s focused on the enlightenment and first sermon of Śākyamuni as moments when *prajñā* was paramount; they focused on *mudrā*s that, likewise, in the context of these scenes signify *prajñā*; and they also employed a variety of symbols, such as the *dharmacakra* and the *pustaka*, to represent *prajñā*.

We have seen in the last chapter that Buddhists during this time also began to represent the *Prajñāpāramitā* texts and discourse as a deity. As I have argued in the last chapter, the development of Prajñāpāramitā as a deity is directly linked to what has frequently been called "the cult of the book," to the discourse - which has its roots in the earliest examples of the *Prajñāpāramitā* genre - that extols the physical text of the *Prajñāpāramitā* as an object of veneration. Thus,

[1]Benoytosh Bhattacharyya, *Indian Buddhist Iconography*, p. 220.

of the various symbols that I have discussed as signifying *prajñā*, none is more resonant than the book.

In this chapter I examine what I would say is a kind of iconographic explosion of books across northeast India in the later, that is tenth-century onward, Pāla period. Not only are several central deities typically represented with books - Prajñāpāramitā and Cundā, and occasionally Tārā, as we have just seen, as well as Avalokiteśvara and Mañjuśrī, who I shall discuss here - but the book itself begins to be represented on its own in sculptures.

In an important sense, what we see in the later Pāla period, particularly in the eastern reaches of the Pāla sphere of influence, is the culmination of the early cult of the book first articulated in the *Prajñāpāramitā* texts. The book here is indeed physically represented as an *object*, *per se*, to be venerated. However, these later representations take the earlier cult of the book discourse to its logical conclusion. As we saw in the previous chapter, there is a crucial amalgamation of the *rūpa*- and *dharmakāya*s at play in this discourse: the book becomes significant not simply as a *container* of the *dharma* (that is, as *rūpakāya*), but also *as* the *dharma* (that is, as *dharmakāya*). As we also saw in the last chapter, however, the *Prajñāpāramitā* discourse maintains what seems to be an intentional ambiguity with regard to the nature of the book and its veneration, a creative tension between an object to be *looked at* (the physical book), and a set of teachings to be learned (the *dharma*).

With the images that I shall discuss in this chapter, we see, as it were, not so much the resolution of this tension but the full synthesis of the *rūpa*- and *dharmakāya*s, and, perhaps more importantly, of vision and wisdom. Nearly a millennium after the appearance of the *Prajñāpāramitā* genre we see the full fruition of its self-referential "cult of the book" discourse; the book, the essence of which is *prajñā*, is represented in the sculpture of the later Pāla period *not* as a container significant because of the *dharma* it contains, but as a container *qua container*, an object set up on a pedestal and venerated.

I. The Book Condensed

> The mystical efficacy of the incantations as adopted by Brahmanism was doubtless enhanced by the introduction of the art of writing, about this time.... Hence the reduction of the oral spells to writing must have enormously intensified their mystery, and also tended to popularize them by fixing them in visible and permanent form and thus rendering them portable, less costly and more freely available for use as amulets.... When the "Word" of Buddha, after being transmitted orally for some generations, was first reduced to writing in India in the then still somewhat novel sacred characters ("the abode of the Gods") this must have tended to enhance its sacred reputation, and to invest the books in which it was inscribed with the character of being materially sacred in themselves. This doubtless is the origin of the custom common in Buddhist countries of carrying in procession the volumes of scriptures round areas or persons infested by disease - the books are used as fetish-charms.
>
> L.A. Waddell [2]

Part of what underlies the focus on the text *as a text* in the later Pāla period, and the sculptural representations of books, and particularly books being venerated, is the emergence of an overall focus in Buddhism on books during this time. A great deal has been written over the years about the rise of literacy in the West, and the impact writing, and more particularly printing, has had on Western culture. The development of widespread printing, and the consequent easy dissemination of information, created something of a cultural revolution.[3] Scholars writing about the Indian Buddhist context have

---

[2] L.A. Waddell, "The 'Dhāranī' Cult in Buddhism, its Origin, Deified Literature and Images," *Ostasiatische Zeitschrift* (1912): 155-95, pp. 162 and 176.

[3] See, for instance, Jack Goody *The Domestication of the Savage Mind* (Cambridge, 1977); J. Goody and I.P. Watt, "The Consequences of Literacy," Comparative Studies in History and Society 5 (1963): 304-15; J. Goody, "Literacy and the Non-Literate," in R. Disch, ed., The Future of Literacy (Englewood Cliffs, 1973); J. Goody, *The Interface Between the Written and the Oral*

also taken up this issue - sometimes, as in the quotation above, in a rather bizarre manner - and have in particular paid close attention to the relationship between the oral and the written.[4]

Clearly, Buddhism during the Pāla period was a largely monastic/scholastic endeavor,[5] and, as such, was intimately associated with the production and, more importantly, the exegesis of texts. As Donald Lopez has pointed out, there was "a self-conscious scholastic entity that thought of itself as the Mahāyāna and which devoted a good deal of energy to surveying what was by then a rather large corpus" of texts, attempting "through a variety of hermeneutical machinations to craft the myriad doctrines contained there into a system."[6] Not only were Pāla period Buddhists intimately associated with texts, however; they were, it would seem, somewhat obsessed with them. As José Cabezón puts it, scholastic Buddhists tended toward the textually *proliferative*: "More textually inclusive than exclusive, they prefer to analyze and systematize rather than to limit what is at their disposal."[7] This proliferative character of monastic culture - this seeming obsession with exegesis - has, of course, resulted in a tremendous mass of written material, *śāstra*s, commentaries, sub-commentaries, and scholars of Buddhism have tended to focus on sorting out this written material, and on sorting out how contemporary Buddhists sorted out this written material; they have, in a sense, engaged in the

---

(Cambridge, 1987); E.L. Eisenstein, "Some Conjectures about the Impact of Printing on Western Society," Journal of Modern History 40 (1968): 1-56; W. Ong, Orality and Literacy: The Technologizing of the Word (London: Methuen, 1982); and Henri-Jean Martin, The History and Power of Writing (Chicago: University of Chicago Press, 1994).

[4]See S. Collins, "Notes on Some Oral Aspects of Pali Literature," Indo-Iranian Journal 35 (1992): 121-35; S. Collins, "On the Very Idea of the Pali Canon," Journal of the Pali Text Society 15 (1990): 89-126; G. MacQueen, "Inspired Speech in Early Mahāyāna Buddhism;" José Ignacio Cabezón, Buddhism and Language: A Study of Indo-Tibetan Scholasticism (Albany: SUNY, 1994), especially Chapter 5; and Donald S. Lopez, Jr., "Authority and Orality in the Mahāyāna," Numen 42 (1995): 21-47.

[5]I should note that this distinction, between the scholastic and monastic, is not really relevant to the Indian context; there was, unlike in the medieval Christian West, no clear difference between the two. For a particularly insightful discussion of this point, see José Ignacio Cabezón, *Buddhism and Language*.

[6]D. Lopez, "Authority and Orality," p. 24.

[7]José Cabezón, *Buddhism and Language*, p. 21.

same sorts of exegetical praxis that seems to have so thoroughly occupied Indian Buddhists.

Writing (and no doubt also, still, reciting) new texts, however, was not the only way this proliferative, text-centric character manifested itself. Consistent with the *visual* emphasis we have already explored - recall Beyer's "wave of visual theism" - Buddhists during the Pāla period also were concerned with *seeing* texts. The written word became a significant object in itself, and not just the *sound* of the word being spoken, as in a *mantra*, say, but also the written word as an object to be seen, to be ensconced in *stūpa*s, and to be "set up and venerated."

One way Buddhists during the Pāla period did this, in an extension of the kind of "cult of the book" ideology I have discussed in the previous chapter, was by treating the written text as a relic in its own right. Perhaps the most prominent example of this is the thousands of "*dhāranī* stones" that have been found enshrined inside *stūpa*s throughout northeastern India.[8] Xuanzang, in the seventh century, provides one of the first accounts of this practice: "It is a custom in India to make little *stūpa*s of powdered scent made into paste; their height is about six or seven inches, and they place inside them some written extract from a *sūtra*; this they call a *dharma-śarīra* (*fa-sh-li*)."[9] We find a similar account in Divākara's seventh-century translation of the "Sūtra on the Merit of Building a Stūpa Spoken by the Buddha": "[O]r else if one deposits the twelve section scripture, which is the storehouse of the Tathāgata's *dharma*, down to even one

---

[8]Such "stones," sometimes call *sācchas*, are usually in fact small clay seals - that is, lumps of clay with part of a text, and often an image of some sort, stamped on while wet and then allowed to dry. Such "stones" have been found throughout Buddhist India, as well as in Sri Lanka and at many places in Burma. See Hiranand Sastri, *Nālandā and Its Epigraphical Material*; see also H. Sastri, "The Clay Seals of Nālandā," *Epigraphica Indica* 21 (1931-32): 72ff. For a general discussion of these clay sealings, see Simon Lawson, "A Catalogue of Indian Buddhist Clay Sealings in British Museums," Ph.D. Dissertation, Oxford University, 1982.

[9]S. Beal, *Si-yu-ki*, vol. 2, p. 146. See also Yijing, who says that such sealings were put in *stūpa*s: "...the priests and the laymen in India make *k*aityas (i.e.) stupas) or images with earth...they put in the images of *k*aityas two kinds of *sarira*s (relics). (1) The relics of the Great Teacher. (2) The Gatha of the Chain of Causation." J. Takakusa., trans., *A Record of the Buddhist Religion as Practised in India and the Malay Archipelago*, pp. 150-51. The vast majority of these clay sealing date to the 9-10th centuries, although some have been found to date significantly earlier; see Debala Mitra, *Buddhist Monuments* (Calcutta: Sahitya Samsad, 1971), p. 84.

four line verse, this person's merit will be as great as the *brahma* heaven."[10]

The first issue here, then, is the nature of these so-called *dhāranī* sealings.[11] The term *dhāranī* comes from the Sanskrit root *dhr*, "hold" or "contain": a *dhāranī* is thus a short verse, a kind of condensed *sūtra*, said to contain or to hold the essence of the larger text from which the verse was drawn. They are "a short mnemonic string of words, holding...the meaning succinctly of an intention which in normal speech would need to be much more prolix."[12] *Dhāranīs* are, of course, a central component in *tantric* practices, but they are also certainly common in even the earliest strands of the Mahāyāna, and need not be seen as necessarily having *tantric* associations.[13] According to the *Mahāprajñāpāramitopadeśa*, *dhāranīs* enable a person "to assemble various good *dharmas* and maintain them without losing them."[14] Alex Wayman, discussing the *tantric* context of *dhāranīs*, quotes a rather cryptic text,[15] but one that nonetheless provides a nice description of *dhāranīs* that holds equally for the non-*tantric* context: "The character of *dhāranī*-s is to hold the Buddha-dharmas; its holding is called 'holding dharmas' and 'virtue'."[16] *Dhāranīs* are also frequently said to hold certain "magical" powers; L.A. Waddell, for instance, in addition to the "fetish-charms" description I have already quoted, emphasized this aspect of such formulas, calling them a "luck-compelling talisman to encompass all

[10]Quoted in Daniel Boucher, "The *Pratītyasamuppādagātha* and Its Role in the Medieval Cult of the Relics," p. 9.

[11]For one of the few general discussions of *dhāranīs*, see L.A. Waddell, "The Dhāranī Cult in Buddhism."

[12]David Snellgrove, *Indo-Tibetan Buddhism*, vol. I, p. 122.

[13]See Gregory Schopen's sharply and concisely worded discussion of this in his "The Bodhigarbhālaṅkāralaksa and Vimalosnīsa Dhāranīs in Indian Inscriptions." *Wiener Zeitschrift für die Kunde Südasiens* 29 (1985): 119-50, p.147. For a discussion of the *tantric* context of *dhāranīs*, see Agehananda Bharati, *The Tantric Traditions* (Delhi: Hundustan Publishing Corp., 1993), Chapter 5.

[14]Quoted in Hirakawa Akira, *A History of Indian Buddhism from Śākyamuni to Early Mahāyāna*, edited and trans. by Paul Groner (Hawaii: University of Hawaii Press, 1990), p. 301.

[15]See Alex Wayman, *The Buddhist Tantras: Light on Indo-Tibetan Esotericism* (New York: Samuel Weiser, 1973); Wayman calls it the "Initiation Preliminary," and refers to it, with a striking lack of bibliographic specificity, as a text "I have in my possession," p. 64.

[16]Ibid., p. 65.

worldly desires, to achieve miracles and mystically for spiritual advancement by short cuts to Bodhisatship or to Nirvāṇa itself."[17] My interest here, however is not so much in the talismanic qualities of such texts, as it is in their *dharmaśarīra* nature, although the two are necessarily linked.

A great many of these clay seals, no doubt the majority of them, are inscribed with the so-called "Buddhist Creed," the well-known *Pratītyasumutpādagāthā*: *ye dharmā hetuprabhavā hetum teṣāṃ tathāgatho hy avadat teṣāṃ ca yo nirodha evam vādī mahāśramaṇaḥ.*[18] This verse was ubiquitous in the Pāla milieu: not only is it found on thousands of clay sealings, but also on a great many sculptures from the period as well.[19] Daniel Boucher has suggested that this verse, from a very early time, was taken as the very essence of the *dharma.* Boucher quotes, for instance, the Chinese recension of a text, the *Śālistambasūtra*, translated in the third century, that picks up a familiar equation: "He, monks, who sees the *pratītyasamupāda* sees the *dharma*; he who sees the *dharma* sees the Buddha."[20] Again, we see here the dual nature of *seeing*, which is at once a physical act, as in gazing on an object, and at the same time a cognitive act, as in comprehending some aspect of the doctrine.

Not all clay sealings found in Pāla environs, however, are stamped with the *Pratītyasamutpādagāthā.* Some bear the impression of Śākyamuni (usually displaying the *bhūmisparśamudrā*), or Avalokiteśvara, or Mañjuśrī, or simply the *dharmacakra* flanked by

---

[17]L.A. Waddell, "The Dhāraṇī Cult in Buddhism," pp. 155-56. Gregory Schopen, in a more recent article, notes that *dhāraṇīs* are part of a broader doctrine "in which 'the text or book as a source of sacred power' is a fundamental preoccupation." See Schopen, "The Text on the 'Dhāraṇī Stones from Abhayagiriya': A Minor Contribution to the Study of Mahāyāna Literature in Ceylon," *Journal of the International Association of Buddhist Studies* 5 (1982): 100-08, p. 105.

[18]"Those things (*dharmas*) that arise from a cause, the Tathāgata has explained their cause, as well as that which is the cessation of them; thus has the great renunciant taught."

[19]Simon Lawson has gone so far as to say that it "drove Buddhism" during the Gupta and Pāla periods. See S. Lawson, "Votive Objects from Bodhgaya," in Janice Leoshko, ed., *Bodhgayā, Site of Enlightenment* (Bombay: Mārg, 1988), p. 68.

[20]Daniel Boucher, "The Pratītyasamutpādagāthā and Its Role in the Medieval Cult of the Relics," p. 2. See also Louis de La Vallée Poussin, *Bouddhisme, Études et Matériaux: Théorie des Douze Causes*, p. 70, for the Sanskrit.

two deer.[21] Furthermore, some of these sealings are stamped with verses other than the *Pratītyasamutpādagāthā*; for instance, Gregory Schopen has written about a *dhāraṇī* text found on stones from Abhayagiriya in Sri Lanka, Nālandā, and various sites in Orissa, the *Sarvatathāgatādhiṣṭhāna-sūtra*. "[I]f someone made a copy of it," this *sūtra* states, "and put it into a *stūpa*, that *stūpa* would become a *stūpa* of the relics of the 'essence' of *vajra* of all *Tathāgata*s."[22] Indeed, where this text is - and where, presumably, a portion of this text is - there are "hundreds of millions of *Tathāgata*s, inspeakably many relics of *Tathāgata*s, the 84,000 pieces of *Dharma*, etc...."[23] Again, the ideological position here favors texts over relics, for it is the texts that give rise to, and are the source of, all of the *tathāgata*s.[24] These small, inscribed clay seals, then, seem to have been seen and treated as equivalents of the larger texts from which their verses were taken, and as such, they too were seen as superior to bodily relics.[25]

The question, of course, is what such *dhāraṇī*s have to do with the sculptural representation of books, and, more importantly, with the visual representation of *prajñā*; there is, I must admit, no concrete or conclusive evidence linking these two practices. There hardly ever is such evidence in the study of Indian Buddhism. Nevertheless, what we do clearly see here is a focus on texts - and specifically *dhāraṇī*s

---

[21]See, for instance, Simon Lawson, "Dhāranī Sealings in British Collections," in Janine Schotsmans and Maurizio Taddei, eds. *South Asian Archaeology 1983*, vol. 2 (Naples: Isitituto Universitario Orientale, 1985), in particular figs. 3-5.

[22]Gregory Schopen, "The Text on the 'Dhāranī Stones from Abhayagiriya'," p. 104. See also A. Ghosh, "A Buddhist Tract in a Stone Inscription in the Cuttack Museum." *Epigraphica Indica* 26 (1941): 171-74.

[23]Ibid., p. 105.

[24]For more on this ideology in *dhāranī* texts, see Gregory Schopen, "The Bodhigarbhālaṅkāralaksa and Vimalosnīsa Dhāranīs." In the *Bodhigarbhālaṅkāralaksa dhāranī*, for instance, we encounter: "If some monk or nun or lay man or woman, or some other son or daughter of good family, after writing this Dhāranī and making a *caitya*, were to put this Dhāranī into that *caitya*, although that person had made (only) one *caitya*, he would (in effect) have made a hundred thousand. He might also do worship with heavenly flowers...but this is not the worshipping of only the *caitya*: the Jewel of the Buddha, the Jewel of the Dharma, and the Jewel of the Community would also (in effect) be worshipped with those articles of worship," pp. 133-34.

[25]Indeed, according to Schopen, there is evidence that these *dhāranī*s, these condensed "text essences" were "different from and superior to *chos sku'i riṅ bsrel*, or 'relics of the *dharmakāya*;" see Schopen, ibid., pp. 125-28.

as condensed texts or "text essences" - that resonates with the early "cult of the book" discourse that runs throughout the *Prajñāpāramitā*. *Dhāraṇī* sealings are not significant because of the profound messages contained in the few verses with which they are stamped, but rather, they are significant as condensations and representations of the larger text from which they are drawn and, by extension, the full teachings of the Buddha. These short verses stamped on clay are thus like little nuggets of *prajñā*, material objects that embody something much more significant than the material out of which they are made.

There are extant versions of *Prajñāpāramitā dhāraṇīs*, although to my knowledge these were rarely enshrined in *stūpas* during the Pāla period. Simon Lawson, however, has discussed a particularly interesting, and relatively long *dhāraṇī*, first discovered by Alexander Cunningham at Bodhgayā,[26] which he believes is linked to one such *Prajñāpāramitā dhāraṇī*. On its face, the *dhāraṇī* in question seems to be addressed to Śākyamuni and company. The text, as Lawson prints it, begins: "*Oṃ namo bhagavate vipula vadana kāñchan ākshipta ketu purvva tathāgatāya namo bhagavate Śākya Munaye tathāgatāyārhate samyak sambuddhāya tad yathā...,*" which can be translated as, "Honor to the Blessed One! To the Tathāgata, who is preceded by the splendorous ray cast from the gold of his joyous face! Honor to Blessed Śākyamuni, to the Tathāgatas, to the Arhats, and to the fully enlightened Buddha, in this way...."[27] After this initial invocation addressed to Śākyamuni, however, the text appears to shift referents: *oṃ bodhi bodhi bodhi sarva tathāgata gocara dhara dhara hara hara prahara prahara mahābodhi citta dhare...,*" or, "Oṃ Enlightenment! Oh, bearer of the thought of the great enlightenment, the bearer and supporter of all of the Tathāgatas!"[28] To whom is *this* praise directed? Lawson suggests that this verse is, in fact, addressed to Prajñāpāramitā.

Lawson's argument is in part based on the fact that, except for the initial obeisance to Śākyamuni - and I might add to the Tathāgatas

---

[26]See Alexander Cunningham, *Mahābodhi, or the Great Buddhist Temple at Buddha-Gayā* (London: W.H. Allen, 1892).
[27]Simon Lawson, "Dhāraṇī Sealings in British Collections," p. 713.
[28]Ibid., my translation.

and to the Arhats and to the fully-enlightened Buddha - (up to *tad yathā*), the rest of the *dhāranī* is in the feminine vocative.[29] "Lip-service has been paid to Gautama, but this female gets most of the praise. A clue to her identity may be found in the words *citta dhare* in the middle of line four above.... They call to mind the ideal of perfect wisdom, worshipped in the form of the female *bodhisattva* Prajñāpāramitā."[30] Although I am not entirely convinced by Lawson's argument - among other things, he glosses over the fact that "*prajñāpāramitā*" does not even appear in the verse - his discussion raises the possibility of an interesting equation between the *dhāraṇī*, relics, and the *Prajñāpāramitā*. As we have seen, the text is better than the relics, since it is the source of the Tathāgatas; the *dhāraṇī*, by extension, serves as, if not exactly an object better than the text, one that is at least equivalent to it. Again, as in the *Prajñāpāramitā* discourse, the emphasis seems to be placed more on the *container* than on the *contents*, and although these small clay sealings cannot, of course, explicitly state these various layers of discourse, they do provide an opportunity for metapractical reflection on these layers.

This emphasis on what we might call "textual objects" that begins in the eighth century and continues into the Pāla period is the foundation, I would suggest, for the representation of books in sculptures. Or, to put it another way, the practice of stamping such verses in clay, carrying them about, and ensconcing such *dhāraṇī* stones in *stūpa*s constitutes the *habitus* of the sculptural representation of texts. Again, let me recall Bourdieu's conception of *habitus*: "The habitus is the universalizing mediation which causes an individual agent's practices, without either explicit reason or signifying intent, to be none the less 'sensible' and 'reasonable.'"[31] The *habitus* provides an orientation, and perhaps more importantly *meaning* to practices and structures that are not specifically stated or explained, but which are nonetheless, as Bourdieu emphasizes, both sensible and reasonable.

---

[29]This point, as argued by Lawson, is somewhat confusing, since he has printed the *dhāraṇī* with the compounds broken up, thus obscuring their gender. Thus the long compound that I have translated above would be better printed as, "*sarvatathāgatagocaradharadharaharahara-praharapraharamahābodhicittadhare*".

[30]Lawson, "Dhāranī Sealings in British Collections," p. 714.

[31]P. Bourdieu, *Outline of a Theory of Practice*, p. 79.

In this sense, then, it is perhaps to be expected that there are no explicit links between *dhāraṇī* seals and representations of books or, for that matter, between the representations of books and the *signification* of *prajñā*, since such associations were simply the *givens* of the contemporary field of practice.

Thus Pāla-period Buddhists recognized and responded to such objects and to such representations because of a common *habitus*. Bourdieu's discussion of this point focuses specifically on social practices, but his point is equally applicable to intellectual and "devotional" practices as well, for the *habitus* is "laid down in each agent by his earliest upbringing, which is the precondition not only for the co-ordination of practices but also for practices of co-ordination, since the corrections and adjustments the agents themselves consciously carry out presuppose their mastery of a common code...."[32] It is this sort of *habitus*, this broad field of practices - which must certainly include a "common code" that was at least partially constituted by the myriad oral and written orientations to such practices that are now lost - that enabled Pāla period Buddhists to recognize and to respond to the sculptural representation of books. In this sense, this *habitus* is constituted by precisely the data I have thus far discussed in this study: the early discourse on presence and absence, the early *Nikāya* conception of images, the supremacy of *prajñā* in Śākyamuni's attainment of enlightenment, the *Prajñāpāramitā* emphasis on the cult of the book, and so on. Such representations of books, again, were resonant with a range of meanings; most significantly, though, they were resonant with *prajñā*.

II. Holding and Beholding the Book

I have already discussed, in Chapter Four, the representation of several female figures who are closely associated with *prajñā*, and who characteristically hold the book. I turn now to two of their book-holding male counterparts, Mañjuśrī and Avalokiteśvara, to their

[32]Ibid., p. 81.

associations with *prajñā*, and to a more focused examination of the significance of these books.

II.A Mañjuśrī.

> He is three faced - white, blue, and yellow; he is six-armed. With his right hands he bears an arrow, [makes] the *varadamudrā*, and bears a sword; with his left hands he bears the bow, a blue lotus, and the *Prajñāpāramitā* book.
>
> *Nispannayogāvalī*[33]

> Just as Avalokiteśvara is said to incarnate all the Buddha's compassion, so Mañjuśrī manifests the other "wing" of Enlightenment - wisdom.
>
> Paul Williams[34]

Mañjuśrī is intimately involved with *prajñā* from the point at which he appears in the earliest stratum of *Prajñāpāramitā* texts, indeed, more so than perhaps any other Buddhist figure, with the exception of Prajñāpāramitā herself. As with Prajñāpāramitā, Mañjuśrī is often discussed as a source of the Buddhas; for instance, the *Fang-Po Ching*, an incomplete translation of the *Ajātaśatrukauktyavinodana*, Mañjuśrī is referred to as the "mother *and* father" of all of the Buddhas.[35] In another text extant only in Chinese, part of the *Mahāratnakūtasūtra*, this is said about Mañjuśrī: "Whatever Bodhisattva Mañjuśrī teaches is beneficial to sentient beings. Hundreds of thousands of (millions of) billions of Buddhas never accomplished this in the past, nor are they doing it at present, nor will

---

[33]*Nispannayogāvalī*, p. 48; *pītanīlaśuklasavyetaravaktaḥ ṣaḍbhujo dakṣinaiḥ khaḍgavara-dabānān vāmaiḥ prajñāpāramitā-pustakanīlābjadhanuṃsi bibhrānaḥ*

[34]Paul Williams, *Mahāyāna Buddhism: The Doctrinal Foundations* (London: Routledge, 1989), p. 238.

[35]See Hirakawa Akira, *A History of Indian Buddhism*, p. 251.

they do so in the future."[36] About this particular passage, Garma C.C. Chang remarks, "Mañjuśrī, who embodies the wisdom of all Buddhas, is shown here as being of more benefit to sentient beings than is the Buddha. The reason for this seeming overstatement is to stress the fact that *only the transcendental wisdom of prajñāpāramitā, which Mañjuśrī embodies*, can conquer demons, and not magical formulas, spells, or other thaumaturgical techniques."[37]

My aim here is not to elaborate on such textual descriptions of Mañjuśrī; nor, for that matter, do I propose an exhaustive study of his iconography and the diversity of his sculptural forms in India.[38] Rather, in keeping with my overall focus in this study, I wish to consider the ways in which this essential aspect of Mañjuśrī's character, his embodiment of *prajñā*, is expressed *visually*. In this regard, two iconographic elements are especially important: 1. The book, which, as in the case of Prajñāpāramitā, Cundā, and Avalokiteśvara, is sometimes held aloft, sometimes clutched close to the chest, and, more frequently, perched atop one or more lotuses; and 2. The sword, which, as we have seen, conveys the sense of *prajñā* as slashing through ignorance and delusion.

Although Mañjuśrī's textual origins are very early indeed, dating to the earliest genre of Mahāyāna texts,[39] it is not until the sixth or seventh century that Mañjuśrī begins to be sculpturally depicted.[40] Furthermore, it is not until another century or so later that Mañjuśrī becomes *visually*, as opposed to just textually, linked with *prajñā*. So,

[36]Garma C.C. Chang, ed., *A Treasury of Mahāyāna Sūtras*, p. 53.

[37]Ibid., p. 71, note 17, emphasis added.

[38]For a masterful, though by no means flawless, study of this topic, see Marie-Thérèse de Mallmann, *Étude iconographie sur Mañjuśrī*, Publications de l'École Française d'Extrême-Orient, vol. 55 (Paris: École Française d'Extrême-Orient, 1964). For a more general, though equally exhaustive, study of Mañjuśrī, see Étienne Lamotte, "Mañjuśrī," *T'oung Pao* 78 (1969): 1-96.

[39]Mañjuśrī figures prominently, for instance, in the *śuramgamasamādhi Sūtra*, first translated into Chinese in the second century, as well as in texts such as the *Aṅgulimālīya Sūtra*, where he is described as being a Buddha with his own *buddhaksetra*. For an extensive discussion of Mañjuśrī's textual origins, see Étienne Lamotte, "Mañjuśrī."

[40]See Geri Malandra, *Unfolding a Mandala*, pp. 75-90; see also de Mallmann, *Étude iconographie sur Mañjuśrī*, pp. 18-19. Malandra's discussion is particularly important here, in that she is justifiably critical of de Mallmann's dismissal of the relevance of early Mañjuśrī images.

for instance, at Ellora, admittedly outside of the strict Pāla region - although certainly not, I think, beyond the bounds of the Pāla sphere of influence - it is not until what Geri Malandra calls "the second phase of work" on the caves, beginning in the late seventh century, that Mañjuśrī is depicted holding his characteristic symbol, the book.[41] We see something similar in the Pāla milieu as well, although it is more difficult to place, exactly, since the Pāla sites are significantly more fragmentary than those at Ellora. At Nālandā, for instance, an early Mañjuśrī, a seated stucco image on the Great Stūpa of Site Three, an image dated to the seventh century, has no representation of a book;[42] the same is true with a slightly later standing image at Nālandā, from Site Eight, which Frederick Asher conjectures is modelled after the earlier image.[43] In these early images, the sword is also absent. By the beginning of the Pāla period, however, and extending into the twelfth century, Mañjuśrī's "embodiment" of *prajñā* is consistently represented in sculptures through the employment of the symbols of the book and the sword.

Mañjuśrī is sculpturally depicted in literally dozens of forms;[44] in the vast majority of surviving Pāla-period stelae, the book *is* represented. For instance, a common way of depicting Mañjuśrī is standing, with the book perched conspicuously atop a *nīlotpala* held in his left hand, such as the tenth-century figure from Bodhgayā, now in the Patna museum. Although, as Janice Leoshko has pointed out, such images are relatively unusual at Bodhgayā,[45] such images seem to have been scattered fairly evenly throughout the Pāla region.

Of the surviving Pāla-period images, seated images are perhaps most prevalent, and such images seem, in comparison to standing images, more markedly to emphasize the book and, thus, *prajñā*. For instance, there are numerous ninth/tenth century bronze

---

[41]Malandra, *Unfolding a Mandala*, p. 101.
[42]See Asher, *Art of Eastern India*, pl. 71, pp. 46-48.
[43]Ibid., pl. 164, p. 48.
[44]For an extensive list of Mañjuśrī attributes and forms, see de Mallmann, *Étude iconographique sur Mañjuśrī*, particularly pp. 23-46.
[45]See Janice Leoshko, "Sculpture of the Pāla and Sena Period," p. 259, where she writes: "The lack of many images of Mañjuśrī and the virtual absence of such images after the tenth century at Bodhgayā is puzzling."

images found at Kurkihār (fig. 5) that depict a seated Mañjuśrī holding a book aloft in his left hand, and a small ball, perhaps a piece of fruit, in his right hand (which also displays the *varadamudrā*). In this image, there is a kind of *dual emphasis* on *prajñā*, in that in addition to the book, the piece of fruit in the right hand can be seen as a representation of Mañjuśrī's offering of the fruit (*phala*) of enlightenment.[46] This sort of dual emphasis of *prajñā* is evident in other images of Mañjuśrī as well. For instance, there is a tenth-century stone image from Nālandā (fig. 6) that is particularly saturated with *prajñā*, echoing both images of Śākyamuni and Prajñāpāramitā that I have already discussed; in this image, Mañjuśrī sits cross-legged, displaying the *dharmacakrapravartanamudrā*, flanked by two book-topped lotuses.

Several of the small bronze Mañjuśrī images from Kurkihār and elsewhere also doubly emphasize *prajñā*, representing Mañjuśrī with both the sword and the book. A ninth-century Nālandā image, now in the National Museum, New Delhi (fig. 7), is especially striking in this regard: Mañjuśrī holds the sword aloft with his right hand, poised to slash through ignorance and delusion, while clutching the *Prajñāpāramitā* book to his chest with his left hand.[47] Although, again, such images are not overly abundant in the Pāla milieu, they are also not rare, and they persist throughout the Pāla period. A noteworthy image in this regard is a six-armed, three-faced eleventh-century image now in the Indian Museum, Calcutta (fig. 8). In the upper left hand, Mañjuśrī holds a book to his chest; and in his upper right hand he holds a large sword; in another left hand he holds a bow, while in one right hand he holds an arrow. The precise significance of these latter implements is unclear, although these weapons may be used to defeat such figures as the Māras, and thus may indirectly

---

[46]This is the suggestion of Huntington and Huntington, *Leaves from the Bodhi Tree*, p. 274; although I can find no textual evidence to support such a claim, it makes good sense, and certainly ties in nicely with Mañjuśrī role as the embodiment *and* bestower of *prajñā*.

[47]See N.K. Bhattasali, *Iconography of Buddhist and Brahmanical Sculptures in the Dacca Museum* (Dacca: Dacca Museum Committee, 1929), pp. 28-29, and pl. VII.b, for an iconographically similar twelfth-century image. Bhattasali describes this image in this way: "The god has the sword of knowledge in his right hand raised to cleave the darkness of ignorance, while he presses the book of Saving Wisdom (Prajñāpāramitā) against his breast with his left hand," p. 28.

signify Mañjuśrī's incisive *prajñā*.[48] Finally, his remaining right hand forms the *varadamudrā*, again perhaps signifying his offering of enlightenment. Taken together, these iconographic details very clearly, I think, emphasize *prajñā*.

Finally, a rather late Mañjuśrī, now at the Bagiya Sahitya Parishad, warrants mention here (fig. 9). This stele depicts a seated Mañjuśrī with two arms, in a fairly typical pose; the right arm forms the *varadamudrā*, while the left holds a lotus. What makes this image especially interesting is a particular detail relating to the book resting on the lotus: here a sword extends from the book, presenting a kind of condensed visual expression of the way in which the *prajñā* contained within the text slices through ignorance and clears the way to enlightenment.

II.B. Avalokiteśvara

> The manuscript, perhaps, came to be associated with him later with the growth of his cult. The superimposition of the aspect of *jñāna* on important cult deities appears to have been a common occurrence. Its attribution is quite apposite as it symbolizes "*prajñā*" which dispels ignorance and leads to enlightenment.
>
> Pratapaditya Pal [49]

Approaching the Great Stūpa at Nālandā, an eighth-century Buddhist would have encountered a most remarkable image of Avalokiteśvara: he stands over five feet, with multiple arms, surrounded by a host of

---

[48]This would hold true, certainly, for a figure such as Mārīcī, popular in the Pāla milieu. For a general discussion of bow symbolism, see, for instance, Gösta Liebert, *Iconographic Dictionary of Indian Religions*, Studies in South Asia Culture, vol. 5 (Leiden: E.J. Brill, 1976), p. 73. In the *Sādhanamālā*, however, the Vajrānaṅga form of Mañjuśrī holds a bow of flowers loaded with an arrow of a red lotus bud, leading Bhattacharyya (and others) to conjecture that this is really "the Buddhist God of Love;" see B. Bhattacharyya, *The Indian Buddhist Iconography*, p. 114-15. The point of this sexual imagery and language, however, is clearly metaphorical, as is of course common in the later *tantric* texts: the pursuit of love, and sex, is really the pursuit of *prajñā*.

[49]Pratapaditya Pal, "The Iconography of Amoghapāśa Lokeśvara," Part II, *Oriental Art* 13 (1967): 20-28, p. 26.

figures (fig. 10). This is truly one of the most spectacular images to have been found at Nālandā - indeed, to have been found in all of Northeast India. This image has made quite an impression on several scholars; Debjani Paul, for instance, writes: "The composition is extremely crowded yet perfectly ordered. For symmetry, balance, rhythm and harmony it has rarely any parallel. In fact, one would be hard put to find a matching example - let alone surpassing - of the present piece in Indian sculpture in qualitative achievement."[50]

There can be little doubt that such an image would also have made quite an impression on the contemporary Buddhist standing before it. Not only is Avalokiteśvara's massive size visually arresting, affecting a life-like presence, but the complexity and detail of the iconographic program surely would have been impressive. What, though, would our eighth-century Buddhist have seen in all of these details? Although, of course, there is no way to answer this question with anything like certainty, I want to argue that one thing he or she would have beheld is *prajñā*.

Avalokiteśvara, with his great compassion, is perhaps the most paradigmatic of Bodhisattvas, and certainly the most prevalent in medieval Indian Buddhist sculpture, represented in innumerable images in dozens of different forms.[51] He is not, however, typically associated with *prajñā* in the many texts that praise him, nor, for that matter, by the many scholars who have written about him.[52] Rather, it is Avalokiteśvara's great compassion that is generally emphasized; he is, to put it succinctly, the very embodiment of *karuṇā*. Thus in texts such as the *Saddharmapuṇḍarīka*, and particularly the

[50]Debjani Paul, *The Art of Nālandā*, p. 27.

[51]For a general discussion of Avalokiteśvara, see C.N. Tay, "Kuan-Yin: The Cult of Half Asia," *History of Religions* 16 (1976): 147-152; for a more iconographically oriented study, see Marie Therese Mallmann, *Introduction à l'étude d'Avalokiteśvara*, Anales du Musee Guimet, Bibliotheque d'études, LXVII (Paris: Civilisations du Sud, 1948); see also L.A. Waddell's very early study, "The Indian Buddhist Cult of Avalokita and his Consort, Tārā, the Saviouress," *Journal of the Royal Asiatic Society* (1894): 51-89.

[52]However, Har Dayal, in his *The Bodhisattva Doctrine in Buddhist Sanskrit Literature* (Delhi: Motilal Banarsidass, 1932), in discussing the compound "*Avalokiteśvara*" notes: "A tentative suggestion may be offered: the word *avalokita* may mean "wisdom," as it is employed in the *Mtu.* [*Mahāvastu*] to denote the essence of Buddha's Enlightenment. In that case, the name would mean 'Lord of Wisdom," p. 48. Although such an analysis might nicely fit my thesis here, I find it simply too fanciful to take seriously.

Kārandavyūha (in which he has higher status than even the Buddha), he is said, out of his compassion for the suffering of all sentient beings, to refuse *nirvāna* until all beings attain enlightenment; he grants children to the barren; he visits the various hells to free those entrapped there; he protects the faithful from *yaksa*s and *rāksasa*s and from malicious bandits, and so on. It is to Avalokiteśvara, for example, that Faxian appeals to save him from shipwreck and pirates during his voyages to and from India.[53]

This apotropaic conception of Avalokiteśvara is emphasized in several early sculptures of the *bodhisattva*, which depict Avalokiteśvara as the guardian of the faithful, saving them from the same perils described in the texts. At Kānheri, for instance, in cave 90, there is a sixth-century image of Avalokiteśvara, accompanied by Tārā and Bhrkutī, along with ten perils from which he protects his devotees.[54] Similarly, in Cave Seven at Aurangabad there is a seventh-century image with eight perils.[55] In images from the Pāla milieu this overt emphasis on the compassionate, savior nature of Avalokiteśvara remains prominent, conveyed by a variety of iconographic details.

However, a subtle but significant shift seems to take place with Avalokiteśvara in the Pāla period; *prajñā* enters the picture. This is not to say that Avalokiteśvara somehow becomes *primarily* associated with *prajñā*. He does not. Indeed, it is important to point out here that the vast majority of Avalokiteśvara images from the Pāla period do *not* include the book and do *not* overtly seem to have anything to do with the representation of *prajñā*. But the spectacular large image from Nālandā, in spite of its unusual nature, serves, I think, as a good representation of a change that *does* seem to take place in the Pāla period in terms of what we might call Avalokiteśvara's iconographic scope. This subtle shift is consistent, furthermore, with what I have been arguing is a persistent concern with *prajñā* in the sculpture of the Pāla period.

---

[53]See James Legge, *A Record of Buddhist Kingdoms*, p. 112.

[54]See S. Huntington, *The Art of Ancient India*, p. 264, for an illustration of this image, as well as a brief discussion of it.

[55]Ibid, p. 266.

The image from Nālandā is certainly visually complex. Avalokiteśvara is here twelve-armed, surrounded by a host of smaller figures, including two seated Buddhas at the top of the stele (perhaps Amoghasiddhi and Ratnasambhava), two small seated female figures in the middle of the stele, and at the bottom Tārā and Bhṛkuṭī, as well as a small Hayagrīva, and a ghoulishly emaciated figure, the *preta* Sūcīmukha. I shall first turn my attention to Avalokiteśvara himself, and then discuss these iconographic details.

The twleve-armed form of Avalokiteśvara is not common in Indian sculpture. There is a single *sādhana* in the *Sādhanamālā* that describes a twelve-armed form of Avalokiteśvara, *Māyājālakramāvalokiteśvara*, although this description does not iconographically correspond with the Nālandā image.[56] In addition to the Nālandā image, only a few other similar images survive.[57] The objects in the twelve arms seem to represent a kind of iconographic amalgamation of a wide variety of Avalokiteśvara forms. Thus, for instance, this image holds a *pāśa*, or noose, the iconographic "signature" of Amoghapāśa Avalokiteśvara; the noose binds the various Māras and other malicious beings, and, therefore, helps Avalokiteśvara protect and aid the faithful in their progress toward enlightenment.[58] This image also holds a lotus and displays the *varadamudrā* with one hand, again both extremely common details in other, less complex images, and he holds a variety of other items that are common on other stelae. One item that the Nālandā image holds, however, does not, I believe, appear on any Avalokiteśvara images prior to this one: in one of his upper left hands, he prominently holds a book.[59] Indeed, not only does

---

[56]The various items held by the Nālandā deity are different and, perhaps more significantly, the form in this text is five-faced; see *Sādhanamālā*, p. 86. See also B. Bhattacharya, *The Indian Buddhist Iconography*, p. 139-40; and also Marie-Thérèse de Mallmann, *Introduction a l'iconographie du tântrisme bouddhique*, p. 111.

[57]See Pratapaditya Pal, "The Iconography of Amoghapāśa Lokeśvara," Parts I and II; see also Janice Leoshko's article, "The Appearance of Amoghapāśa in Pāla Period Art," in A.K. Narain, ed., *Studies in Buddhist Art of South Asia*, pp. 127-35.

[58]For an excellent discussion of the iconographic significance of Amoghapāśa's implements, see Leoshko, ibid.

[59]In the *Sādhanamālā*, the Sadaksarī form of Avalokiteśvara does hold a book; see *Sādhanamālā*, p. 36. There are other *textually* described images with a book as well; see R.O Meisezahl, "Amogha-pāśa, Some Nepalese Representations and Their Vajrayanic Aspects," *Monumenta Serica* 26 (1967): 272. However, there are no corresponding images prior to the eighth or ninth century.

he hold a book; the small seated female figure to the right of his waist also holds a book, a point to which I shall return shortly.

Several later images from the Pāla milieu seem to be modelled, if not exactly on the image itself, at least on aspects of this early image. A ninth-century image found in the vicinity of Mahāsthāngarh provides a good illustration of this point.[60] Avalokiteśvara here is six-armed, and flanked by Tārā and Bhrkūtī; in the upper left hand, where we might expect the *pāśa*, however, is a book. Again, Avalokiteśvara is clearly not primarily conceived as a "*prajñā* deity," and it would be quite a stretch to suggest that the *śilpins* and patrons responsible for this image wished, specifically, to emphasize *prajñā*. However, it is, I think, significant - and consistent with my larger thesis - that Avalokiteśvara's iconographic scope is expanded in the Pāla period to include, at times, an unambiguous reference to *prajñā*.

We see evidence of this expansion of Avalokiteśvara's iconographic scope in several Pāla-period stelae. For instance, in the Patna Museum there is a seated, six-armed image from Gayā, dated to the tenth century, with Avalokiteśvara holding a book in one of his left hands. This is not an isolated example; although images of Avalokiteśvara holding a book are by no means ubiquitous in the Pāla period, images such as these have been found throughout the Pāla milieu.[61] Thus although *prajñā* is not a primary part of Avalokiteśvara character, there does seem to develop in the Pāla period a sense of Avalokiteśvara as in some way a conveyor, or perhaps more in character, a *protector* of *prajñā*.[62] Furthermore, the presence of the book as signifying this connection is supported by other iconographic details on these stelae. For instance, the *aksamāla*, or rosary, that Avalokiteśvara often holds in such images is frequently said to be used

---

[60]S. Huntington, *Pāla-Sena Schools*, pl. 198.

[61]There is a similar image in the H.P. Podder collection, one now *in situ* at Bodhgayā, and another at the Patna Museum, just to mention a few images that conform to the same basic iconographic program.

[62]See also J. Leoshko, "The Iconography of Buddhist Sculptures," pls. 50 and 241; see also M. Ghosh, *Development of Buddhist Iconography in Eastern India: A Study of Tārā, Prajñās of Five Tathāgatas and Bhrikutī* (Delhi: Munshiram Monoharlal Publishers Pvt. Ltd., 1980), pl. 49.

in counting out the verses of the text; it is thus an aid in the development of *prajñā*.[63] Avalokiteśvara also sometimes is represented with a sword, which, as we have seen, is a common visual metaphor for *prajñā*. Likewise, the presence of Tārā and Bhrkūtī also involves *prajñā*.

Tārā is of course an extremely prominent figure throughout the Buddhist world, and as I have noted, the most commonly depicted female figure in the Pāla period.[64] As her name implies, Tārā is the great saviouress, the guide.[65] She saves sentient beings from suffering and she is called, for instance, *jagat-tāriṇī*, the "deliverer of the world," in the Vipulaśrīmitra inscription from Nālandā.[66] Tārā is frequently depicted with Avalokiteśvara in Pāla-period sculpture, and seems most obviously to be an aspect, or an extension, of his compassionate and protecting nature, although Tārā too is associated with *prajñā*. Mallar Ghosh writes that, similar to Avalokiteśvara, to "her original function as a protectress came to be added the aspects of *jñāna* and *prajñā* for dispelling the ignorance of sentient beings and for leading them to salvation and enlightenment."[67]

Far less is known about Bhṛkūṭī's specific character.[68] She too, however, seems to reflect Avalokiteśvara's relationship with *prajñā*; Ghosh, for instance, has said that Bhṛkuṭī, as one of Avalokiteśvara's companions, reflects "the practice of wisdom of the Bodhisattva."[69] In the *Sādhanamālā*, there is description of

---

[63]See Conze, "The Iconography of the Prajñāpāramitā," Part I, pp. 47-48. Mallmann, in *Introduction à l'étude d'Avalokiteśvara*, p. 20, remarks that the rosary functions "sorte de boulier destiné à compter les formules d'invocation."

[64]Studies of Tārā abound; see Hiranand Sastri, *The Origin and Cult of Tārā*, Memoirs of the Archeological Survey of India, no. 20 (Calcutta: 1925); Stephan Beyer, *The Cult of Tārā: Magic and Ritual in Tibet* (Berkeley: University of California Press, 1973), for a sweeping study of her cult; see Ghosh, *Development of Buddhist Iconography*, pp. 6-90, for a good discussion of Tārā origins and iconography; for a specific discussion of Tārā in the Pāla period, see Janice Leoshko, "The Iconography of Buddhist Sculptures," pp. 282-97.

[65]Frequently taken to mean "star," *Tārā* is a causative form of the Sanskrit root *tr*, "pass, cross."

[66]N.G. Majumdar, "Nālandā Inscription of Vipulaśrīmitra," *Epigraphica Indica* 21 (1931-32): 97-101.

[67]Mallar Ghosh, *Development of Buddhist Iconography*, p. 32; see also Geri Malandra, *Unfolding a Maṇḍala*, pp. 92-96..

[68]For the fullest study of the deity to date, see Mallar Ghosh, ibid., pp. 145-80.

[69]Ibid., p. 155; Tārā, in this sense, would then be a reflection of Avalokiteśvara's *karuṇā*.

Khasarpana Avalokiteśvara that notes that Bhṛkuṭī has the matted hair (*jaṭākalāpinī*) of an ascetic, perhaps a reference to her ascetic character that enables her to cultivate *prajñā.*[70] She tends to be conceived of as an angry, or *krodha* deity, and also typically posses a third eye, perhaps, again speculatively, the eye of wisdom.

A particularly intriguing detail on the large Nālandā stele is the small female figure to Avalokiteśvara's right, who holds the book (fig. 11). This is undoubtedly Prajñāpāramitā, although the way in which she holds the book, high in her left hand, is unusual; more typically the book rests atop one or both of the lotuses she holds. Prajñāpāramitā is also not typically associated with Avalokiteśvara, although her presence here is consistent with my point about the broadening of Avalokiteśvara's iconographic scope to include *prajñā*, and the more general emphasis on *prajñā* in Buddhist sculptural and discursive practice in the Pāla period.

III. Setting Up the Text

> We prescribe that the icons of our Lord...are to be venerated and shown the same honour as is accorded to the Books of the Gospels.
>
> Anti-Photionic synod of 869[71]

> Wherever a son or daughter of an elite family, having copied the *Prajñāpāramitā*, and having made it into a book [and] venerated it, will set it up....
>
> *Aṣṭasāhasrikāprajñāpāramitā*[72]

---

[70]*Sādhanamālā*, pp. 39-41; see also p. 341. M. Ghosh conjectures that she was "originally a *sāttvika* goddess dedicated to an ascetic life and rising above the worldly matter," Mallar Ghosh, *Development of Buddhist Iconography*, p. 158.

[71]Quoted in H. Belting, *Likeness and Presence*, p. 150.

[72]*Aṣṭasāhasrikāprajñāpāramitā*, p. 42; *yatra khalu punaḥ kauśika kulaputro vā kuladuhitā va imāṃ prajñāpāramitāṃ likhitvā pustakagatāṃ kṛtvā pūjāpūrvagaṃ sthāpayiṣyati.....*

In the previous chapter, I examined a passage from the *Aṣṭasāhasrikāprajñāpāramitā* that states that if someone will set up a *Prajñāpāramitā* book, and if the gods and humans come to that place and see the book, those gods and humans will worship the text. In that passage, as I have noted above, it is clear that it is a *written* book that is to be looked at and to be venerated. However, as I also noted, there is a tension in this and other similar passages between seeing and knowing, between the conventional knowledge that comes from seeing an object, and the penetrating wisdom that allows one truly to know the nature of such an object.[73] The first question I wish to address here, then, is what exactly it means to say that a book has been or will be "set up," and what this setting up of the text has to do with *seeing* and with *prajñā*.

To begin, the word in question is *sthāpayiṣyati*, the future causative form of the Sanskrit verbal root *sthā*, which most simply means "stand." In the form in which it occurs in this passage, it would most literally be translated, then, as "will cause to be stood" - hence my translation, "will set up." The semantic range of *sthā*, however, is somewhat broader than this, and it can also mean something like "establish." Thus "*sthāpayiṣyati*" could mean that it is really the doctrine, the *contents* of the text, that will be established, an interpretation which, as we have seen in the examination of the context of the phrase "*sa pṛthivīpradeśaś caityabhūto bhavet,*" is certainly within the realm of possibilities. As I have argued in the last chapter, however, the context of the passage - and indeed the general thrust of the *Prajñāpāramitā* discourse - makes it clear that what this passage is about is a *physical* book that is to be seen and to be venerated *as such*. The question thus remains: What does it mean to *set up* a book?

In a passage that occurs earlier in the same chapter of the *Aṣṭasāhasrikā*, there is a description of the veneration of the text that sounds very much as if the book is, quite literally, set up on some kind of alter-like structure and venerated in the same way that an image might be worshipped.

---

[73]I have also made note of this tension in Chapter Four, with Buddhaghosa's distinction, articulated in the *Visuddhimagga*, between *saññā*, *viññāṇa*, and *paññā*.

> Blessed One, [what if] some person, the son or daughter of an elite family, having written out the *Prajñāpāramitā*, and having made it into a book, set it up; and what if that person were to honor, worship, think about, adore, and pay reverence to it, with various *pūjās* and many forms of worship, and with flower lamps all around, with heavenly flags, bells, banners, umbrellas, garments, powders, ointments, garlands, perfume, incense, and flowers....[74]

There is, as far as I know, no evidence contemporary with the first redactions of this text that would indicate that this is anything more than a *highly motivated* rhetorical statement about the status of the book. In other words, although we know that Buddhists treated *parts* of books with great reverence, as *dharmaśarīra*, it is simply unclear from the passage, and the context in which it appears, whether or not *real* Buddhists - Buddhists "on the ground" - actually treated books in this manner. Nearly a millenium after the fact, however, this passage (and others similar to it) seems to begin to be taken *quite literally*, and sculptures begin to be constructed that include images of the book *set up* on a pedestal and venerated in a manner almost identical to that described in the above passage.

One of the earliest examples of such a representation that survives is found on a fragment of a *bhūmisparśamudrā* Buddha image from outside of the Pāla milieu proper, from Kiching, in Orissa, that dates to the ninth century (fig. 12). The book here is very clearly *set up* on an altar-like pedestal. Surrounding the book are three figures; to the book's left is a bearded man, kneeling, seeming to be offering the book some object; to the right of the book is a standing female figure, in one hand holding a *caurī* (a "fly whisk"), in the other a two-tiered lamp; and, kneeling below the book, is another female figure making the *añjali* gesture of veneration and respect toward the

---

[74]*Aṣṭasāhasrikāprajñāpāramitā*, p. 28; *yo bhagavan kulaputro vā kuladuhitā vā imāṃ prajñāpāramitāṃ likhitvā pustakagatāṃ kṛtvā sthāpayet, enāṃ ca divyābhiḥ puṣpadhūpagandhamālyavilepanacūrṇacīvaracchatra-dhvajaghaṇṭhāpatākābhiḥ samantācca dīpamālābhiḥ, bahuvidhābhiśca pūjābhiḥ satkuryāt gurūkuryāt mānayet arcayet apacāyet.....*

pustaka. A similar scene is represented on the base of a *bhūmisparśamudrā* image from Ratnagiri, now in the Patna museum.[75] On this image, the book is set up on a stand, with several kneeling devotees, some making the *añjali* gesture, others offering garlands. Another *bhūmisparśamudrā* Buddha image, an eleventh-century stele (fig. 13), again from Orissa (Chanduar), has a similar, though more simple depiction of the book. Here, there is only a single human figure, kneeling in the same manner as in the earlier image. In this later image, the book is set up on what appears to be a kind of folding stand.[76]

Although this iconographic motif seems to have been more prevalent in Orissa, for reasons that are not at all clear, it is far from anomalous in the Pāla milieu proper. Indeed, this is a quite common visual trope from the ninth century onward, and it is by no means confined to images of the Buddha. There are, for instance, numerous images from Bodhgayā that include the book set up on a pedestal. The exact iconographic details vary considerably from image to image: the book is sometimes on a pedestal, sometimes on a stand; there are sometimes multiple worshippers, sometimes only one; the book is sometimes part of a what seems to be a larger ritual context, sometimes represented alone. Nevertheless, despite such iconographic variety, the book as an object set up and venerated is extremely common.

For instance, a Tārā image now in the Dacca Museum (fig. 14) includes a very prominent book on a pedestal - indeed, the book is almost as large as the figures who venerate it - and a seated figure holding a *vajra*, and two *cintamāni*, or "wish-fulfilling gems," a motif we see on several other such images. For instance, an image of

---

[75]See Parmeshwari Lal Gupta, *Patna Museum Catalogue of Antiquities* (Patna: 1965), pp. 87-88; see also Debala Mitra, *Ratnagiri (1958-61)*, two vols. Memoirs of the Archaeological Survey of India, no. 80 (Delhi: Director General, Archaeological Survey of India, 1981 and 1983), pp. 426-28, and pl. CCCXXV, A.

[76]The pedestal and the folding stand are equally common, and it is impossible to tell whether or not they represent two different modes of veneration. In fact, very little has been written on the nature of these ritual accouterment; by far the most extensive discussion of this subject is found in Claudine Bautze-Picron's excellent article, "Between Men and Gods: Small Motifs in the Buddhist Art of Eastern India, an Interpretation," in K.R. van Kooij and H. van der Veere, eds, *Gonda Indological Studies*, vol. 3 (Groningen: Egbert Forsten, 1995), pp. 59-79

Śākyamuni displaying the *bhūmisparśamudrā*, now in the Dacca Museum (fig. 15) includes on its base not only the *cintamāṇi*, but all seven jewels of the *Cakravartin*, including at the far right a similar book set up on a pedestal and again being venerated by the bearded male figure.[77]

The exact nature of images such as these is, I must say, something of a mystery. First, it is unclear whether the comparative prevalence of such images in Bangladesh and Orissa represents a particular doctrinal and ritual specificity, focused on books as objects. It is also impossible to say, exactly, what sort of ritual is represented by these images - or, for that matter, whether they *even* represent real rituals - since, as I have mentioned, as far as I know there is no surviving corroborating textual evidence about the ritual veneration of books.[78]

Nevertheless, the visual significance of such iconographic details should not be underestimated. Such details would have been at eye level for the Buddhists beholding them, and as such, perhaps these images were intended to serve, in part, as *visual metaphors* - in other words as *signifiers* - impressing upon the Buddhist looking at them the value of the book and the *prajñā* it contains. Indeed, it is perhaps significant in this regard that the book usually occurs at the *base* of the image, a kind of *visual reminder* that the central figure -

---

[77]See also N.K. Bhattasali, *Iconography of Buddhist and Brahmanical Sculptures*, p. 30, and pl. VIII. Bhattasali is also stymied by the specific identity of this figure, and describes him as: "A squatting bearded man with a skull-cap holding up to the Buddha [really to the book] something like a torch and a censer with his hands: looks like a priest." See also Claudine Bautze-Picron, "Between Men and Gods," pp. 61-62; here the author, drawing on the *Mañjuśrīmūlakalpa* and Tāranātha's History, suggests that these distinctive conical caps may have been adopted by some *panditas* in the Pāla period. For a brief discussion of the seven gem motif, see Mirielle Bénisti, *Contribution à l'étude du stūpa bouddhique indien: les stūpa mineurs de Bodh-Gayā et de Ratnagiri*, Publications de l'École Française D'Extrême-Orient, vol. 75 (Paris: École Française D'Extrême-Orient, 1981).

[78]We know, however, that books are frequently paraded out in public during festivals in South Asia. Todd Lewis, for instance, tells me that during the *cakan dyo* festival, a gold-inscribed copy of the *Prajñāpāramitā*, housed in a pallanquin, is carried in procession, accompanied by an entourage including musicians, along with an image of Dīpankara Buddha around Kathmandu. See also David Gellner's "'The Perfection of Wisdom': A Text and its Use in Kuā Bāhāh, Lalitpur Nepal," in S. Lienhard, ed., *Change and Continuity in the Nepalese Culture of the Kathmandu Valley* (Turin: Edizioni dell' Orso, 1996). For a discussion of the other ritual objects represented on such *stelae*, see Bautze-Picron, "Between Men and Gods," especially pp. 64-66.

Tārā, Avalokiteśvara, the Buddha - is supported by *prajñā*. Or perhaps these iconographic details were intended to have a *mimetic character*, in much the same way, say, that the worshippers at the bottoms of other stelae seem to be there as figures to be emulated.[79] We see this latter possibility particularly clearly on a lintel fragment (fig. 16) from Bodhgayā, which seems to emphasize the ritual accoutrement involved in venerating the book; along with the book, which seems to be draped in some kind of cloth and which is being venerated by four kneeling figures, there are also two other items - two lamps, or perhaps a lamp and a jug - which seem to be intentionally oversized, almost as if they were intended to be *prescriptive*.[80] In other words, perhaps these scenes involving the veneration of the book served as visual clues to correct practice.

Whatever the exact nature of these images of books, it seems clear that, first, they were an important facet of the visual representation and presentation of *prajñā*, and, further, it also seems that these images function in a decidedly *metapractical* manner. By this I mean that such images at once function as components of ritual practice and, at the same time, visual reflections on the nature of such practice.

Furthermore, such images only fully make sense when situated in the broader *habitus* of the complex of ideas relating to the visual representation of *prajñā*, the "schemes of perception, thought, and actions....whose limits are set by the historically and socially situated conditions," that I have been examining throughout this study, including the equation of the *rūpa-* and *dharmakāyas*, the discourse on the presence of the Buddha in images, the relationship of the book as object and the book as container of the *dharma*, and so on. Indeed, the metapractical nature of such images, and the degree to which proper *recognition* of them, and response to them, is dependent on the *habitus* in which they are situated, is particularly evident when we consider

---

[79]Here I am thinking, in particular, of the *dharmacakrapravartanamudrā* images where the figures on the base are often depicted listening to the teaching of the Buddha, thus presenting a kind of devotional mirror image to the practitioner.

[80]See also the Dacca *bhūmisparśamudrā* Buddha image, above, for another close up of this motif.

that these are not, after all, actual books - that could be venerated *and* learned - but *representations* of books. In other words, although oral recitation of the text was perhaps part of the ritual context, we are dealing here with an unambiguously *visual* context, in which the text, and the *prajñā* that is its essence, is primarily *to be seen*.

Chapter Seven

SEEING AND KNOWING

> An individual literary feature, or an individual clothing feature, possesses meaning *because it is perceived as part of a whole cluster of meanings*; and, in each case, this type of whole must be a more or less explicit guess about the kind of utterance or the kind of dress that is being interpreted. Unless interpreters make a guess about the kind of meaning they confront they have no way of unifying their transient encounters with the details.
>
> Paul Connerton[1]

In the preceding chapters, I have examined a great many individual *visual* features relating to *prajñā*, and, furthermore, I have argued that these various pieces of evidence do, in fact, conglomerate into something like a whole. Thus, for instance, as we have seen in the last chapter, an individual representation of a book set up on a pedestal fits into, and indeed only makes sense *as part of*, a much broader context that includes: the early discourse on the presence and absence of the Buddha and the essential equation of seeing the Buddha and seeing the *dharma*; the centrality of *prajñā* in both the *Nikāya*s and the Mahāyāna, particularly its discursive elevation in the *Prajñāpāramitā* genre; and, perhaps most saliently, the discourse concerning the superiority of the book as an object of veneration, and the actual representation of Prajñāpāramitā both as a deity and as a book *per se*.

Connerton is correct, of course, in saying that understanding and interpreting *the whole* in such a case is a more or less explicit guess. Indeed, what I have done in this study is a bit like what a paleontologist does in constructing a model of a dinosaur: out of a few bones, or even bone fragments, a whole animal is constructed, but this whole is based on a range of guesses; in reality, of course, we have no way to know, with any certainty, what an ichthyosaur really looked like. In the same way, we can never really know what, exactly,

---

[1]Paul Connerton, *How Societies Remember* (Cambridge: Cambridge University Press, 1989), p. 12, emphasis added.

a specific Buddhist might have seen in, or thought about, a specific image.

This does not, I think, mean that the preceding chapters have been mere guesswork (even educated guesswork). On the contrary, the visual and textual data I have assembled and analyzed here not only demonstrates that *prajñā* was a central part of Buddhist discourse *and* practice during the Pāla period, but also that the *visual* representation and presentation of wisdom--as opposed to only the textual/intellectual discourse that is so frequently the object of our inquiries--was of great importance to Pāla-period Buddhists. That is, Pāla-period Buddhists did not only want to *think* about the Buddha; they also wanted to *see* him, and to be in his presence (and, as I have argued, to think about the nature of this presence). Indeed, it is the amalgamation of these two faculties, *seeing* and *knowing*, that is at the root of Pāla-period visual practice. But it is worth asking, at least, what, exactly, is going on here, with this amalgamation of vision and wisdom, of *dṛṣṭi* and *prajñā*? How is it that a sculpture, a *mere* piece of stone, can articulate such a complicated and complex message?

The obvious answer is that it simply cannot. However, let me return to the notion of *metapraxis* that I discussed in the first chapter of this book, an idea that has, perhaps more implicitly than explicitly, run throughout this study. First, recall what Kasulis says about metapraxis: "[M]eta-practical reflection arises out of questions about the purpose and efficacy of the religious praxes.... Metapractical reflection inquires into the purpose and efficacy of the practice in terms of these participatory and transformative functions.... Metapraxis analyzes and evaluates that happening."[2]

As I have argued here, images of the Buddha are perhaps best understood as instances of metapraxis; they provide an opportunity to reflect on the nature of the Buddha's absence and presence, and, furthermore, they are at once part of the process of, and a "statement" about, the formulation of proper practice in light of this absence and presence. In other words, images are exceedingly complex things: an image of the absent Buddha not only in some way makes him present--

[2]Kasulis, "Philosophy as Metapraxis," p. 178.

with all of the complexity that this concept entails--but such an image also gives rise to, or at least encourages, critical reflection on the complexly intertwined nature of both the Buddha's absence and his presence and the centrality of *prajñā* in the Buddha's own attainment of enlightenment and the practitioner's progress toward this same goal. Thus, for instance a Pāla-period image of Śākyamuni displaying the *bhūmisparśamudrā* provides an opportunity to consider the process through which Śākyamuni conquered Māra, that is overcame *death* itself, and attained enlightenment, a process that has at its very heart *prajñā*.

Such an image, as I have argued, cannot be taken in isolation, but must be seen in the context of a broad *habitus*. Early sculptures must be seen in the context of the early textual discourse about being in the presence of the Buddha, and the development of *paññā* as a result of this presence; later sculptures, specifically Pāla-period images, likewise must be seen in the context, first, of both the earlier sculptures and the earlier *Nikāya* discourse, as well as in the context of the later, contemporary comments on, and developments of, that discourse in the Mahāyāna texts. All of this, these complex competing and overlapping discourses, is what constitutes the field of praxis, and perhaps more significantly, *meta*praxis, in which the visual representation of *prajñā* is located. It is important, though, that the nature of this *habitus* is, as Bourdieu makes clear, that it is not *explicitly* stated, but rather constituted by, in Bourdieu's words, the *self evident givens* of the socio-cultural milieu in which it occurs. Thus one of my central aims throughout this study has been to tease out some of these givens, to attempt to make *explicit* the ways *prajñā* was visually represented and received during the Pāla period.

There is, of course, a real danger of overdetermination here, of positing complexity where it did not perhaps originally lie. In this regard, I have erred on the side of the complex, but I have done so, I think, with sufficient warrant. For one fundamental aspect of images--Buddhist, Hindu, Christian, ancient, medieval, modern--that I hope I have clearly demonstrated here is that they are every bit as multivalent as texts. A particularly clear example of this is evident in representations of Prajñāpāramitā as a deity, for as I have demonstrated, images of Prajñāpāramitā must be seen within a larger context, a discursive and ritual *field* of practice that includes the *Nikāya* discussions of presence, images of the Buddha, the textual discourse on the superiority of the book as an object of veneration, and so on. Such images, really, function as what we might call *meta-practical objects*: they provide, at once, an opportunity for *practice* - veneration of both the deity Prajñāpāramitā and the *Prajñāpāramitā* book - as well as an opportunity for reflection on such practice - such as the nature of such veneration, the reality of *śunyatā*, the true *dharmakāya*, and the superiority of the *Prajñāpāramitā* book and discourse *vis-à-vis* the earlier formulations of the *dharma*. This is not to say that all Pāla-period Buddhists would have seen and thought about such issues; nor is it to say that this is all there is to such an image. Rather, I have attempted to tease out the range of the possibilities of the *habitus* of such images, a *habitus* which necessarily entails the intent (or *intents*, as is probably more accurate) of those responsible for the construction of such an image as well as the various ways in which such images would or could have been received.

In the last chapter of this study, I examine what I argue is the culmination of the Pāla-period representation of *prajñā*: the sculptural representation of the book *as* book, set up on a pedestal, and venerated. Here, again, we can see the image as an instance of metapraxis, a further reflection on the synthesis of the *rūpakāya* and the *dharmakāya*, on the relationship between the container (the book) and the contained (the *dharma*), and the synthesis of the faculties of vision (*dṛṣṭi*) and wisdom (*prajñā*). Furthermore, I think it is here that what Bourdieu means by *habitus* becomes particularly clear: here we see a system that functions to structure proper practice, a system of "schemes of perception, thought and action...whose limits are set by the historically and socially situated conditions of its production."[3] Such a *habitus*, as Bourdieu further emphasizes, "structures new experience in accordance with the structures produced by past experiences...."[4] In this specific case, this orientation explicitly *and* implicitly, consciously *and* unconsciously, includes, among other

---

[3]Pierre Bourdieu, *The Logic of Practice*, pp. 54-55.
[4]Ibid., p. 60.

things, the complex of discourses on presence and absence, on the nature of *prajñā*, and on the relationship between the relics and the texts.

In Chapter Four, I noted that there is "an important tension between conventional vision and wisdom evident in the *Aṣṭasahāsrikā*: in order to see the true Buddha, and not just his mere form, one must develop *prajñā*; but it is also *through* the very act of seeing the Buddha that *prajñā* can be cultivated." This is, though, a creative tension, and we see it running throughout the tradition. We see it in the account of the first sermon in the *Dhammacakkapavatana Sutta*, where the Buddha, recounting the experience of enlightenment to the *bhikkhu*s, tells them that there arose in him both vision (*cakkhu*) and wisdom (*paññā*). We also see it, of course, in the well-known formula from the *Nikāya*s, "He who sees me, he sees the *dhamma*...." And we see this tension between seeing and knowing, vision and wisdom, running throughout the Mahāyāna; recall, for instance, Eckel's remark concerning both Bhāvaviveka and Xuanzang: "Vision functions for them as a metaphor for the process of enlightenment itself." As Eckel aptly puts it, "To see something is to know it more directly than to hear about it through words."[5]

There is, of course, much that I have left out here, and much, much more to be learned about the place of images in the medieval Buddhist world. For instance, even with Schopen's ground-breaking work, we know comparatively little about the mechanisms of production and control of such images - who paid for them, who made them, who regulated and proscribed their proper use, and so on. There is also much more to be learned about how images such as the ones I have been discussing actually functioned in the various ritual contexts in which they were used, and also how the perception and use of these images has changed as these contexts changed. Indeed, to a certain extent I have frozen these images in the time and space of the Pāla milieu, despite the fact that many of them continue to be situated in a constantly evolving *habitus*.

---

[5]M.D. Eckel, *To See the Buddha*, p. 141 and p. 149.

Richard Davis, in his recent study of the ways in which Hindu images frequently undergo transformation, has reminded us that images in India, be they Hindu, Buddhist, or Jain, are rarely "fixed in stone," but rather change identities as the contexts in which they are situated change. As Davis puts it at the end of his book, "The lives of the Indian images we have followed through history are made and remade through their encounters with differing audiences, who reciprocally bring with them different ways of seeing and acting toward the images they encounter."[6]

This sort of ongoing transformation can be seen in the modern contexts in which many Pāla-period images are now situation. A particularly interesting example, and by no means the only one, is the image of Śākyamuni at Bodhghayā, which I have argued in the preceding pages was, for the ninth or tenth century viewer/participant, saturated with the presence of the Buddha and the *prajñā* of which he was the embodiment. Such an image, however, affected a vastly different sort of presence, and evoked a very different set of associations, six or seven hundred years later, by which time Bodhghayā was inhabited not by Buddhist monks, nor visited by more than a handful of Buddhist pilgrims; it was, instead, controlled by a lineage of Śaiva priests, and patronized by Vaisṇava pilgrims intent on taking *darśana* of Lord *Visṇu.* The identity of this same image, however, changed again toward the end of the nineteenth century, when the Buddhist presence at Bodhgayā was reasserted by Anagarika Dharmapala and his followers, who attempted to claim the site, and its image, as exclusively Buddhist. Despite these competing and conflicting claims, though, the Pāla-period images of Śākyamuni are still *in situ*, and they are daily venerated equally by Hindu pilgrims as Visnu and Buddhist pilgrims as the Buddha.[7]

---

[6]Richard Davis, *Lives of Indian Images* (Princeton: Princeton University Press, 1997), p. 263.
[7]See my "When is the Buddha not the Buddha? The Hindu/Buddhist Battle over Bodhgayā and the Buddha Image," *Journal of the American Academy of Religion* 66.4 (1998).

REFERENCES

Primary Sources in Pāli and Sanskrit

Abhisamayālaṇkāra-Prajñāpāramitā-Upadeśa-Śāstra. Th. Stcherbatsky and E. Obermiller, eds. Minato-ku, Japan: Meicho-Fukyū-Kai, 1977.

Anguttara Nikāya. Richard Morris and E. Hardy, eds. 5 vols. London: Pali Text Society, 1955-61.

Astasāhasrikāprajñāpāramitā. P.L. Vaidya, ed. Buddhist Sanskrit Texts, no. 4. Dharbhanga: Mithila Institute, 1960.

Atthasālinī: Buddhaghosa's Commentary on the *Dhammasangani*. E. Muller, ed. London: Pali Text Society, 1979.

Bodhicaryāvatāra. Buddhist Sanskrit Texts, no. 12. P.L. Vaidya, ed. Darbhanga: Mithila Institute, 1960.

Buddhavasmsa and Cariyāpiṭika. N.A. Jayawickrama, ed. London: Pali Text Society, 1975.

Commentary on the Dhammapada. H.C. Norman, ed. 4 vols. London: Pali Text Society, 1906-14.

Dīgha Nikāya. 3 vols. T.W. Rhys Davids and J. Estlin Carpenter, eds. London: Pali Text Society, 1949-1960.

The Gilgit Manuscript of the Aṣṭdaśasāhasrikāprajñāpāramitā: Chapters 55 to 70 Corresponding to the 5th Abhisamaya. Edward Conze, ed. Roma: Istituto Italiano per il Medio ed Estremo Oriente, 1962.

The Gilgit Manuscript of the Aṣṭdaśasāhasrikāprajñāpāramitā: Chapters 70 to 82 Corresponding to the 6th, 7th, and 8th Abhisamayas. Edward Conze, ed. Roma: Istituto Italiano per il Medio ed Estremo Oriente, 1962.

Guhyasamāja Tantra or Tathāgataguhyaka. Gaekwad's Oriental Series, no. 53. Benoytosh Bhattacharyya, ed. Baroda: Oriental Institute, 1931.

Jātakā: Together with its Commentary. 6 vols. V. Fausboll, ed. London: Pali Text Society, 1962-64.

Lalistavistara. P.L. Vaidya, ed. Buddhist Sanskrit Texts, ṇo. 1. Darbhanga: Mithila Institute, 1958.

Majjhima Nikāya. 3 vols. V. Treckner and Robert Chalmers, eds. London: Pali Text Society, 1960-64.

Monorathapūranī: Buddhaghosa's Commentary on the Anguttara Nikāya. 5 vols. Max Walleser and Hermann Kopp, eds. London: Pali Text Society, 1924-56.

Milindapañha. V. Treckner, ed. London: Pali Text Society, 1962.

Nispannayogāvalī. B. Bhattacharyya, ed. Gaekwad's Oreintal Series, no. 59. Baroda: Oriental Institute, 1949.

Prajñā-Pāramitā-Ratna-Guṇa-Saṃcaya-Gāthā. Akira Yuyama, ed. Cambridge: Cambridge University Press, 1976.

Prajñā-Pāramitā-Ratna-Guṇa-Saṃcaya-Gāthā. E. Obermiller, ed. Minato-ku, Japan: Meicho-Fukyū-Kai, 1977.

Sādhanamālā. 2 vols. B. Bhattacharyya, ed. Gaekwad's Oriental Series, nos. 26 and 41. Baroda: Oriental Institute, 1925 and 1928.

Samantapāsādikā: Buddhaghosa's Commentary on the Vinaya Pitaka. 5 vols. J. Takakusu and M. Nagai, eds. London: Pali Text Society, 1924-38.

Samyutta Nikāya. 5 vols. Leon Feez, ed. London: Pali Text Society, 1960.

Śikṣāsamuccaya of Śāntideva. Buddhist Sanskrit Texts, no. 11. P.L. Vaidya, ed. Dharbhanga: Mithila Institute, 1961.

Sumangala-vilāsinī: Buddhaghosa's Commentary on the Digha Nikāya. 3 vols. T.W. Rhys Davids, J. Estlin Carpenter, and W. Stede, eds. London: Pali Text Society, 1886-1932.

Suvikrāntavikrāmi-Paripṛcchā Prajñāpāramitā-Sūtra. Ryusho Hikata, ed. Fukuoka, Japan: Kyushu University, 1958.

Vimāna-vatthu, E.R. Gooneratne, ed. London: Pali Text Society, n.d.

Vinaya Pitaka. 5 vols. Hermann Oldenberg, ed. London: Pali Text Society, 1964.

Viṣnudharmottara-purāna. Priyabala Shah, ed. Gaekwad's Oriental Series, no. 130. Baroda: Oriental Institute, 1958.

Secondary Sources and Translations

Acharya, P. "A Critical Study of the History of Bengal and Orissa for the Period Roughly from 1070 A.D. to 1220 A.D." *Orissa Historical Research Journal* 14 (1966): 9-34.

Akira, Hirakawa . *A History of Indian Buddhism from Śākyamuni to Early Mahāyāna*, Paul Groner, ed. and trans. Hawaii: University of Hawaii Press, 1990.

Almond, Philip. *The British Discovery of Buddhism.* Cambridge: Cambridge University Press, 1988.

Argan, Giulio Carlo. "Ideology and Iconology." In W.J.T. Mitchell, ed., *The Language of Images*, 15-23. Chicago: University of Chicago Press, 1980.

Armstrong, Robert Plant. *The Affecting Presence: An Essay in Humanistic Anthropology.* Urbana: University of Illinois Press, 1971.

_____. *The Powers of Presence: Consciousness, Myth, and Affecting Presence*. Philadelphia: University of Pennsylvania Press, 1981.

_____. *Wellspring: On the Myth and Source of Culture* Berkeley: University of California Press, 1975.

Asad, Talal. *Genealogies of Religion: Discipline and Reasons fo Power in Christianity and Islam*. Baltimore: The Johns Hopkins University Press, 1993.

Asher, Frederick M. *The Art of Eastern India, 300-800 AD.* Minneapolis: University of Minnesota Press, 1980.

_____. "Bihar Sculpture, 6th-8th Centuries." Ph.D. Dissertation, University of Chicago, 1975.

_____. "The Former Broadley Collection, Bihar Sharif." *Artibus Asiae* 32 (1970): 105-24.

_____. "Vikramasila Mahavihara." *Bangladesh Lalit Kalā* 1 (1975): 107-13.

Bagchi, P.B. *India and China: A Thousand Years of Cultural Relations*. Calcutta: Saraswat Library, 1981.

Bagchi, P.C. "The Eight Great Caityas and Their Cult," *Indian Historical Quarterly* 17 (1941): 223-35.

Bandyopadhyay, Bimal. *Metal Sculptures of Eastern India*. Delhi: Sundeep Prakashan, 1981.

Banerji, Rakhal Das. "The Bangarh Grant of Mahi-Pala I: The 9th Year." *Epigraphica Indica* 14 (1917-18): 324-30.

_____. *Eastern Indian School of Mediaeval Sculpture*. Archaeological Survey of India, New Imperial Series, 47. Delhi: Manager of Publications, 1933.

_____. *The Pālas of Bengal*. Memoirs of the Asiatic Society of Bengal, vol. 5. Calcutta: The Asiatic Society, 1915.

_____. *History of Orissa from the Earliest Times to the British Period*. 2 vols. Calcutta: R. Chatterjee, 1930-31.

Banerji-Sastri, Ananta Prasad. "Ninety-three Inscriptions on the Kurkihar Bronzes." *Journal of Bihar and Orissa Research Society* 26 (1940): 236-51, 299-308.

Bapat, P.V. *Vimuttimagga and Visuddhimagga: A Comparative Study*. Calcutta: J.C. Sarkhel, 1937.

Bautze-Picron, Caudine. "Between Men and Gods: Small in the Buddhist Art of Eastern India, an Interpretation." In K.R. van Kooij and H. van der , eds., *Function and Meaning in Buddhist Art: Proceedings of a Seminar Held at Leiden University, 21-24 October 1991*, pp. 59-79. Groningen: Egbert Forsten, 1995.

Barua, Benimadhab. *Gaya and Buddha-Gaya*. 2 vols. Calcutta: Chuckervertty Chatterjee and Co., 1931-34.

Barua, Dipak Kumar. *Buddha Gaya Temple: Its History*. Buddha Gaya: Buddha Baya Temple Management Committee, 1975.

_____. *Viharas in Ancient India: A Survey of Buddhist Monasteries*. Calcutta: Indian Publications, 1969.

Beal, Samuel. *A Catena of Buddhist Scriptures from the Chinese*. London: Trübner and Co., 1871.

_____. *The Life of Hiuen-tsiang*. London: Kegan Paul, Trench, Trübner and Co., 1914.

_____. Si-Yu-Ki: *Buddhist Records of the Western World Translated from the Chinese of Hiuen Tsiang* (AD 629). London: Trübner, 1884.

Bell, Catherine. *Ritual Theory, Ritual Practice*. New York: Oxford University Press, 1992.

Belting, Hans. *Likeness and Presence: A History of the Image Before the Era of Art*, Edmund Jephcott, trans. (Chicago: University of Chicago Press, 1994

Bénisti, Mirielle. *Contribution à l'étude du stūpa bouddhique indien: les stūpa mineurs de Bodh-Gayā et de Ratnagiri*. Publications de l'École Française D'Extrême-Orient, vol. 75. Paris: École Française D'Extrême-Orient, 1981.

Bernet-Kempers, August Johan. *The Bronzes of Nalanda and Hindu-Javanese Art*. Leiden: E.J. Brill, 1933.

Beyer, Stephan. *The Cult of Tārā: Magic and Ritual in Tibet*. Berkeley: University of California Press, 1973.

_____. "Notes on the Vision Quest in Early Mahāyāna." In Lewis Lancaster, ed., *Prajñāpāramitā and Related Systems: Studies in Honour of Edward Conze*, pp. 329-40. Berkeley: Berkeley Buddhist Studies Series, 1977.

Bhandarkar, Devadatt Ramkrishna. Ed. *BC Law Volume*. 2 vols. Calcutta: Indian Research Institute, 1945; Poona: Bhandarkar Oriental Research Institute, 1946.

Bharati, Agehananda. *The Tantric Traditions*. Delhi: Hindustan Publishing Corp., 1993.

Bhattacharyya, Benoytosh. *The Indian Buddhist Iconography*. Calcutta: Firma K.L. Mukhopadhyay, 1958.

_____. "The Home of Tantric Buddhism." In Devadatta Ramkrishna Bhandarkar, ed., *B.C. Law Volume*, pp. 354-61. Calcutta: Indian Research Institute, 1945.

_____. *An Introduction to Buddhist Esoterism*. Mysore: OUP, 1932.

_____. "Notes on the *Guhyasamajatantra* and the Age of the Tantras." *Indian Historical Quarterly* IX (1933):1-10.

_____, ed. *Two Vajrayana Works*. Gaekwad's Oriental Series. Baroda: Oriental Institute, 1929.

Bhattacharyya, Dipak Chandra. *Tantric Buddhist Iconographic Sources*. New Delhi: Munshiram Manoharlal, 1974.

_____. *Studies in Buddhist Iconography*. Delhi: Manohar, 1978.

Bhattacharya, Gouriswar. "Four Interesting Votive Slabs from Bihar-Bengal." *Oriental Art* 33 (1987): 84-94.

Bhattasali, Nalini Kanta. *Iconography of Buddhist and Brahmanical Sculptures in the Dacca Museum*. Dacca: Dacca Museum Committee, 1929.

Birnbaum, Raoul. *Studies on the Mysteries of Manjusri*. Boulder: Society for the Study of Chines Religions, 1983.

Bond, George. *The Word of the Buddha*. Colombo: M.D. Gunasena and Co., 1982.

Boucher, Daniel. "The Pratītyasamutpādagathā and Its Role in the Medieval Cult of the Relics." *Journal of the International Association of Buddhist Studies* 14 (1992): 1-27.

Bourdieu, Pierre. *The Field of Cultural Production: Essays on Art and Literature*, Randal Johnson, ed. New York: Columbia University Press, 1993.

_____. *Outline of a Theory of Practice*. Cambridge: Cambridge University Press, 1977.

_____. *The Logic of Practice*. Stanford: Stanford University Press, 1990.

Brandon, S.G.F. *Man and God in Art and Ritual: A Study of Iconography, Architecture and Ritual Action as Primary Evidence of Religious Belief and Practice*. New York: Scribners, 1975.

Broadley, Alexander Meyrick. "The Buddhist Remains of Bihar." *Journal of the Asiatic Society of Bengal* 41 (1872): 209-312; *Asiatic Society of Bengal, Proceedings* (1872): 119-20.

Brown, Peter. *The Cult of the Saints: Its Rise and Function in Latin Christianity*. Chicago: University of Chicago Press, 1981.

Brown, Robert L. "Bodhgaya and South-East Asia." In Janice Leoshko, ed., *Bodhgayā, the Site of Enlightenment*. Bombay: Marg, 1988, 101-24.

Buchanan, Susan L. "A Study of Pāla Patronage," M.A. Thesis, Ohio State University, 1975.

Burgess, James. "Buddhist Mudras." *Indian Antiquary* 26 (1897): 24ff.

REFERENCES

Burks, Arthur. "Icon, Index, and Symbol." *Philosophy and Phenomenological Research* 9 (1949): 673-89.

Burnouf, Eugène. *Introduction à l'histoire du Buddhisme indien.* Paris: Imprimerie Royal, 1844.

Bynum, Caroline Walker. "Image, Text and Context in the Study of the Middle Ages." Unpublished manuscript.

Cabezón, José Igancio. *Buddhism and Language: A Study of Indo-Tibetan Scholasticism.* Albany: State University of New York Press, 1994.

_____, ed. *Buddhism, Sexuality, and Gender.* Albany: State University of New York Press, 1992.

_____. "Mother Wisdom, Father Love: Gender-based Imagery in Mahāyāna Buddhist Thought." In José Igancio Cabezón, ed. *Buddhism, Sexuality, and Gender*, pp. 181-99. Albany: State University of New York Press, 1992.

Camille, Michael. *The Gothic Idol: Ideology and Image-Making in Medieval Art.* New York: Cambridge University Press, 1989.

_____. "Seeing and Reading: Some Visual Implications of Medieval Literacy and Illiteracy." *Art History* 8 (185): 26-49.

Campany, Robert. "'Aśokan Stūpas,' Images, and the Cult of Relics in Early Medieval China." Paper presented to the 1995 session of the A.A.R. Seminar on Buddhist Relic Veneration.

Cassidy, Brendan, ed. *Iconography at the Crossroads: Papers from the Colloquim Sponsored by the Index of Christian Art, Princeton University, 23-24 March 1990.* Princeton: Department of Art and Archaeology, Princeton University, 1993.

Chandra, Lokesh, ed. *The Art and Culture of South-East Asia.* New Delhi: Academy of Indian Culture and Aditya Prakashan, 1991.

Chandra, Ramaprasad. "Art in Orissa." *Journal of the Royal Asiatic Society* 82 (1933): 101-28.

_____. *Exploration in Orissa. Memoirs of the Archaeological Survey of India*, No. 44. Calcutta: Archaeological Survey of India, 1930.

Chang, Garma C.C., ed. *A Treasury of Mahāyāna Sūtras: Selections from the Mahāratnakūta Sūtra.* University Park: Penn State University Press, 1983.

Chaudhary, Radha Krishna. *Select Inscriptions of Bihar.* Patna: Shanti Devi, 1958.

Chaudhury, Binayendra N. *Buddhist Centres in Ancient India.* Calcutta: Sanskrit College, 1969.

Chauduri, K.N. *Trade and Civilisation in the Indian Ocean: An Economic History from the Rise of Islam to 1750*. Cambridge: Cambridge University Press, 1985.

Ch'en, Kenneth. *Buddhism In China: A Historical Survey*. Princeton: Princeton University Press, 1964.

Chimpa, Lama and Alaka Chattopadhyaya, trans. *Tāranātha's History of Buddhism in India*. Simla: Indian Institute of Advanced Studies, 1970.

Chipp, Herschel B. *Theories of Modern Art*. Berkeley: University of California Press, 1968.

Chowdhury, Abdul Momin. "Bengal at the Rise of the Pālas." *Journal of the Asiatic Society of Pakistan* 10 (1965): 35-53.

_____. *Dynastic History of Bengal (c.750-1200 A.D.)*. Dacca: Asiatic Society of Pakistan, 1967.

Clark, Walter Eugene. *Two Lamaistic Pantheons*. 2 vols. Cambridge: Harvard University Press, 1937.

Coedes, George. "Note sur une stele Indienne d'epoque Pala decouverte a Ayudhya (Siam)." *Artibus Asiae* 22:1-2 (1959): 9-14.

_____. *The Indianized States of Southeast Asia*, ed. Walter F. Vella and trans., Susan Brown Cowing. Honolulu: East-West Center Press, 1968.

Collins, Steven. "*Nirvāṇa*, Time, and Narrative." *History of Religions* 31 (1992): 215-46.

_____. "Notes on Some Oral Aspects of Pali Literature." *Indo-Iranian Journal* 35 (1992): 121-35.

_____. "On the Very Idea of the Pali Canon." *Journal of the Pali Text Society* 15 (1990): 89-126.

_____. *Selfless Persons: Imagery and Thought in Theravāda Buddhism*. Cambridge: Cambridge University Press, 1982.

_____. "Some Remarks on Time in Two Pali Texts." Unpublished paper presented at the University of Chicago, March 1994.

Connerton, Paul. *How Societies Remember*. Cambridge: Cambridge University Press, 1989.

Connolly, Peter, ed. *Perspectives on Indian Religion: Papers in Honour of Karel Werner*. Bibliotheca Indo-Buddhica, no. 30. Delhi: Sri Satguru Publications, 1986.

Conze, Edward, trans. *Aṣṭasāhasrikā Prajñāpāramitā*, Bibliotheca Indica, no. 284. Calcutta: The Asian Society, 1958.

_____. *Buddhist Meditation.* London: George Allen and Unwin Ltd., 1956.

_____. *Buddhist Thought in India.* London: George Allen and Unwin, Ltd., 1962.

_____. "The Iconography of the Prajnaparamita," Parts I and II. *Oriental Art* 1 (1949-50): 47-52, and 2 (1950-51): 104-09.

_____. *Materials for a Dictionary of the Prajñāpāramitā Literature.* Tokyo: Suzuki Research Foundation, 1973.

_____. *The Perfection of Wisdom in Eight Thousand Lines and its Verse Summary.* Bolinas: Four Seasons, 1973.

_____. "Prajñā and Sophia." *Oriental Art* 1 (1948): 196-97.

_____. *The Prajnaparamita Literature.* The Hague: Mouton and Co., 1960.

_____. "Remarks on a Pala Manuscript." *Oriental Art* I (1949): 9-12.

_____. "Tantric Prajnaparmaita Texts." *Sino-Indian Studies* 5 (1956): 101.

_____. *Thirty Years of Buddhist Studies.* Columbia: University of South Carolina Press, 1968.

Coomaraswamy, Ananda. "The Indian Origin of the Buddha Image." *Journal of the American Oriental Society* 46 (1926): 165-70.

_____. "The Origin of the Buddha Image." *Art Bulletin* 9 (1927): 1-43.

_____. "*Samvega,* 'Aesthetic Shock." *Harvard Journal of Asiatic Studies* 7 (1942-43): 174-79.

Cunningham, Alexander. *Mahābodhi or the Great Buddhist Temple under the Bodhi Tree at Buddha-Gaya.* London: W.H. Allen, 1892.

Dallapiccola, ed. *The Stupa: Its Religious, Historical and Architectural Significance.* Weisbaden: Granz Steiner, 1980.

_____, ed. *Shastric Tradition in Indian Arts.* 2 vols. 1990.

Das, Sarat Chandra. *Indian Pandits from the Land of Snow.* Calcutta: Baptist Mission Press, 1893.

Dasgupta, Shashi Bhusan. *Eastern Indian Manuscript Painting.* Bombay: D.B. Taraporevala Sons and Co., 1972.

_____. *An Introduction to Tantric Buddhism.* Calcutta: University of Calcutta, 1958.

_____. *Obscure Religious Cults.* Calcutta: University of Calcutta, 1969.

Davis, Richard. *Lives of Indian Images.* Princeton: Princeton University Press, 1997.

Dayal, Har. *The Bodhisattva Doctrine in Buddhist Sanskrit Literature.* Delhi: Motilal Banarsidass, 1932.

De, Sushil Kumar. "The Buddhist Tantric Literature (Sanskrit) of Bengal." *New Indian Antiquary* 1 (1938-39): 1-23.

_____. "Sanskrit Literature under the Pala Kings of Bengal." *New Indian Antiquary* 5 (1939): 263-82.

REFERENCES

Dehejia, Vidya. "Aniconism and the Multivalence of Emblems." *Ars Orientalis* 21 (1992): 45-66.

_____. "Bodhgaya and Sri Lanka." In Janice Leoshko, ed., *Bodhgayā, the Site of Enlightenment*, pp. 89-100. Bombay: Marg, 1988.

_____. *Early Stone Temples of Orissa*. New Delhi: Vikas Publishing House Pvt. Ltd., 1979.

_____. "On Modes of Visual Narration in Early Buddhist Art." *The Art Bulletin* 72 (1990): 374-92.

Dikshit, K.N. *Excavations at Paharpur, Bengal*. Memoirs of the Archeological Survey of India, vol. 55. Delhi: Manager of Publications, 1938.

Dohanian, Diran K. *The Mahayana Buddhist Sculpture of Ceylon*. New York: Clarendon Press, 1977.

Dreyfus, H.L., and P. Rabinow. *Michel Foucault: Beyond Structur-alism and Hermeneutics*. Chicago: University of Chicago Press, 1982.

Dutt, Nalinaksha. *Buddhist Sects In India*. Calcutta: Firma KLM, 1977.

_____. *Buddhism in Orissa*. Cuttack: Orissa Mission Press, 1958.

Dutt, Sukumar. *Buddhist Monks and Monasteries of India: Their History and their Contribution to Indian Culture*. Delhi: Motilal Banarsidass, 1962.

Eastman, Alvan C. "Some Steles of the Pala Period Containing the Eight Miracles of Buddha with Notes on the Variations." *Art in America and Elsewhere* 18:6 (October 1930): 271-83; 19:1 (December 1930): 23-33.

Eckel, Malcom David. *Jñānagharbha's Commentary on the Distinction Between the Two Truths*. Albany: State University of New York, 1987.

_____. "The Power of the Buddha's Absence: On the Foundations of Mahāyāna Buddhist Ritual." *Journal of Ritual Studies* 4 (1990): 61-95.

_____. *To See the Buddha*. San Francisco: Harper/Collins, 1992.

Ehara, N.R.M, and Soma Thera and Kheminda Thera, trans. *The Path of Freedom (Vimuttimagga)*. Colombo: Roland D. Weerasuria, 1961.

Eisenstein, E.L. "Some Conjectures about the Impact of Printing on Western Society." *Journal of Modern History* 40 (1968): 1-56

Evans-Pritchard, E.E. *Nuer Religion*. London: Oxford University Press, 1956.

Fabri, Charles L. *History of The Art of Orissa*. New Delhi: Orient Longman Ltd., 1974.

Fleet, J.F. "Sanskrit and Old-Canarese Inscriptions." *Indian Anitiquary* 10 (1881): 185-90.

Foucher, A. *The Beginnings of Buddhist Art and Other Essays in Indian and Central Asian Archaeology.* Paris: Paul Geuthner, 1917.

_____. *Etudes sur l'iconographie bouddhique de l'Inde d'après des documents nouveaux.* 2 vols. Bibliothèque de l'Ecole des hautes études: Sciences religieuses, vol. 3, pts. I-II. Paris: Ernest Leroux, 1900-05.

_____. "L'Origine greque de l'image du Bouddha." *Annales du Musee Guimet.* Calon-sur-Saone: Bibliotheque de vulgarisation, 1913.

Freedberg, David. *The Power of Images: Studies in the History and Theory of Response.* Chicago: University of Chicago Press, 1989.

Gadamer, Han-Georg. *Truth and Method.* New York: Seabury Press, 1975.

Geertz, Clifford. *The Interpretation of Cultures.* New York: Basic Books, 1973.

Gellner, David. "'The Perfection of Wisdom': A Text and its Use in Kuā Bāhāh, Lalitpur Nepal." In S. Lienhard, ed., *Change and Continuity in the Nepalese Culture of the Kathmandu Valley*, 223-40. Turin: Edizioni dell' Orso, 1996.

Getty, Alice. *The Gods of Northern Buddhism: Their History and Iconography.* New York: Dover Publications, 1928.

Ghosh, A. "A Buddhist Tract in a Stone Inscription in the Cuttack Museum." *Epigraphia Indica* 26 (1941): 171-74.

Ghosh, Mallar. *Development of Buddhist Iconography in Eastern India: A Study of Tārā, Prajñās of Five Tathāgatas and Bhṛikutī.* Delhi: Munshiram Monoharlal Publishers Pvt. Ltd., 1980.

Giles, H.A., trans. *The Travels of Fa hsien.* London: 1966.

Gold, Anne. *Fruitful Journeys.* Berkeley: University of California Press, 1988.

Gombrich, Richard. "The *Kosala-Bimba-Vaṇṇanā.*" In Heinz Bechert, ed., *Buddhism in Ceylon and Studies on Religious Syncretism in Buddhist Countries*, 281-303. Symposium zur Buddhismusforschung, I, Akademie der Wissenschaften, Göttingen, Philogish-Historische Klasse, Dritte Folge, no. 108. Göttingen: Vandenhoeck and Ruprecht, 1978.

_____. *Precept and Practice: Traditional Buddhism in the Rural Highlands of Ceylon.* Oxford: Clarendon Press, 1971.

Goody, Jack, and I.P. Watt. "The Consequences of Literacy." *Comparative Studies in History and Society* 5 (1963): 304-15.

_____. *The Domestication of the Savage Mind.* Cambridge: Cambridge University Press, 1977.

_____. *The Interface Between the Written and the Oral.* Cambridge: Cambridge University Press, 1987.

_____. "Literacy and the Non-Literate." In R. Disch, ed., *The Future of Literacy.* Englewood Cliffs: Prentice Hall, 1973.

Gosh, Amalandanda. "A Buddhist Tract in a Stone Inscription in the Cuttack Museum." *Epigraphia Indica* 26 (1941): 171-74.

Granoff, Phyllis. "A Portable Buddhist Shrine from Central Asia." *Archives of Asian Art* 22 (1968): 81-95.

Griffiths, Paul. *On Being Buddha: The Classical Doctrine of Buddhahood.* Albany: State University of New York Press, 1994.

Gross, Rita M., ed. *Beyond Androcentrism: New Essays on Women and Religion.* Missoula: Scholars Press, 1977.

Grousset, Rene. "L'Art Pala et Sena dans l'Inde esoterieure." In *Etudes d'orientalisme publiees par le Musee Guimet a la memoire de Raymonde Linossier.* 2 vols., vol. 1: 277-85. Paris: Librairie Ernest Leroux, 1932.

Grünwedel, Albert. *Buddhist Art in India*, A.C. Gibson, trans. London: Susil Gupta, 1901.

Gupta, Parmeshwari Lal, ed. *Patna Museum Catalogue of Antiquities.* Patna: Patna Museum, 1965.

Gutmann, Joseph, ed. *No Graven Images: Studies in Art and the Hebrew Bible.* New York: Katv, 1971.

Gyatso, Janet, ed. *In the Mirror of Memory: Reflections on Mindfulness and Remembrance in Indian and Tibetan Buddhism.* Albany: State University of New York Press, 1992.

_____. "Letter Magic: A Peircean Perspective on the Semiotics of Rdo Grub-chen's Dhāraṇī Memory." In Gyatso, ed. *In the Mirror of Memory: Reflections on Mindfulness and Remembrance in Indian and Tibetan Buddhism*, pp. 173-214. Albany: State University of New York Press, 1992.

Habibullah, A.B.M., ed. *Nalini Kanta Bhattasali Commemoration Volume.* Dacca: Dacca Museum, 1966.

Hall, Kenneth R. *Maritime Trade and State Development in Early Southeast Asia.* Honolulu: University of Hawaii Press, 1985.

Haque, Enamul. *The Iconography of the Hindu Sculptures of Bengal, up to circa 1200 A.D.* Ph.D. dissertation, University of Oxford, 1973.

REFERENCES

Harrison, Paul. "Buddhānusmrti in the Pratyutpanna-Buddha-Sammukhāvasthita-Samādhi-Sūtra." *Journal of Indian Philosophy* 6 (1978): 35-57.

_____. "Commemoration and Identification in *Buddhānusmṛti.*" In Janet Gyatso, ed. *In the Mirror of Memory: Reflections on Mindfulness and Remembrance in Indian and Tibetan Buddhism*, pp. 215-38. Albany: State University of New York Press, 1992.

_____. "Is the *Dharma-kāya* the Real 'Phantom Body' of the Buddha?" *Journal of the International Association of Buddhist Studies* 15 (1992): 44-94.

_____. *The Samādhi of Direct Encounter with the Buddhas of the Present.* Tokyo: The International Institute for Buddhist Studies, 1990.

Hazra, Kanai Lal. *Royal Patronage of Buddhism in Ancient India.* Delhi: D.K. Publications, 1984.

Hixon, Lex. *Mother of the Buddhas: Meditation on the Prajnaparamita Sutra.* Wheaton: Quest Books, 1992.

Hock, Nancy. "Buddhist Ideology and the Sculpture of Ratnagiri, Seventh through Thirteenth Centuries." Ph.D. Dissertation, University of California, Berkeley, 1987.

Holt, John C. *Buddha in the Crown: Avolokitesvara in the Buddhist Traditions of Sri Lanka.* Oxford University Press:. New York, 1991.

Hopkins, Jeffrey, and Lati Rinpoche, trans. *The Precious Garland and the Song of the Four Mindfulnesses.* London: George Allen and Unwin, 1971.

Huntington, C.W. *The Emptiness of Emptiness: An Introduction to Early Indian Mādhyamika.* Honolulu: University of Hawaii Press, 1989.

_____. "The System of Two Truths in the *Prasannapadā* and the *Madhyamakāvatāra*: A Study in Madhyamaka Soteriology." *Journal of Indian Philosophy* 11 (1983): 77-107.

Huntington, John C. "Cave Six at Aurangabad: A Tantrayāna Monument?" In J. Williams, ed., *Kalādarśana: American Studies in the Art of India*, pp. 47-55. New York: Oxford and I.B.H. Publishers, Co., with A.I.I.S., 1981.

_____. "The Origin of the Buddha Image: Early Image Traditions and the Concept of Buddhadarśanapunyā." In A.K. Narain, ed., *Studies in Buddhist Art of South Asia*, pp. 24-58. New Delhi: Kanak Publications, 1985.

_____. "Pilgrimage as Image: the Cult of the Astamahāpratihārya," part 1, *Orientations* 18 (1987); part 2, *Orientations* 18 (1987): 56-68.

_____. "Sowing the Seeds of the Lotus: A Journey to the Great Pilgrimage Sites of Buddhism, Part I." *Orientations* 16 (1985): 46-61.

_____. "Sowing the Seeds of the Lotus: A Journey to the Great Pilgrimage Sites of Buddhism, Part II [Rsipatana and Mrgadāva]." *Orientations* 17 (1986): 28-43.

_____. "Sowing the Seeds of the Lotus: A Journey to the Great Pilgrimage Sites of Buddhism, Part III [Śrāvastī and Sāṅkāsya]." *Orientations* 17 (1986): 28-40.

_____. "Sowing the Seeds of the Lotus: A Journey to the Great Pilgrimage Sites of Buddhism, Part IV [Vaiśali]." *Orientations* 17 (1986): 28-40.

_____. "Sowing the Seeds of the Lotus: A Journey to the Great Pilgrimage Sites of Buddhism, Part V [Kuśinagara]." *Orientations* 17 (1986): 46-58.

Huntington, Susan L. "Aniconism and the Multivalence of Emblems: Another Look." *Ars Orientalis* 22 (1993): 111-56.

_____. *The Art of Ancient India.* Weatherhill: New York, 1985.

_____. "Early Buddhist Art and the Theory of Aniconism." *Art Journal* 49 (1990): 401-08.

_____. "The Origin and Development of Stone and Bronze Sculpture in Bihar and Bengal, ca. 8th-12th Centuries." Ph.D. Dissertation, UCLA, 1972.

_____. *The "Pala-Sena" Schools of Sculpture.* Studies in South Asian Culture, vol. 10. Leiden: 1984.

_____. "Pre-Pala and Pala Period Sculptures in the Rockefeller Collection." *Apollo* (November 1983): 370-78.

_____. "Some Bronzes from Fatehpur, Gaya." *Oriental Art* 25 (1979): 240-47.

_____, and J.C. Huntington. *Leaves from the Bodhi Tree: The Art of Pala India and its International Legacy.* Dayton: The Dayton Art Institute, 1990.

Hurvitz Leon. "Hsüan-tsang (602-664) and the *Heart Scripture.*" In Lewis Lancaster, ed., *Prajñāpāramitā and Related Systems: Studies in Honour of Edward Conze*, pp. 103-21. Berkeley: Berkeley Buddhist Studies Series, 1977.

Ingalls, D.H.H., trans. *An Anthology of Sanskrit Court Poetry - Vidyakara's Subhasitaratnakosa.* Harvard Oriental Series, vol. 44. Cambridge: Harvard University Press, 1965.

Jaini, Padmandabh S. "On the Buddha Image." In A.K. Narain, ed., *Studies in Pali Buddhism: A Homage Volume to the Memory of Bhikkhu Jagdish Kashyap*, pp. 183-88. Delhi: 1979.

_____. "*Prajñā* and *dṛṣṭi* in the Vaibhāsika Abhidharma." In Lewis Lancaster, ed., *Prajñāpāramitā and Related Systems: Studies in Honour of Edward Conze*. Berkeley: Berkeley Buddhist Studies Series, 1977.

Joshi, Lalmani. *Studies in the Buddhistic Culture of India*. Delhi: Motilal Banarsidas, 1967.

_____. "Religious Changes in Late Indian Buddhist History." *Buddhist Studies Review* 8 (1991): 45-64, and 9 (1992): 153-68.

Kajiyama, Y. "Stupas, the Mother of Buddhas, and Dharma-body." In A.K. Warder, ed., *New Paths in Buddhist Research*, pp. 9-16. Durham: Acorn Press, 1985.

Kasulis, Thomas P. "Philosophy as Metapraxis." In Frank Reynolds and David Tracy, eds., *Discourse and Practice*. Albany: State University of New York Press, 1992.

Kielhorn, F. "The Dinajpur Copper-Plate Inscription of Mahipala." *Journal of the Asiatic Society of Bengal* 61 (1892).

_____. "Khālimpur Plate of Dharmapāladeva." *Epigraphica Indica* 7 (1896-97): 243-54.

King, Winston. *Theravāda Meditation: The Buddhist Transformation of Yoga*. University Park, PA: Pennsylvania State University Press, 1980.

Kinnard, Jacob N. "Reevaluating the Eighth-Ninth Century Pāla Milieu: Icono-Conservatism and the Persistence of Śākya-muni." *Journal of the International Association of Buddhist Studies* 19.2 (1997): 281-300.

_____. "When is the Buddha not the Buddha? The Hindu/Buddhist Battle over Bodhgayā and the Buddha Image." *Journal of the American Academy of Religion* 66.4 (1998).

Klimburg-Salter, Deborah E., et al. *The Silk Route and The Diamond Path Esoteric Buddhist Art on the Trans-Himalayan Trade Routes*. Los Angeles: U.C.L.A. Art Council, 1982.

Kramisch, Stella. "Pala and Sena Sculpture." In Barbara Stoller Miller, ed., pp. 204-240. *Exploring India's Sacred Art: Selected Writings of Stella Kramisch* Philadelphia: University of Pennsylvania Press, 1983.

van Kooij, K.R., and H. van der Veer, eds., *Function and Meaning in Buddhist Art: Proceedings of a Seminar Held at Leiden University, 21-24 October 1991*, pp. 59-79. Groningen: Egbert Forsten, 1995.

Kuraishi, Muhammad Hamid. *A Short Guide to the Buddhist Remains Escavated at Nalanda*. Calcutta: Government of India, Central Publications Branch, 1931.

Lalou, Marcelle. *Iconographie des etoffes peintes (pata) dans le Manjusrimulakalpa*. Paris: Libraire Orientaliste Paul Guethner, 1930.

Lamotte, Étienne. *La Concentration de la Marche Héroïque (Sūrangamasamādhisūtra)*, Mélanges Chinois Bouddhique, vol. 13. Bruxelles: 1965.

_____. *History of Buddhism from the Origins to the Śaka Era*, Sara Webb-Boin, trans. Publications de l'Institut Orientaliste de Louvain, vol. 36. Louvain-la-neuve: Institut Orientaliste, 1988.

_____. "Mañjuśrī." *T'oung Pao* 78 (1969): 1-96.

_____. "Vajrapani en Inde." In *Melanges de Sinologie offerts a Monsieur Paul Demieville*. Biblioteque de l'Institut des Hautes Etudes Chinoises 20. Paris: Press Universitaires de France, 1966.

Lancaster, Lewis R.. "An Early Mahayana Sermon About theBody of the Buddha and the Making of Images." *Artibus Asiae* 36 (1974): 287-291.

_____. "Literary Sources for a Study of Barabudur," *Barabadur: History and Significance of a Buddhist Monument*. Berkeley: Berkeley Buddhist Studies Series, 1981.

_____, ed. *Prajñāpāramitā and Related Systems: Studies in Honour of Edward Conze*. Berkeley: Berkeley Buddhist Studies Series, 1977.

Law, Bimala Charan, ed. and trans. *The Dāthāvamsa (A History of the Tooth-Relic of the Buddha*. Lahore: Motilal Banarsidass, 1925.

Lawson, Simon. "A Catalogue of Indian Buddhist Clay Sealings in British Museums." Ph.D. Dissertation, Oxford University, 1982.

_____. "Dhāranī Sealings in British Collections." In Janine Schotsmans and Maurizio Taddei, eds., *South Asian Archaeology 1983*, vol. 2. Naples: Instituto Universitario Orientale, 1985.

_____. "Votive Objects from Bodhgaya." In Janice Leoshko, ed., *Bodhgayā, Site of Enlightenment*. Bombay: Marg, 1988.

Legge, James. *A Record of Buddhistic Kingdoms*. New York: Dover Publications, 1965.

Leoshko, Janice. "The Appearance of Amoghapāśa in Pāla Period Art," in A.K. Narain, ed., *Studies in Buddhist Art of South Asia*, pp. 127-35. New Delhi: Kanak Publications, 1985.

_____. ed. *Bodhgayā: The Site of Enlightenment*. Bombay: Marg, 1988.

_____. "Buddhist Images from Telhara, a Site in Eastern India. *South Asian Studies* 4 (1988) 89-97.

_____. "The Case of the Two Witnesses to the Buddha's Enlightenment." *Marg* 39 (1988): 39-52.

_____. "The Iconography of Buddhist Sculptures of the Pāla and Sena Periods from Bodhgaya." Ph.D. Dissertation, The Ohio State University, 1987.

Lessing, Ferdinand D., and Alex Wayman, translators. *Mkhas grub rje's Fundamentals of the Buddhist Tantras*. New York: Samuel Weiser, 1980.

Liebert, Gösta. *Iconographic Dictionary of Indian Religions*. Studies in South Asia Culture, vol. 5. Leiden: E.J. Brill, 1976.

Lohuizen-de Leeuw, J.E. van. "The Dhyāni-Buddhas of Barabudur." *Bijdragen Tot de Tall-, Land- enVolkenkunde* 121 (1965): 389-416.

_____. "New Evidence with Regard to the Origin of the Buddha Image." In Herbert Hartel, ed., *South Asian Archaeology 1979*, pp. 377-400. Berlin: Dietrich Reimer Verlag, 1981.

_____. "The Pattikera Chundā and Variations of her Image." In *Nalini Kanta Bhattasali Commemoration Volume*, pp. 119-43. A.B.N. Habibullah, ed. Dacca: Dacca Museum, 1966.

_____. "The Recent Excavations at Pāhārpur." *South Asian Archeology, 1983*, 741-50. Naples:

Lopez, Donald S. Jr. "Authority and Orality in the Mahāyāna." *Numen* 42 (1995): 21-47.

Losty, Jeremiah P. *The Art of the Book in India*. London: The British Library, 1982.

_____. "Bengal, Bihar, Nepal: Problems of Provenance in 12th-century Illuminated Buddhist Manuscripts, Part One." *Oriental Art* 35 (1989): 86-96; Part Two, *Oriental Art* 35 (1989): 140-49.

Lüders, H., and K.L. Janert. *Mathura Inscriptions*. Gottingen: 1961.

Macdonald, Ariane, ed. and trans. *Le mandala du Manjusrimulakalpa*. Collection Jean Przyluski, III. Paris: Adrien-Maisonneuve, 1962.

MacQueen, Graeme. "Inspired Speech in Early Maḥāyāna," Parts I and II. *Religion* 11 (1981): 306-19, and 12 (1982): 49-65.

Macy, J.R. "Perfection of Wisdom: Mother of All Buddhas." In Rita M. Gross, ed. *Beyond Androcentrism: New Essays on Women and Religion*. Missoula: Scholars Press, 1977.

Majumdar, Gayatri Sen. *Buddhism in Ancient Bengal*. Calcutta: Navana, 1983.

Majumdar, N.G. *Nālandā Copper-plate of Devapāladeva*. Rajshahi: Monographs of the Varendra Research Society, 1926.

_____. "Nālandā Inscription of Vipulaśrīmitra." *Epigraphica Indica* 21 (1931-32): 97-101.

Majumdar, Ramesh Chandra. *Ancient Indian Colonization in South-East Asia*. The Maharaja Sayajirao Gaikwad Honorarium Lecture, 1953-54. Baroda: Maharaja Sayajirao Univeristy of Baroda Press, 1955.

_____. "The Date of the Khadga Dynasty of Bengal." *Journal of the Asiatic Society of Bengal* 29 (1923): 32.

_____. *History of Ancient Bengal*. Calcutta: G. Bharadwaj & Co., 1971.

_____, ed. *The History of Bengal, Volume I: The Hindu Period*. Dacca: University of Dacca, 1943.

Malandra, Geri. "The Mahabodhi Temple." In J. Leoshko, ed., *Bodhgayā, the Site of Englightenment*, pp. 10-28. Bombay: Marg, 1988.

_____. *Unfolding a Mandala: The Buddhist Cave Temples at Ellora*. Albany: State University of New York, 1993.

Mallmann, Marie-Thérèse de. *Étude iconographie sur Mañjuśrī*. Publications de l'École Française d'Extrême-Orient, vol. 55. Paris: École Française d'Extrême-Orient, 1964.

_____. *Introduction l'étude d'Avalokiteśvara*. Analles du Musee Guimet, Bibliotheque d'etudes, vol. 57. Paris: Presses Universitaires de France, 1967.

_____. *Introduction a l'iconographie du tântrisme bouddhique*. Paris: Libraire Adrien-Maisonneuve, 1975.

Marcus, Margaret F. "Sculptures from Bihar and Bengal." *Bulletin of the Cleveland Museum of Art* (1967): 240-62.

Marion, Jean-Luc. *God Without Being*, Thomas Carlson, trans. Chicago: University of Chicago Press, 1991.

Martin, Henri-Jean. *The History and Power of Writing*. Chicago: University of Chicago Press, 1994.

Meisezahl, R.O. "Amoghapāśa, Some Nepalese Representations and Their Vajrayanic Aspects." *Monumenta Serica* 26 (1967): 272.

Mettinger, Tryggve N. D. *No Graven Image? Israelite Aniconism in its Ancient Near Eastern Context*. Stockholm: Almqvist and Wiksell, 1995.

REFERENCES

Michalski, Sergiusz. *The Reformation and the Visual Arts: The Protestant Image Question in Western and Eastern Europe*. London: Routledge, 1993.

Miles, Margaret. *Image As Insight*. Boston: Beacon Press, 1985.

Mitchell, W.J.T. *Iconology: Image, Text, Ideology*. Chicago: University of Chicago Press, 1986.

_____, ed. *The Language of Images*. Chicago: University of Chicago Press, 1980.

Mitra, Debala. "Ashtamahabhaya Tara." *Journal of the Asiatic Society. Letters and Science* 23 (1957): 19-22.

_____. *Buddhist Monuments*. Calcutta: Sahitya Samsad, 1971.

_____. *Bronzes from Achutrajpur, Orissa*. Delhi: Agam Prala Prakashan, 1978.

_____. *Bronzes from Bangladesh: A Study of Buddhist Images from District Chittagong*. Delhi: Agam Prala Prakashan, 1982.

_____. "Iconographic Notes." *Journal of the Asiatic Society of Bengal Letters* 1 (1959): 37-39.

_____. "The Indian Museum Inscriptions from Ratnagiri Orissa." *Indian Historical Quarterly* 34 (1958): 163-166.

_____. *Ratnagiri (1958-1961)*. 2 vols. Memoirs of the Archaeological Survey of India, no. 80. Delhi: Director General, Archaeological Survey of India, 1981 and 1983.

_____. "Ratnagiri Plates of Somavamsi-Karna." *Epigraphica Indica* 33 (1959-60): 263-68.

_____. "A Temple of the Buddhist God Mahakala." *Indian Historical Quarterly* 39 (1958): 1-5.

Mitra, S.K. *East Indian Bronzes*. Calcutta: Centre of Advanced Study in Ancient Indian History and Culture, Calcutta University, 1979.

Moxey, Keith. "The Politics of Iconology." In B. Cassidy, ed. *Iconography at the Crossroads: Papers from the Colloquim Sponsored by the Index of Christian Art, Princeton University, 23-24 March 1990*, 29-30. Princeton: Department of Art and Archaeology, Princeton University, 1993.

Mukherjee, Prabhat. *The Buddhist Remains of Orissa*. Cuttack: Government of Orissa, 1964.

_____. *Buddhist Sculptures and Monuments of Orissa*. Cuttack: Mahabodhi Society, n.d.

_____. *Lalitgiri, Udayagiri and Ratnagiri*. Bubhanewswar: Mahabodhi Society, 1957.

Mukherji, R.R., and S.K. Maity. *Corpus of Bengal Inscriptions Bearing on History and Civilizations of Bengal.* Calcutta: K.L. Mukhopadhyay, 1967.

Mullick, C.C. *Nalanda Sculptures: Their Bearing on Indonesian Sculptures.* Delhi: Pratibha Prakashan, 1991.

Mus, Paul. *Barabudur: Esquisse d'une histoire du bouddhisme fondée sur la critique arhéologique textes.* Hanoi: Imprimerie d'Extrême Orient, 1935.

_____. "Le Buddha Pare. Son origine Indienne. Cakyamuni dans le Mahayanisme moye." *Bulletin de le'Ecole Francaise d'Extreme-Orient* 28 (1928): 153-278.

_____. "The Iconography of an Aniconic Art." *RES* 14 (1987): 5-28.

Nakamura, H. "The Astamahasthanacaityastotra." In *Indianisme et Bouddhisme: Melanges offerts a Mgr. Etienne Lamotte*, Publications de l'Institut Orientaliste de Louvain, 23. Louvain-la-Neuve, 1980, pp. 259-66.

Ñānamoli Bhikkhu. *The Path of Purification (Visuddhimagga).* Colombo: Buddhist Publication Society, 1975.

Narain, A.K. "First Images of the Buddha and Bodhisattvas: Ideology and Chronology." In A.K. Narain, ed., *Studies in Buddhist Art of South Asia*, 1-21. New Delhi: Kanak Publications, 1985.

_____. *Studies in Buddhist Art of South Asia.* New Delhi: Kanak Publications, 1985.

_____, ed., *Studies in Pali Buddhism: A Homage Volume to theMemory of Bhikkhu Jagdish Kashyap.* Delhi: 1979.

Newman, John. "Vajrayana Deities in an Illustrated Indian Manuscript of the *Astasahasrika-Prajnaparamita.*" *Journal of the International Association of Buddhist Studies* 13 ():117-32.

Nikam, N.A., and Richard McKeon, eds. *The Edicts of Asoka.* Chicago: University of Chicago Press, 1959.

Niyogi, Puspa. *Buddhism in Ancient Bengal.* Calcutta: Kali Press, 1980.

_____. "Cundā - a Popular Buddhist Goddess." *East and West* 27 (1977): 299-310.

_____. "Dynastic and Regional Affiliations of Buddhism in Ancient Bengal," *Journal of Ancient Indian History* 9 (1975-76): 120-67.

_____. "Organization of Buddhist Monasteries in Ancient Bengal and Bihar." *Journal of Indian History* 54 (1976): 273-98.

Obermiller, E., trans. *History of Buddhism (Chos-hbyung) by Bu-ston*, vol. 2. Tokyo: Suzuki Research Foundation, 1965.

Ong, Walter. *Orality and Literacy: The Technologizing of the Word.* London: Methuen, 1982.

Pal, Pratapaditya. *The Art of Tibet.* New York: The Asia Society, 1969.

_____. *The Arts of Nepal.* 2 vols. Leiden/Koln: EJ Brill, 1974-78.

_____. "The Iconography of Amoghapāśa Lokeśvara," Part II. *Oriental Art* 13 (1967): 20-28

_____. *Nepal: Where the Gods are Young.* New York and Tokyo: The Asia Society in association with John Weatherhill, 1975.

_____, and Julia Meech-Pekarik. *Buddhist Book Illuminations.* New York: Ravi Kumar Publishers, 1988.

Pandey, Deena Bandhu. *The Dharmacakrapravartana in Literature and Art.* Delhi: Oriental Publishers, 1978.

Panofsky, Erwin. *Studies Iconology: Humanistic Themes in the Art of the Renaissance.* New York: Oxford University Press, 1939.

Pathak, V.S. "The Crowned Buddha and the Adamantine Throne." *Journal of the Asiatic Society* 3 (1961): 81-84.

Patil, D.R. *The Antiquarian Remains in Bihar.* Patna: Jayaswal Research Institute, 1963.

Paul, D. *The Art of Nālandā: Development of Buddhist Scultpure 600-1200 A.D.* Leiden: EJ Brill, 1987.

Peirce, C.S. "The Icon, Index, and Symbol." In Charles Hartshorne and Paul Weis, eds., *Collected Works*, vol. 2. Cambridge: Harvard University Press, 1931-58.

Pelikan, Jaroslav. *The Christian Tradition: A History of the Development of Doctrine*, 5 Volumes, *Volume II: The Spirit of Eastern Christendom (600-1700).* Chicago: University of Chicago Press, 1974.

Poussin, Louis de La Vallée. *Bouddhisme, Études et Matériaux: Théorie des Douze Causes.* Grand: Luzac and Co., 1913.

____. "The Four Classes of Buddhist Tantras." *Journal of the Royal Asiatic Society* (1901): 900-.

Prasad, Ram Chandra. *Archaeology of Champa and Vikramasila.* Delhi: Ramanand Vidya Bhawan, 1987.

Przluski, J. "Le *Parinirvāna* et les funérailles du Buddha." *Journal Asiatique* 11 (1918), 12 (1918), 13 (1919), and 15 (1920)

Rahula, Walpola. *History of Buddhism in Ceylon.* Colombo: M.D. Gunasena and Co., 1956.

____. *What the Buddha Taught.* New York: Grove Press, 1974.

Rath, Asoka Kumar. "The Buddhist Remains in the Cuttack District of Orissa." *Journal of Andhra Historical Research Society* 27 (1961-62): 155-63.

Rawlinson, Andrew. "Visions and Symbols in the Mahāyāna." In Peter Connolly, ed., *Perspectives on Indian Religion: Papers in Honour of Karel Werner*. Bibliotheca Indo-Buddhica, no. 30. Delhi: Sri Satguru Publications, 1986.

Ray, Niharranjan. *Idea and Image in Indian Art*. New Delhi: Mushiram Monoharlal, 1973.

_____. and K. Khandalavala, and S. Gorakshkar. *Eastern Indian Bronzes*. New Delhi: Lalit Kalā Akademi, 1986.

Read, Kay. "Binding Reeds and Burning Hearts: Mexica-Tnochca Concepts of Time and Sacrifice." Ph.D. Dissertation, University of Chicago, 1991.

Ricoeur, Paul. *The Symbolism of Evil*. Boston: Beacon Press, 1969.

Roerich, George N. *Biography of Dharmasvāmin*. Patna: K.P. Jayswal Research Institute, 1959.

_____. *The Blue Annals*, Royal Asiatic Society of Bengal Monograph Series. Delhi: Motilal Banarsidass, 1976.

Roth, Gustav. "The Physical Presence of the Buddha and its Representation in Buddhist Literature." In *Investigating Indian Art*, 291-312. Berlin: Museum für Indische Kunst, 1987.

Sahai, N. *Iconography of Minor Hindu and Buddhist Deities*. New Delhi: Abhinav Publications, 1975.

Sahu, Nabin Kumar. *Buddhism in Orissa* Cuttack: Utkal University, 1958.

_____. "Buddhist Art in Orissa." In *Orissa Past and Present*, pp. 84-88. Edited by Prija and Mukherjee, 1962.

Samtani, N.H. "The *Arthviniścaya-Sūtra* - An Important Buddhist Text Discovered by Rāhul Sānkrtyāyana in Tibet." *Journal of the Bihar Research Society* 47 (1961): 399-400.

Samuel, Goeffrey. *Civilized Shamans: Buddhism in Tibetan Societies*. Washington: Smithsonian Institute Press, 1993.

Sānkrtyāyana, Rāhul. "Sanskrit Palm-Leaf Manuscripts in Tibet." *Journal of the Bihar and Orissa Research Society* 31 (1935): 31-35.

Sarasvati, Sarasi Kumar. "East Indian Manuscript Painting." In *Chhavi: Golden Jubilee Volume*, pp. 243-62. Banaras: Bharat Kala Bhavan, 1971.

_____.Saraswati, S.K. *A Survey of Indian Sculpture*. Calcutta: Sambodhi Publications, 1958.

_____. *Tantrayana Art: An Album*. Calcutta: Asiatic Society, 1977.

Sastri, Haraprasad, trans. *Ramacarita of Sandhyakaranandi*. Memoirs of the Asiatic Society of Bengal, vol. 3. Calcutta: The Asiatic Society, 1910.

REFERENCES

Sastri, Hiranand. "The Clay Seals of Nālandā." *Epigraphica Indica* 21 (1931-32): 72ff.

_____. "The Nālandā Copper-plate of Devapāladeva." *Epigraphica Indica* 17 (1923-24), pp. 310-27.

_____. *Nālandā and its Epigraphical Material*, Memoirs of the Archaeological Survey of India, no. 66. Delhi: Manager of Publications, 1942.

_____. *The Origin and Cult of Tārā*, Memoirs of the Archeological Survey of India, no. 20. Calcutta: 1925.

Sastri, Kali Kumar Datta. *Bengal's Contributions to Sanskrit Literature*. Calcutta: Sanskrit College, 1974.

Saunders, E. Dale. *Mudrā: A Study of Symbolic Gestures in Japanese Buddhist Sculpture*. New York: Pantheon Books, 1960.

Schaff, Philip and Henry Wace, eds. *A Select Library of Nicene and Post-Nicene Fathers of the Christian Church*, second series, vol. 13. Edinburgh: T. and T. Clark, 1989.

Schopen, Gregory. "Archaeology and the Protestant Presuppositions in the Study of Indian Buddhism." *History of Religions* 31 (1991): 1-23.

_____. "The Bodhigarbhālaṅkāralaksa and Vimalosnīsa Dhāraṇīs in Indian Inscriptions." *Wiener Zeitschrift für die Kunde Südasiens* 29 (1985): 119-50.

_____. "Burial '*Ad Sanctos*' and the Physical Presence of the Buddha in Early Indian Buddhism: A Study in theArchaeology of Religions." *Religion* 17 (1987): 193-225.

_____. "On the Buddha and His Bones: The Conception of a Relic in the Inscriptions of Nāgārjunikonda." *Journal of the American Oriental Society* 108 (1988): 527-37.

_____. "On Monks, Nuns and 'Vulgar' Practices: The Introduction of the Image Cult into Indian Buddhism." *Artibus Asiae* 46 (1988) : 153-68.

_____. "The Phrase '*sa pṛthivīpradeśaā caityabhūto bhavet*' in the *Vajracchedikā*: Notes on the Cult of the Book in the Mahāyāna." *Indo-Iranian Journal* 27 (1975): 147-81.

_____. "The Text on the 'Dhāraṇī Stones from Abhayagiriya': A Minor Contribution to the Study of Mahāyāna Literature in Ceylon." *The Journal of the International Association of Buddhist Studies* 5 (1982): 100-08.

_____. "A Verse From the Bhadracaripranidhana in a 10th Century Inscription Found at Nalanda." *Journal of the International Association of Buddhist Studies* 12 (1989), pp. 149-57.

Singhal, Sudarshan Devi. "Iconography of Cundā." In Lokesh Chandra, ed., *The Art and Culture of South-East Asia*, pp. 385-410. New Delhi: Academy of Indian Culture and Aditya Prakashan, 1991.

Sinha, Bindeshwar Prasad. *Dynastic History of Magadha circa 450-1200 A.D.*. New Delhi: Abhinav, 1977.

Sircar, Dinesh Chandra. "Comments on the Chronology in Dr. R.C. Majumdar's *History of Ancient Bengal*." *Journal of the Asiatic Society* 18 (1976): 97-98.

Slusser, Mary. *Nepal Mandala*. Two volumes. Princeton: Princeton University Press, 1982.

Smith, Jonathan Z. *Imagining Religion*. Chicago: University of Chicago Press, 1982.

_____. *Map Is Not Territory*. Leiden: E.J. Brill, 1978.

_____. *To Take Place: Toward Theory in Ritual*. Chicago: University of Chicago Press, 1987.

Smith, William Robertson. *Lectures in the Religion of the Semites*. London: Adam Black, 1889.

Snellgrove, David. "Buddhism in North India and the Western Himalayas - Seventh to Thirteenth Centuries." In *The Silk Route and Diamond Path*, pp. 64-82. Edited by Deborah E. Klimburg-Salter. Los Angeles: UCLA Art Council, 1982.

_____. *Buddhist Himālaya*. Oxford: Bruno Cassirer, 1957.

_____. *The Hevajra Tantra*. London: Oxford University Press, 1959.

_____, ed. *The Image of the Buddha*. Paris: UNESCO, 1978.

_____. *Indo-Tibetan Buddhism*, two volumes. Boston: Shambhala Publications, 1987.

_____. "Indo-Tibetan Liturgy and its Relationship to Iconography." In *Mahayanist Art After A.D. 900*. Colloquies on Art and Archaeology in Asia No. 2. London: Percival David Foundation of Chinese Art, 1972.

Soper, Alexander. *Literary Evidence for Early Buddhist Art in China*. Ascona, Switzerland: Artibus Asiae Publishers, 1959.

Sperber, Dan. *Rethinking Symbolism*. Cambridge: Cambridge University Press, 1975.

Srivastava, Balram. *Iconography of Sakti*. Delhi: Chaukhambha Orientalia, 1978.

_____. *The Nature of Indian Aesthetics, with Special Reference to Silpa*. Varanasi: Chaukhamba Orentalia, 1985.

Stadtner, Donald M.. "New Approaches to South Asian Art." *Art Journal* 49 (1990): 359-62.

Stewart, Mary. "Nālandā Mahāvihāra." Ph.D. Dissertation, Cambridge University,

Streng, Frederick. *Emptiness: A Study in Religious Meaning*. New York: Abingdon Press, 1967.

Strong, John. "*Gandhakuṭī*: The Perfumed Chamber of the Buddha." *History of Religions* 16 (1977): 390-406.

_____. *The Legend and Cult of Upagupta: Sanskrit Buddhism in North India and Southeast Asia*. Princeton: Princeton University Press, 1992.

Takakusu, J., trans. *A Record of the Buddhist Religion as Practised in India and the Malay Archipelago (A.D. 671-695), by I-tsin*. Oxford: The Clarendon Press, 1896.

Tambiah, Stanley J. "A Performative Approach to Ritual." *Proceedings of the British Academy* 65 (1979): 113-69.

_____. *The Buddhist Saints of the Forest and the Cult of Amulets*. Cambridge: Cambridge University Press, 1984.

_____. "Famous Buddha Images and the Legitimation of Kings." *RES* 4 (1982): 5-19.

Tay, N. "Kuan-Yin: The Cult of Half Asia." *History of Religions* 16 (1976): 147-152.

Templeman, David. "Tāranātha the Historian." *Tibet Journal* 6 (1981): 41-46.

Trainor, Kevin. *Relics, Ritual, and Representation in Buddhism: Rematerializing the Sri Lankan Theravāda Tradition* Cambridge: Cambridge University Press, 1997

Tucci, Giuseppi. *The Theory and Practice of the Maṇḍala*. London: Rider and Company, 1961.

Underwood, Frederic B. "Buddhist Insight: The Nature and Function of *Paññā* in the Pali Nikāyas." Ph.D. Dissertation, Columbia University, 1973.

Waghorne, Joanne Punzo. "Dressing the Body of God: South Indian Bronze Sculpture in its Temple Setting." *Asian Art* 3 (1992): 9-34.

Waddell, L.A. "The 'Dhāraṇī' Cult in Buddhism, its Origin, Deified Literature and Images." *Ostasiatische Zeitschrift* (1912): 155-95.

_____. "The Indian Buddhist Cult of Avalokita and his Consort, Tārā, the Saviouress." *Journal of the Royal Asiatic Society* (1894): 51-89.

Waley, Arthur. "Did the Buddha Die of Eating Pork?" *Mélanges chinois et bouddhiques* 1 (1932): 352-54.

Warder, A.K. *Indian Buddhism*. Delhi: Motilal Banarsidass, 1970.

REFERENCES

Wayman, Alex. *The Buddhist Tantras: Light on Indo-Tibetan Esotericism.* New York: Samuel Weiser, 1973.

_____. "The Buddhist Theory of Vision." In George Elder, ed., *Buddhist Insight: Essays by Alex Wayman*, pp. 153-61. Delhi: Motilal Banarsidass, 1984.

_____. *Chanting the Names of Mañjuśrī. The Mañjuśrī-nāma-saṃgīti.* Boston: Shambala, 1985.

_____. "Notes on the Sanskrit Term *Jñāna*." *Journal of the Asian Oriental Society* 75 (1955): 253-68.

_____. "Regarding the Translation of the Buddhist Terms *Saññā/Samjñā, Viññāna/Vijñāna*." O.H. de A. Wijesekera, ed., *Malalasekera Commemoration Volume*, pp. 325-35. Colombo: Malalasekera Commemoration Volume Editorial Committee, 1976.

_____. "Studies in Yama and Māra." *Indo-Iranian Journal* 3 (1959): 44-73, 112-31.

Williams, Joanna Gottfried. *The Art of Gupta India: Empire and Province.* Princeton: Princeton University Press, 1982.

_____. "Sārnāth Gupta Steles of the Buddha's Life." *Ars Orientalis* 10 (1975): 171-92.

Williams, Paul. *Mahāyāna Buddhism: The Doctrinal Foundations.* London: Routledge, 1989.

Wiltshire, Martin G. "The 'Suicide' Problem in the Pāli Canon." *Journal of the International Association of Buddhist Studies* 6 (1983): 124-40.

Winternitz, M. "Notes on the Guhyasamaja-Tantra and the Age of the Tantras." *The Indian Historical Quarterly* 9 (1933): 1-10.

Woodward, Hiram W. Jr. "The Life of the Buddha in the Pala Monastic Environment." *The Journal of the Walters Art Gallery* 48 (1990): 13-27.

Yün-hua, Jan. "Buddhist Relations Between India and Sung China." *History of Religions* 6 (1966): 24-42.

_____. "Buddhist Relations Between Indian and Sung China, Part II," *History of Religions* 6 (1966): 135-68.

Yuyama, Akira. *A Systematic Survey of Buddhist Sanskrit Literature.* H. Bechert, ed. 1979.

INDEX